THE SPANISH
INQUISITION

CECIL ROTH, M.A., PH.D., OXON.

Reader in Jewish Studies at Oxford University

W · W · NORTON & COMPANY

New York · London

First published in the Norton Library 1964

For David

W. W. Norton & Company, Inc., 500 Fifth Avenue, New York, NY 10110
W. W. Norton & Company Ltd., 10 Coptic Street, London WC1A 1PU

ISBN 0-393-00255-1

PRINTED IN THE UNITED STATES OF AMERICA

5 6 7 8 9 0

PREFACE

IT was once asserted by an unkind critic that history does not repeat itself so much as historians repeat one another. Today, the more conventional form is emphatically true. The Spanish Inquisition was until yesterday an antiquarian diversion. The events of the past few years, and above all of the past few months, have converted it into a dreadful warning. The author must request the incredulous reader to believe that, however contrary appearances may seem, this book is based on authorities, manuscript as well as printed, as reliable as he has been able to trace, and is not intended as a satire on present-day conditions.

His thanks are due to Miss Phyllis Abrahams, Mr. J. M. Rich, and Mr. W. S. Samuel, for their helpful collaboration.

CECIL ROTH.

LONDON,
 September, 1937.

FOREWORD

BY an accident of lexicography, the English reader looks for *Inquisition* between *Iniquity* and *Insincerity*. For the last four hundred years or more, this has reflected accurately enough his outlook upon that institution, particularly as it existed in Spain. It happens that during a part of its career the Holy Office directed its attention against English Protestants. Numbers of them were piratical seafaring men, who might well have qualified for the gallows instead of for the stake. Nevertheless, the English attitude was so deeply coloured that the effects may still be discerned. In the course of time, the agitation against the Inquisition merged in and was fortified by that against the Church of Rome and everything connected with Popery; and supplementary anti-Inquisitional anecdotes were appended to successive editions of that great Protestant masterpiece, Foxe's *Book of Martyrs*, which for generations constituted half of the average Englishman's library. Thus the legend of the Inquisition developed: and the great Whig school of historians did nothing to tone down the glaring colours of the original picture.

Meanwhile, the tide was strengthened by two fresh currents deriving from France, and each reflecting an entirely different aspect of the many-sided Gallic genius. The first was the rationalist tradition of the eighteenth century, which had seen its greatest enemy in the Church of Rome and its easiest butt in the Church's most devoted instrument. The second was the taste for highly spiced historical narrative, interspersed as lavishly as possible with erotic anecdotes, in which the French have led the world. These tendencies reinforced the traditional prejudice; with the result that as the nineteenth century advanced there were added to the stereotyped Protestant tirades various works with titles such as *The Secrets of the Inquisition*. In these, the prurient delighted in highly coloured romance (generally with an unhappy ending), displayed against a background of inhuman torture, and interspersed with battles for female virtue, with varying success, against libidinous familiars and their superiors. It is from a medley of such accounts that the average English and American reader of today has derived his impressions. The rising generation mumbles "sadism" and "inferiority complex" over the infernal brew, and imagines that a psychological problem has been solved.

But this is both an error and an injustice. It is impossible to understand the Inquisition and the spirit which infused it—or, indeed, the Middle Ages as a whole—without grasping one salient feature which differentiated that day from ours. Then, men really did believe (not merely professed to believe) that they were endowed by God with immortal souls. They really did believe in a heaven and a hell, in which they were destined to make reckoning for what they had done during their transient terrestrial existence. They believed, too, that Theophany and Incarnation had put them in possession of the key to the eternal verities and indicated the path to heaven—the only path to heaven, all others leading to hell: and they were not willing to see this precious secret endangered or contemned. Today, men have become indifferent or sceptical regarding all this. They may have good reason: but they have no right to confuse their attitude with tolerance.

Granted these premises, it was natural for the man of

the Middle Ages (and the man of the Middle Ages persisted long after the Middle Ages themselves had passed) to be prepared to go to any lengths, and to submit himself to any discipline, in order to safeguard his eternal felicity, and to secure that of others whose eyes were blinded. "Had I sister in a country wherein there were but one heretic, still that one heretic would keep me in fear for her," wrote a great mediæval German mystic, in all sincerity. And it was because mediæval man, and the leaders of mediæval thought, were of a similar opinion that the Holy Inquisition was introduced in the Middle Ages, and continued its sway in Spain until only a century ago. For all the devastating nature of its work, the Inquisition was essentially a Tribunal, bound fully as much by precedent and rule as any Court of Justice. Its ideology was in fact accepted unquestioningly throughout Europe, at the outset at least; its procedure was similar in most ways to that of judicial bodies in other countries: its excesses can be matched, in kind if not in degree, in most parts of the western world. Its premises were moreover unchallenged at that time, and led inexorably to its conclusions.

All that has been said above does not minimise the stark horror of the institution or of its underlying conception. The tragedy of the Inquisition—and in particular of the Inquisition in Spain—is all the greater in view of the patent sincerity, and one may add even the high idealism, which inspired it. It is possible (though the art is rapidly becoming a lost one) to comprehend, without necessarily being in agreement. And to comprehend the Inquisition and the causes which led to its foundation, it is essential to examine, first of all, one aspect of the religious background of fourteenth-century Spain.

CONTENTS

PREFACE

FOREWORD

CHAPTER I

PRIDE AND PRECEDENT: THE SPANISH SCENE

TOWARDS the close of the fourteenth century, while Richard II. was trifling on the throne of England and Charles VI. was raving on the throne of France, a certain Spanish archdeacon named Ferran Martínez was engaged in delivering a series of sermons in the diocese of Seville. It was his remarkable eloquence rather than the novelty of his subject which attracted an audience: for he spoke only on a single theme, one that in every age has provided an easy stalking horse for demagogues religious and civil—the iniquities of the Jews. This scattered section of humanity was not however regarded in that backward civilisation as a people of pariahs, in whose veins there ran a venom that poisoned whatever contribution they made to the common store. Science had not yet progressed so far: and the Archdeacon Martínez based his harangues, frankly and without shame, on ecclesiastical prejudice. The Jews, he urged (his audience had heard it before, but it always sounded novel from those eloquent lips), had been guilty, as a body, of the greatest crime in history. They adhered to a faith that had been rejected in no uncertain manner by the Deity. Their ceremonies were outmoded and impious, rendered those who performed them capable of the most heinous misdoings, and doomed them to eternal punishment in the hereafter. Their fidelity to their ancestral religion was, in fact, a standing affront to Christianity, to Christians, and to Jesus Christ himself.

Martínez had been preaching in this vein ever since

1378. He had been commanded to desist by the King, the Archbishop, the Pope: but their rescripts had no more effect on him than the pleadings of the Jews themselves. For thirteen years, his harangues increased in violence: until at last the inevitable occurred. It is a lesson which is well worth remembering at the present time. That a mob-orator is illogical, ungrammatical and ill-informed does not necessarily rob his words of effect. Even when as a matter of expedience he counsels moderation (which Martínez never did), his words cannot fail to inflame his hearers. And when in the end the inevitable happens, and a murderous popular outbreak takes place, it is ridiculous for him to suggest that this is a spontaneous upheaval, which confirms what he has been preaching all along. The responsibility is directly his, whether in the fourteenth century or in the twentieth.

Martínez would have been ashamed to evade responsibility in any such manner. To be sure, without the advantages and technique of the modern demagogue—the Press, the Radio, and the loud-speaker—it was a long time before his harangues took effect. There was reason, indeed, for this. The Jews were no strangers or newcomers in Spain, any more than they are in Germany today. They had been settled there, demonstrably, ever since the first century, some of them disclaiming on this plausible ground any conceivable responsibility for the Crucifixion. Documentary and archæological evidence demonstrates their numbers at the beginning of the fourth century, long before the coming of the Arabs or even of the Visigoths. The latter indeed had persecuted them, after the light of Roman Catholicism had spread in the Peninsula; but under the Moors they had flourished, as nowhere else in Europe. They constituted so important and so influential a minority that, after a few initial massacres out of sheer habit, the Christians thought it advisable to leave them undisturbed in the territories reconquered from the Crescent. Every Spanish city, therefore, had its prosperous *judería*, or Jewish quarter. There was no question of restricting the inhabitants, as elsewhere, to the degrading occupation of money-lending. They were the craftsmen and the weavers, the goldsmiths and the carpenters: and, when Moors and Christians met on the stricken field, Jewish contingents fought manfully on either side. In this same Seville, there was still preserved the silver key which the Jews had presented to King Ferdinand III., the Conqueror of the city, when he made his triumphant entry in 1248: and his tomb in the Cathedral bore a magniloquent Hebrew inscription.

It was true that, once the Moorish menace was mastered, and the necessity for conciliating the Jewish minority diminished, their position began to deteriorate. It was true that the anti-Jewish legislation inspired by the Vatican had begun to make some headway, though it was generally enacted more rigorously than it was enforced. It was true that in the Civil War in Castile between Pedro the Cruel and his half-brother, Henry of Trastamara, the Jews (like the English) had been so careless as to espouse the side of the loser, and that (unlike the English) they had been left in a position to bear the victor's resentment. Their lot was thus less happy than it had been; but in comparison with that of their coreligionists elsewhere in Europe it was tolerable—even enviable. The Jews had been expelled from England in 1290 by Edward I. *en masse*. His example had been followed in France, sixteen years later, by Philip the Fair. (A few had returned meanwhile, but they were the merest remnant, soon to be chased out again.) The Germans, of course, were too disorganised to carry out any consistent policy. They had, however, already established themselves in their historic rôle, of the Jew-baiters *par excellence* of the world: and they had perpetrated massacres (particularly at the time of the Black Death) which beggared, for fury, system, and comprehensiveness, anything that Europe had as yet known.

The Spanish Jews considered themselves secure from a repetition of anything like this. The activities of Martínez disturbed, but did not alarm, them: and as month after month passed, without any untoward occurrence, they fell into the common error of imagining that what had not happened as yet would never happen at all. It came as a shock to them when at the close of 1390, just before Christmastide, Martínez succeeded in having some Synagogues in the diocese partially destroyed and closed down, on the plea that they had been built without authorisation. The community, alarmed, applied for protection to the Council of Regency then governing Castile in the name of the young King Henry III., which ordered steps to be taken for the protection of the petitioners. Martínez was defiant, now as always: and in the ensuing Lent, with its reminiscences of the Passion, his sermons were as violent and as inflammatory as they had ever been.

On Ash Wednesday (March 15th, 1391) his harangue was particularly effective, and his audience was roused to a high pitch of frenzy. On its way from the church, a turbulent crowd, thirsting with zeal and greed (the two, it may be noticed, are often combined), surged towards the Jewish quarter, which seemed to be in imminent danger of sack. The civil authorities were at last awakened to the necessity of stern measures. Seizing two of the most turbulent members of the mob, they had them flogged. This measure was either too violent or not violent enough. The two sufferers became popular martyrs, and the feel-ings of the rest were embittered. After some further disturbances, order was outwardly restored: but the spirit of unrest still simmered, and Martínez continued his unbridled invective from the pulpit. None who were there lived to know it: but to these seemingly unimportant disorders are to be traced some of the greatest tragedies in history—the darkest page in the dark record of the Jewish people, one of the saddest episodes in the history of human thought, and the ultimate decline of Spain from the high status to which her achievements and her genius entitled her—everything, in a word, which is associated with the term "The Spanish Inquisition."

For some weeks after that fatal Ash Wednesday, disaffection smouldered, the ominous calm being punctuated by sporadic outrages in the Jewish quarter. Meanwhile, the spirit of unrest spread to Córdova, Toledo, Burgos and elsewhere; while Martínez, delighted at this initial success, continued his inflammatory addresses in every pulpit open to him. The excitement increased day by day, until at length, on June 6th, the storm broke. An infuriated mob rushed upon the *judería* of Seville and put it to sack. An orgy of carnage raged in the city. The dead were numbered by the hundred, if not by the thousand. Every ruffian in the city flaunted the finery sacked from Jewish houses, or boasted the ravishing of a Jewish maiden. Through some curious process of mass psychology—a phenomenon as unmistakable as it is mysterious—the infection spread from one city to the other, and throughout Spain onslaughts on the Jews became the order of the day.

The fury raged that summer and autumn throughout the Peninsula, from the Atlantic to the Mediterranean and from the French frontier to the Straits of Gibraltar. At several places, the entire Jewish community was exterminated in a frenzy of slaying. At Córdova, the ancient Jewish quarter, where Moses Maimonides had first seen the light, was reduced to ashes. Toledo was the scene of a ghastly massacre on the fast-day when the Jews were mourning the breach of the walls of Jerusalem two thousand years before. Seventy other towns in Castile witnessed similar scenes of horror.

In Aragon, notwithstanding the measures taken by the authorities to quell the disorders at their outset, the example was generally followed. In Valencia, the lead was given by a crowd of hysterical boys: and within a few days not a single professing Jew was left alive in the entire kingdom. At Barcelona, despite the half-hearted protection given by the civic authorities, the whole community was wiped out. From Catalonia, the disorders spread to the Balearic Islands, where an exterminatory massacre took place on August 2nd at Palma. Outbreaks were prevented only in the kingdom of Granada—still under the rule of the barbaric Moslems—and, thanks to the strenuous efforts of the Crown, in Portugal. Elsewhere in the Peninsula, hardly a single community escaped. The total number of victims was estimated at as many as 50,000: and, considering the prosperous state of Spanish Jewry before that date, this figure is well within the bounds of possibility.

There was in all this nothing which the historian can regard with surprise. From one point of view, the outbreak was no more than an early illustration of that innate violence of character ("sadism," it would be termed in the current pseudo-scientific jargon) which has distinguished Spanish life throughout history, and rendered Spanish civil wars noteworthy for their ferocity in the annals of the human race. Nor was such an outbreak unusual as far as the Jews were concerned. Something of the same sort, though necessarily on a smaller scale, had taken place even in England in 1189 and the following year: there had been similar occurrences in other European countries: and ever since the First Crusade, the tragic record of German Jewry had been punctuated by bloody outbreaks on a vast scale, in comparison with which this Spanish fury was almost of minor consequence. But the massacres of 1391 were accompanied by a phenomenon hitherto unexampled. Elsewhere, it occasionally happened that in a similar contingency a handful of individuals forgot that suffering was the badge of all their tribe, and submitted to baptism in order to save their lives. These redeemed souls were eagerly welcomed, in that age of militant Christianity. The neophytes were considered and treated as being equal in all things to their neighbours, and became amalgamated in the general community: with the result that, in those Central European countries in which the Jewish settlement is of longest duration, there can be few families in whose veins there does not run some tincture of the blood of these enforced proselytes of many centuries ago.

Such conversions were, nevertheless, comparatively rare. On the whole, when faced with the alternatives of apostasy or death, the vast majority of Jews unflinchingly chose the latter. They met their end with a hymn of praise upon their lips: and they qualified thus for the world's truest nobility. The same had generally taken place in Spain during previous outbreaks. But, in 1391, for some mysterious reason, the case was different. For the first and only time in the whole course of their long history, the morale of the Jewish people—or of a considerable portion of it—broke. Faced with the alternatives of apostasy or death, a large—a very large—number chose the former.

What was the reason? It is impossible to tell. Perhaps there was something in the soft, scented air of the Iberian Peninsula which predisposed its Jewish denizens to a lesser fortitude than that which was traditional with their brethren elsewhere; for as long back as Visigothic times, and again during one of the Moslem persecutions in the thirteenth century, something of the same sort had occurred, though on a far smaller scale. Possibly, the recent disasters and expulsions throughout Europe had made Spanish Jewry despair of their future after all those long centuries. Their immemorial residence in the country made them think of themselves solely as Iberians: their philosophical interests and rationalising tendencies had minimised the cleavage between the various faiths: their intimate social and business relations with their fellow-countrymen made the step of conversion seem less drastic: and to many of these cultured men of affairs free enjoyment of their goods and chattels appeared to be well worth an occasional mass. Moreover, this was, like all mediæval persecutions, essentially religious in motivation—titularly, at least: and the most frenzied mob gave over its howling and was filled with a genuine spiritual satisfaction if it saw the opportunity of saving the soul of one of its victims, by escorting him to the priest for baptism.

Whatever the reason, and whatever the psychological process which accompanied it, the massacres of 1391 changed the whole face of Spanish Jewry. Throughout the Peninsula, large bodies of Jews accepted baptism *en masse* in order to escape death. In Barcelona alone, those who saved their lives by this means are said to have been numbered by thousands. In Valencia, it was considered miraculous that the supply of holy chrism in the Churches held out. In some places, the Jews did not wait for the application of compulsion, but anticipated the attack and came forward spontaneously, clamouring for admission to the true faith. Nor was it only the semi-apathetic ordinary members of the community who acted in this way, but in some cases the entire body, led by their Rabbis, their scholars, and their lay-leaders. All told, the number of conversions in Aragon and Castile alone was reckoned at the improbable figure of two hundred thousand. It was a phenomenon unique in the whole of Jewish, as it was in the whole of Spanish, history.

This remarkable triumph for the Church emboldened some of its more fiery advocates to renewed endeavours. The outbreak at Valencia had been due to the eloquence of Fray Vincent Ferrer, afterwards to enter the roll of Catholic saints. In subsequent years, he did not relax his efforts: and he travelled about from place to place, preaching to the Jews and endeavouring to secure their conversion. Cowed and disheartened as they were, he achieved a success greater than he had hoped for in his wildest dreams. In 1411 he began a veritable Crusade in Castile, from end to end. In one township after the other, he appeared in the synagogue bearing a Scroll of the Law in one arm and a crucifix in the other, with an unruly mob at his heels to add force to his arguments: and everywhere many persons allowed themselves to be won over. On a single day, in Toledo, he is said to have gained four thousand converts. In the Bishopric of Segovia, the remnants of Judaism were almost entirely destroyed. Subsequently, he returned to Aragon, where his labours for the faith continued. By the time he ended his campaign, a couple of years later, he is said to have gained thirty-five thousand additional converts.

Thus, from the close of the fourteenth century, a completely new state of affairs existed in Spain, in the religious sphere. By the side of those who still openly professed their Judaism, now sadly decreased in wealth and numbers, there were vast numbers of "*conversos*," totalling according to some reports hundreds of thousands. Some of them were indeed sincere enough: for example, Paul de Santa Maria, who, as Solomon Levi, had at one time been a Rabbi, but subsequently rose to the dignity of member of the Council of Regency of Castile and Bishop of Burgos —in which office he was succeeded (an unusual prodigy) by his son. There were doubtless many others, who had not been over-sincere in their attachment to Judaism, and found little difficulty in accommodating themselves equally well, or ill, to their new religion. But the vast majority had accepted Christianity only to escape death, and remained at heart as Jewish as they had ever been. They took their children to church to be baptised, though they hastened to wash off the traces of the operation as soon as they returned home. They would go to a priest to be married, but they were not content with the ceremony and arranged another in the privacy of their houses afterwards. Occasionally, as a matter of form, they would go to be shriven: but their confessions were so blatantly unreal that on one occasion a priest is said to have begged one of his clients for a fragment of his garment, as a relic of so blameless a soul.

Behind this outward sham, the recent converts remained for the most part nearly as Jewish as they had ever been. Their disbelief in the dogmas of the Church was notorious, and not always concealed. They kept all the traditional Hebraic ceremonies, in some cases down to the least details. For the most part, they married exclusively among themselves. They consorted familiarly with their former coreligionists, often continuing to live in the same quarter. On occasion, they furtively frequented the synagogues, for the illumination of which they superstitiously sent gifts of oil. Alternatively, they would form religious associations with titularly Catholic objects, and under the patronage of some Catholic saint, using them as a cover for observing their ancestral rites. By descent, in belief, and largely in practice, they remained as they had been before the conversion. They were Jews in all but name, and Christians in nothing but form. Moreover, they were able to transmit their point of view to their children, who, though as time went on they were born in the dominant faith and baptised at birth, were as little sincere in their Christianity as their fathers had been. In Jewish life, they were known as *Anusim*, or the Forced Ones. But, as they went through the streets, the "pure-blooded" Spaniard would scowl after them. "Marrano," he would mutter, with expectoratory contempt. (The word is an old one meaning "swine," in both its literal and its figurative sense.) Like many other names first applied in contempt, this has now come into general currency; and the term is associated with one of the most remarkable chapters of heroism and romance that history can shew.

On the other hand, one great change had come about for these Marranos as a result of their nominal conversion. Previously, as Jews, they had been weighed down by the innumerable restrictions which were applied to unbelievers by the code of that period, civil as well as ecclesiastical. They were compelled to live in their own separate quarter. They were not supposed to occupy a position which might afford them any vestige of authority over true believers. They were excluded, thus, from any official appointment in the state. By recent legislation, they were forbidden to be styled "Don," or to shave their beards, or to wear any but the coarsest clothing, or to ride on horseback as hidalgos did. They were supposed to wear at all times a badge of shame, to distinguish them from ordinary folk. Intermarriage or sexual intercourse with Christians was considered little less abominable than incest, and was punished as such—and the penalties for incest were of the severest. They were not supposed to hold real estate. While the Spanish Jews were never subjected to limitations quite so galling and so oppressive as was the case in Northern Europe (in parts of which the tendency has remained), the range of their business activities was narrowly restricted. This repressive code was seldom or never enforced in every detail (it is a commonplace that mediæval legislation enunciated an ideal, rather than laid down a positive rule of conduct). Nevertheless, at the best the Jews were hampered by a long series of galling restrictions; they were excluded from the professions, and on the whole from government service; and their economic life was severely limited.

On the other hand, these restrictions were based on purely religious motives. Once a Jew went over to the dominant religion, they lapsed automatically: and henceforth, the tens of thousands of Jews converted to Christianity in 1391 and the succeeding years ("New Christians," was the technical term, to distinguish them from the "Old Christians" whose fathers and fathers' fathers had been brought up in the Faith) found no obstacles whatsoever in their way. Needless to say, they availed themselves whole-heartedly of their opportunities. It was as though a tree-trunk, long held under water by some aquatic growth, were suddenly released during a storm, and came forcing its way to the surface, sweeping away all obstacles that kept it back. With the removal of the social and religious disabilities from which they had previously suffered, the social and economic progress of the recent converts and their descendants became phenomenally rapid. However questionable their sincerity, it was now impossible—indeed, it was uncanonical—to exclude them on the score of their creed from any walk of life. The Law, the administration, the army, the universities were all overrun by recent converts of more or less dubious sincerity, or by their immediate descendants. They pushed their way into the municipal councils, into the legislatures, into the judiciary. A good many of them even entered the Church. There is extant an extraordinary letter of recommendation written early in the fifteenth century by the community of Saragossa to introduce a certain friar of Jewish birth, who was going to preach a Holy War against the Moors. Their coreligionists were begged to believe that, notwithstanding appearances, he was favourable to them at heart!

The wealthier of them intermarried with the highest nobility of the land, few impoverished counts or nobles being able to resist the lure of their gold. Within a couple of generations, there was barely a single aristocratic family in Aragon, from the royal house downwards, which was free from some Jewish admixture or alliance. Half the important offices at Court were occupied by *conversos*, or their children, or else their close relatives. In 1480, for example, both the supreme court of justice of that kingdom and the Cortes were presided over by persons of Jewish extraction. Conditions were much the same in Castile. In the whole of Spain, it was only in Catalonia that the process was to some degree restricted, though the boast that Catalan blood was never polluted by admixture cannot be substantiated.

One or two instances, out of very many, may be cited here. A Jewish merchant of Calatayud, Noah Chinillo, who was converted in consequence of the preaching of Vincent Ferrer and assumed the name of Santángel,

counted among his descendants before the close of the
century a Bishop, many prominent politicians and magistrates, and that Luis de Santángel who was Secretary to
the Household and more responsible than any other man
for the fact that Christopher Columbus at last received the
royal patronage. The De La Caballeria family contributed, besides a few prominent clerics, the Vice-Chancellor of the Kingdom of Aragon, the Comptroller General
of the royal household, a Treasurer of the Kingdom of
Navarre, an Admiral, a Vice-Principal of the University
of Saragossa, and (most typical of all) a prominent anti-
Semitic writer. Don Juan Pacheco, Marquis of Villena
and Grand Master of the Order of Santiago (who was
virtually king-maker in Castile in the middle of the
fifteenth century, and at one time aspired to the hand of
the Infanta Isabella, subsequently Queen of Spain),
was a descendant on both sides of the former Jew, Ruy
Capon. His brother, Don Pedro Giron, was Grand Master
of the Order of Calatrava: while the Archbishop of Toledo
was his uncle. Seven at least of the principal prelates
of the kingdom were of Jewish extraction, as well as the
Treasurer. In intellectual life, conditions were similar.
The revival of vernacular literature at the court of Juan II.
of Aragon was due in considerable measure to the genius
of persons of Jewish blood, while the Castilian poets who
flourished at the same period made a practice of taunting
one another in their pasquinades on their Ghetto origin.
It is hardly an exaggeration to say that before much more
than a generation had elapsed, the *conversos* had en-
riched—or, as others alleged, dominated—the intellectual
life of Spain in every branch.

The people looked on, uncomprehending. In the
Marranos, they could see only hypocritical Jews, who had
lost none of their unpopular characteristics, pushing their

way into the highest positions in the state. Their natural ability and acumen had attracted them in large numbers to the financial administration, from which, as Jews, they had previously been nominally excluded. Throughout the country, they farmed the taxes, thus becoming identified in the popular mind with the royal oppression, of which they were in fact the principal victims. A hidalgo of ancient lineage could not restrain his jealousy when he saw the scion of a family still known in the *judería* forcing himself into high office at Court, snapping up all the best matrimonial alliances for his daughters and procuring high advancement in the Church for his sons. This jealousy was accentuated by an angry realisation of the religious infidelity of these questionable neophytes, or a high proportion of them. A typical satire of the period was directed by a penurious poet against a wealthy Marrano, Alfonso Fernandez (formerly known as Samuel), who had been so unwise as to refuse him alms. The other revenged himself by circulating a fictitious will, in which Fernandez was represented as leaving one penny to Holy Church and a hundred ducats to poor Jews, to enable them to rest on the Sabbath. He bequeaths his shirt to a synagogue-beadle at Salamanca, to recite prayers for the repose of his soul. He orders a crucifix to be placed at his feet in the coffin, a copy of the Koran on his breast, and a scroll of the Law of Moses at his head!

This witty effusion typifies the manner in which the *conversos* were generally regarded. Their problem was in fact almost identical with that of the Jews before 1391, accentuated however by a blind resentment of the Marrano hypocrisy and of the golden opportunities which it had furnished. It was in vain that men pointed to New Christians of unquestionable sincerity, or even bigotry—men like the saintly Hernando de Talavera, later Archbishop of Granada and Confessor to Isabella of Castile, or even Juan de Torquemada, Cardinal of San Sisto, the learned uncle of Spain's most fanatical son. Doubts were expressed even concerning religious leaders of this eminence. The problem of the New Christians claimed more and more attention from the leaders of the Spanish Church. General Councils advised measures to check the blasphemous duplicity of these recent adherents to the Catholic faith. All the pulpits in the Peninsula resounded anew to impassioned sermons, calling attention to their misconduct and urging that steps should be taken to check them. Occasionally, there were outbursts of violence, culminating in waves of massacre in 1468 and again in 1473, when Toledo was set in flames and the corpses were piled high in the tortuous streets of Segovia.

Had the Marranos been insincere but not successful, it is doubtful whether the problem would have become so acute. Had they been successful but not insincere, on the other hand, the jealousy and the consequent difficulties would have been much the same. It was thus a social even more than a religious problem: and there is a recent analogy which shews in a striking fashion how far this was the case.

To the incredibly rapid process which we have been examining, of the sudden advance and expansion of the New Christians in Spain, there is only one parallel in history—that which took place in central Europe, and particularly in Germany, four centuries later. Here, too, the Jews had been established from time immemorial, and were as much acclimatised to the environment as it is possible for men to be. Here, too, religious intolerance, translated by the State into law, had long kept them under, forcing them to restrict to the Ghetto what was meant for mankind. Here, too, generation after generation, the

Jews had been compelled to turn keen intellects to petty commercial problems, had sharpened their wits on abstruse Rabbinic studies, had pent up their energies and their abilities until they attained an almost overwhelming force. The release came, in this instance, with the Liberal Revolution of the nineteenth century, which was accompanied by a weakening of traditional values, an undermining of religious forces, and a discarding of ancient forms. Thus, in Germany too, the reservoir was broken, and the accumulated forces rushed forth with irresistible power.

The same phenomenon happened as in fifteenth-century Spain. Those who had been artificially depressed for so long found their true level. They flocked into the professions, from which they had thus far been excluded. They diverted their intellectual powers from the seemingly barren Talmudic exercises to the study of science, medicine, law. They brought a fresh spirit into literature and other arts. They prospered in business. They intermarried with the nobility. That in the process they largely lost their Jewish allegiance, that they were as Teutonic as any of their neighbours in background and in environment, that their ancestors had been living on the Rhineland long before the Germanic tribes finally established themselves there—none of these considerations counted with their neighbours, any more than did the obvious fact that the original artificial impetus decreased progressively from generation to generation. They could see only that a group, sociologically distinct, and traditionally unpopular, had attained a position of disproportionate prominence in the national life: and they resented it with every jealous fibre of their being.

The reactions, in the fifteenth century and in the twentieth, were much the same. In the one instance, the

day of open religious intolerance having passed, the
jealousy was based upon a new theory of race, and was
dignified by the name of Anti-Semitism: in the other, it
was justified by ostensibly religious motives, and made
use of the old instrument (now to be given a new and
more terrible lease of life) which was called the Inquisition.

CHAPTER II

TORQUEMADA

THE Inquisition may be defined as an institution brought into being by the Church for the purpose of dealing with heresy in all its forms. The conception that dissent should be punished by force was indeed almost as old as Christianity itself. As early as the year 385, the pious Emperor Maximus had tortured and executed the heretic Priscillian and some of his followers. At the time, this procedure had aroused a certain degree of criticism: but civilisation was progressing, and in the following century the laws of Theodosius II. (to be followed, a hundred years later, by those of Justinian, "the first Christian Inquisitor") applied the death-penalty, in the last resort, against certain categories of heretics. In the "Dark" Ages, the idea seems to have fallen into desuetude, and ecclesiastics of undoubted learning and sanctity were uncertain as to the proper penalty to be imposed in such cases. Occasionally, to be sure, bigoted rulers or hysterical mobs took the law into their own hands. It was not, however, until the mediæval renaissance was at its height, and Christian Europe had arrived at what it considered to be the state nearest perfection attainable on this earth, that the old conception was finally revived and elaborated.

The history of mediæval heresy followed lines which are only too familiar to the student of modern racial or religious persecution. The first step was the working up, by those who had the power to mould public opinion, of popular hatred of non-conformists; then followed riots and massacres of heretics at the hands of the infuriated

35

populace; and, finally, special tribunals and legislation had to be introduced ostensibly in order to preserve law and order. This was the sequence of events in the thirteenth century, when the unity of the Church was seriously threatened by the development of the Albigensian movement, which was particularly strong in the south of France, but had begun to spread into adjacent districts. The heresy was apparently stamped out by the so-called Albigensian Crusades from 1209 to 1244, but no sooner had these wars ended in victory for the orthodox party than a fresh problem presented itself. It was discovered that the detested heresy had not been eradicated, but only driven underground; and the idea was conceived that in order to detect and convict heretics it was necessary to employ persons specially qualified for the purpose.

It is true that the Church was not altogether without the means of suppressing heresy. Spiritual courts were attached to every see, and heresy naturally came within their cognisance. Sometimes, also, the bishops would institute what was termed a General Inquisition, when itinerant ecclesiastics would make an "enquiry" (for that is the real meaning of the term) into moral and spiritual affairs in a given district. What was lacking, however, was a body of men able and willing to make use of the existing machinery. Though the Inquisitorial functions of detecting and punishing heresy were vested by virtue of their office in the bishops (a power they always retained), they rarely exercised it, for they were occupied with a mass of other business. For this reason, in the course of the thirteenth century, the Papacy gradually built up the organisation known as the Inquisition—at present termed the "Mediæval" or "Papal," to distinguish it from the Spanish Inquisition which was to attain such gruesome notoriety later on. The same period witnessed the rapid increase of secular legislation against heresy, and it was at this time that death by burning became in most countries the recognised doom of the impenitent heretic. The Dominican Order, which had been founded early in the century as a preaching Order whose activities were directed against heresy, was early associated with the institution: and though it was never formally confided to this, many of the most influential Inquisitors, both now and later, were members of this body.

The Papal Inquisition, which never officially superseded the Episcopal Inquisition, proved infinitely more efficient than the latter. By the end of the thirteenth century, it had developed a system of great thoroughness, with a hierarchy of officials and detailed records, and its arm was notoriously long, so that the very name already struck terror into every wavering heart. It had attained complete independence, and had the support of secular authority, by which its introduction had generally been welcomed; it possessed its own prisons; and it wrapped all its affairs in inviolable secrecy. The use of torture, though long opposed by the Church, was officially authorised by a Papal Bull of 1252. The Inquisitor was maintained by the confiscation of the property of the victim— a particularly forceful argument, in most cases, against acquittal. When a person was arrested, his property was immediately sequestered. The prisoner was not allowed the use of counsel for his defence, and the names of witnesses were concealed from him. We have here all the features which were later to distinguish the Spanish Inquisition, though that institution developed them to a high pitch of ingenuity and perfection.

So, too, with the punishments. The Inquisition nominally dealt, not with acts, but with spiritual affairs, and its titular object was the salvation of souls, which it hoped to bring about by the imposition of penances sufficient to wash away sin. Sentence was passed, not by the Inquisitors alone, but by a larger body containing a number of experts on theological and doctrinal points, including some delegate of the bishop to whose see the accused belonged. Impenitent heretics were generally burned. Relapse, which was frequent in the thirteenth century, was indeed generally punished by imprisonment, but absolute refusal to submit to penance was bound to lead to the stake. The Inquisition did not itself carry out the death penalty, for it was a spiritual body, but handed the victim over to the secular authorities. The public reading and execution of the sentence was an early institution, and soon became a popular spectacle, like anything else which involves the loss of life.

But, though it was powerful and efficient, there were certain weaknesses in the mediæval Inquisition, which led to its decay in the fifteenth century. Above all, it did not cover the whole of the Christian world; Germany was largely free from its interference, and England wholly so. (This country, true to its conservative instincts, preferred to burn its heretics by Act of Parliament, backed up by the Common Law precedent of the thirteenth-century deacon who was converted to Judaism for love of a Jewess and was brought to the stake without further ado.) The only central authority which the mediæval Inquisition acknowledged was that of the Pope, who was generally too deeply absorbed in other affairs to be able to devote much time to it. Thus its influence varied in different countries, and notwithstanding its nominal independence it came to rely very largely on the support of the State. When that was withheld, or became lukewarm, the power of the Inquisition automatically declined.

This is what had occurred in Spain, in parts of which the secular authorities had at one time been particularly zealous in promoting legislation against heresy. It is a remarkable illustration of the persistence of certain national traits, generation after generation, that the first mediæval ruler who is definitely known to have prescribed the stake as a penalty for heretics was Pedro II., King of Aragon, who did so as long back as 1197. In the early part of the thirteenth century, the decrees of his successor Jayme I. had been particularly noteworthy for their severity. It was in the latter's reign that the mediæval Aragonese Inquisition is said to have been founded. Nevertheless, it did not become active until the fourteenth century, when its principal victims were the so-called *Fraticelli* (schismatic Franciscan friars who, in spite of the Pope, persisted in clinging to what they considered the pristine simplicity of the Order, and in finding support for their attitude in Scripture) and converts from Judaism or Islam who showed themselves weak in faith. In Castile, Leon, and Portugal, the Inquisition was potential rather than actual. In the last-named country, various Inquisitors had been appointed from time to time on special occasions during the fourteenth century, but the practice and the idea were allowed to lapse in the fifteenth: in Castile, the Provincial of the Dominican Order was authorised in 1402 by Pope Boniface IX. to appoint or remove Inquisitors, but in actual fact the Inquisition had never functioned, and may be said never to have existed, in that kingdom.

Nevertheless, the model was known, and the idea was constantly before men's minds. With the advance of the fifteenth century, accordingly, clerical zealots and political failures began to agitate for the introduction of this system into Castile in order to cope with what they considered the

problem of the crypto-Jews, the bugbear of the former
and rivals of the latter. The uses of the tribunal as a
pawn in politics were moreover obvious. When, during
the reign of Juan II., the unpopular minister Alvaro de
Luna found himself opposed by a couple of bishops who
happened to be of Jewish extraction, he had obtained
from Pope Nicolas a delegation of Inquisitorial powers to
certain high ecclesiastical dignitaries, who were em-
powered specifically to proceed even against the episcopate. This was an ominous indication of the manner in
which de Luna intended to use the new weapon. For
various reasons, however (of which the most important
was his overthrow and decapitation in 1453), this licence
was never acted upon.

During the reign of Juan's successor, Henry IV. (un-
charitably known as the Impotent), the agitation assumed
a more menacing form. Under the influence of Fray
Alonso de Spina, the most learned anti-Semite of the fifteenth century, the Franciscans began to sue for the
introduction of a special tribunal to cope with the problem,
which they alleged was growing more serious from day
to day. But ecclesiastical rivalries can generally be relied
upon to make themselves manifest: and the Geronimite
Order, under the influence of their saintly General Fray
Alonso de Oropesa (who was of course immediately
alleged to be of Jewish birth), mounted the pulpit in the
defence of the *conversos*, maintaining that such drastic
steps were unnecessary. The other side was momentarily
silenced. But the feeling of bitterness continued in all
classes. Henry IV. was largely supported by the New
Christian elements; and the nobility who had taken up
arms against him revived the agitation. In the Con-
cordat of Medina del Campo, which he concluded with
the insurgents in 1464, the King was constrained to

enjoin the bishops throughout the land to establish a searching enquiry into the conduct of the *conversos,* and to punish rigorously any who might be found guilty of backsliding into the faith of their fathers. In consequence of this, a few victims were tracked down and punished in Toledo and elsewhere, though, to the disappointment of the nobility, they did not include any of the more prominent political figures, against whom their resentment was really directed.

Isabella the Catholic, Henry's half-sister, came to the throne in 1465, amid a maze of civil war. Although for some time after her accession her attention was absorbed by more pressing problems, she was surrounded by ecclesiastics and notables who were constantly dinning into her ears the necessity for taking action against the *conversos,* whether on political or on spiritual grounds. Chief among them was a gaunt, sunken-eyed Dominican friar named Thomás de Torquemada, born at Valladolid in 1420, and now at the height of his extraordinary powers. He had been the Queen's confessor when she was still Infanta, and was bitterly opposed to the Jews in spite (or because) of the fact that he was himself said to be of partly Jewish extraction. It was reported, in fact, that long ago he had made Isabella take a vow that, should she reach the throne (a most unlikely contingency, it had then appeared) she would devote herself heart and soul to the extirpation of heresy and the persecution of the Jews. Even he was outdone in virulence by Fray Alonso de Hojeda, Prior of the Dominican Convent of S. Pablo in Seville, who lost no opportunity of urging extreme and if necessary violent measures against the enemies of the Faith. The ruling Pope, Sixtus IV., was less eager, but hopefully invested his legate to Castile with full Inquisitorial authority.

But the time was not yet ripe. Isabella, however pious, was politic: and she was completely under the influence of her husband, Ferdinand of Aragon, who enjoys the distinction of being one of the wiliest and most selfish rulers of all time. The sovereigns would not permit any outside interference in the affairs of their precariously united kingdom, and the attempt ended in failure. Nevertheless, an enquiry was instituted in Seville, and revealed the fact that heresy was widespread throughout Andalusia, and indeed the whole of Castile.

The civil war came to an end in 1477, leaving Isabella a queen and her rival a nun. With the restoration of peace, the former came to Seville, where she remained for over a year, dealing out heavy-handed justice, and seldom appearing more than once in the same attire. The sight of the *conversos* who thronged the court, occupying many of the highest posts, stimulated Fray Alonso to fresh efforts. Still Isabella hesitated, until a chance episode strengthened the fanatics' hands.

On the night of Wednesday, March 18th, 1478, a young cavalier penetrated into the *judería* for the purpose (or in the hope) of carrying on an intrigue with a young Jewess who had captivated his fancy. Gaining admission into the house by stealth, he surprised a number of Jews and *conversos* who had come together for some mysterious celebration. That night was the eve of the Jewish Passover, and it is pretty clear that they had assembled in order to celebrate the traditional *Seder* service. By an unfortunate but by no means uncommon coincidence, it happened to be Holy Week. The accidental conjunction conveyed its own story: and the report immediately spread like wild-fire throughout the city, that these miscreants had gathered in order to blaspheme the Christian religion and its founder, at the season of his Passion.

When the news reached the ears of the Prior of S. Pablo, he saw his opportunity and, hastening to Court, laid the evidence before the scandalised young Queen. This, it is said, finally decided her to take action. The Spanish Ambassadors to the Holy See were immediately instructed to obtain a Bull authorising the establishment of an Inquisition. Pope Sixtus hesitated—prompted not so much by humanity as by the desire to keep the body under his own control. But he could not very well maintain his opposition: and at last, in the following November, a Bull was issued noting with horror the existence of many false Christians in Spain and empowering the Spanish sovereigns to appoint three bishops or other suitable persons learned in theology or the common law, being priests and above the age of forty, whom they might remove or replace at will, to have complete jurisdiction over heresy within the kingdom of Castile. In these seemingly innocuous terms, the Spanish Inquisition was founded.

The victims enjoyed a respite of nearly two years before the tribunal was actually inaugurated. It was only on September 17th, 1480, that commissions were issued to Miguel de Morillo, Master of Theology, and Juan de San Martin, Bachelor of Theology, both friars of the Dominican Order, with instructions to begin their activities forthwith. (They were subsequently assigned the assistance of a Promotor Fiscal, or Prosecutor, and two receivers of confiscations.) On Christmas Day, they arrived in Seville. A solemn procession was arranged for the following Sunday, so as to inaugurate their activities with that pomp which has always constituted an integral part of Catholic zeal.

Seville was one of the principal New Christian centres, but no disturbances had taken place there in recent years. The Marranos, who had long played a prominent part in every facet of local life, determined to resist with all their might, and were confident that they would receive the whole-hearted support of their fellow-citizens. The lead was taken by Diego de Susan, an immensely wealthy merchant, whose fortune was reckoned at ten millions of maravedis—one of the eight persons who had been chosen two years before to support the canopy on the occasion of the baptism of the infant Juan. With him were associated numerous other influential merchants, including several members of the Town Council.

The conspirators held a meeting late one night in S. Salvador—the parish church of that part of the city most favoured by the Marranos, many of whom served on its governing body. An account of the proceedings is preserved in a contemporary record. One of the ringleaders (presumably Diego de Susan himself) delivered an impassioned harangue. "How can they come against us?" he cried. "We are the principal persons of the city, and well liked by the people. Let us assemble our men. If they come to take us, we will set the city in a tumult—we, and our followers, and our associates."

As his voice died away, a voice was heard out of the shadows, the speaker being an old man, more cautious in his outlook, who had been invited to attend. "By my life! To assemble men and to be prepared seems good to me. But the hearts, where are they? Find me the hearts!"

Thus the incipient Inquisition, hardly as yet established, terrorised its victims by the mere mention of its name. In spite of this warning, the conspirators persisted. Each man present promised men, arms, or money: and Pedro Fernandez Benedeva, major-domo of the church and father of one of its clergy, brought sufficient weapons together in his house to arm one hundred men.

At the last moment, the secret was betrayed. Diego de Susan had a daughter, nicknamed "*La Susanna*," whose surpassing beauty had caused her to be known throughout Seville as *La Hermosa Hembre* ("The beautiful woman"). She was carrying on an intrigue with a Christian *caballero* of unimpeachable lineage, to whom she disclosed the secret in a moment of sentimental weakness. As in duty bound, he informed the Inquisitors. Nothing could have served their purpose better, as all the principal citizens of Seville were placed in their power at a single stroke. A series of arrests was carried out, those apprehended including several magistrates and other civic dignitaries. They were hurriedly tried and condemned to death. The outcome was seen on February 6th, 1481, when the first Act of Faith (as it was termed) took place in Seville, six men and women being burned alive. The customary sermon before the last ghastly scene was preached by Alonso de Hojeda, thus privileged to preside over the triumphant outcome of the agitation which had engrossed his heart and mind for so many years. The spectacle was repeated not long after. Hojeda, however, was not present this time: for the pestilence which was to carry off fifteen thousand of the people of Seville had just begun, and he had been one of the earliest victims.

Diego de Susan himself was one of the three persons who suffered the extreme penalty on the second occasion. He went to the stake calm and unperturbed as usual. The halter round his neck was trailing uncomfortably in the mud, and he had to solicit the help of one of the crowd of bystanders. "Be so good as to lift up the end of my African scarf," he requested, urbanely.

A *quemadero*, or Place of Burning, had been constructed for the purpose just outside the city walls, in the Campo de Tablada. At the four corners, huge plaster figures of the four major prophets had been set up, as it were to preside over the sufferings of those among their descendants who dared to remain faithful to their teachings according to their own lights. The cost of this tactful embellishment was defrayed by a local dignitary named Meza, whose zeal won for him the highly lucrative position of Receiver to the Holy Office, to administer the confiscated property. He did not live long to enjoy his emoluments, however, for he too was subsequently discovered to be a Judaiser, and was burned on the pyre which he had helped to adorn.

"*La Susanna*," left destitute on her father's death, was befriended by Rainoldo Romero, titular Bishop of Tiberias, who placed her in a convent. As was only to be imagined, a cloistered life proved completely unsuited to her, and she to it, and she took the first opportunity to escape. She adopted what is technically known as a life of shame, drifting from one lover to another until she, who had been notorious in all Seville for her loveliness, found a last refuge in the arms of a grocer. In the end, she died in want. With her last breath, she gave instructions that her skull should be placed as a warning over the door of the house which had been the scene of her disorderly life, in what was subsequently known as the *Calle de la Muerte* ("Street of Death"). Here it remained for centuries, and it was said that in the middle of the night strange cries of grief and remorse were sometimes heard to issue from the fleshless, grinning jaws. In the course of structural alterations in the middle of the last century, the house was swept away. But the name of " *La Hermosa Hembre* " is still perpetuated hard by, in the Calle Susona; and the romantic Sevillans still imagine that in the Barrio de Santa Cruz, haunted as it is by the shade of Pedro the Cruel seeking for amorous adventure, the voice of the loveliest of Andalusian women may still sometimes be heard uttering shrieks of anguish for her share in the Great Betrayal.

Immediately news had spread of the approaching establishment of the Inquisition, many Marranos had fled from Seville and the immediate neighbourhood into the surrounding territory, in the hope of finding refuge under the protection of the local magnates. Peremptory demands were addressed forthwith to the latter, however great their rank or influence, ordering them to surrender the fugitives. Such was the terror which the new tribunal had already excited that, in most cases, these demands were immediately obeyed. From the Marquisate of Cadiz alone, for example, some eight thousand persons were sent back: and the Marquis was notoriously one of the most refractory of all Castilian noblemen. To such an extent did the number of prospective victims increase, that the Inquisitors removed their headquarters from the Dominican Convent of S. Pablo in the centre of the town (where they had established themselves in the first place at Hojeda's invitation) to the great Castle of Triana, just outside the city walls. The accommodation here should have sufficed for any purpose: but, before long, the dungeons were filled to overflowing with suspects.

During the Plague, even those *conversos* who were of the most blameless reputation were forbidden to leave the city except if they abandoned all their property, so as to prevent any possibility of evasion. The Inquisitors themselves took up their residence during this period at

Aracena, where they found plenty to engage their attention until the pestilence showed signs of diminishing, when they returned to Seville. *Autos* continued without intermission; it seldom happened that a month elapsed in which none was held. Even the dead were not spared, their bones being exhumed and burnt after a mock trial. (This, of course, was no meaningless formality, since condemnation automatically led to confiscation.) By November 4th, 298 persons had been burned, while 98 had been condemned to perpetual imprisonment. Vast numbers of others had come forward spontaneously to confess their guilt on the understanding that they would be dealt with mercifully: but even they were made to parade as penitents. At one of these solemnities, no less than fifteen hundred men and women were exhibited. There were still some among the *conversos* who believed that they might be able to find superior authority willing to protect them. They appealed to the Pope, who, in January, 1482, wrote expressing his disapproval of the excessive severity of the methods employed; but this communication had no effect upon the independent rulers of Spain.

From the beginning the Spanish Inquisition elaborated certain rules of procedure which were followed throughout its existence. A list was drawn up and published of the signs (many of them grotesque) by which a Judaizer could be recognised; from washing the hands before prayer to changing linen on the Sabbath, and from calling children by Old Testament names to turning the face to the wall at the moment of death. Wholesale denunciations were encouraged by the policy of promising a free pardon in return for full confession within a stipulated time, and placed thousands in the power of the dreaded Tribunal. Even the Jews themselves were called upon to help in the work, their rabbis being compelled to enjoin their congregations, under pain of excommunication, to reveal everything in their knowledge concerning Judaizers. The extraordinary delicacy of conscience, which was shown in some instances, is illustrated by an incident which has recently come to light. A certain Rabbi of Saragossa under menace of death had to enjoin his co-religionists publicly to obey the Inquisitors and to tell them all they knew against any Marranos who followed their ancestral practices, under automatic penalty of excommunication. One of the congregation came to him privately and implored exemption from this, since if he told all he knew about Alfonso de la Caballeria, the whole community would be placed in jeopardy. The Rabbi complied; but after the edict of expulsion of 1492 he considered it his duty to go to the authorities and inform them of the episode, since the plea of danger no longer applied! Some persons adopted a very different attitude. Judah ibn Verga, the scholarly head of the community of Seville, who had encouraged many Marranos to revert to their ancestral rites, anticipated arrest by a timely flight to Lisbon. This did not save him, however, for the long arm of the Inquisition ultimately seized him, and he died in prison as a result of the tortures which he underwent.

The volume of work grew apace, meanwhile, and it soon became evident that additional tribunals were necessary. By a papal brief of February 11th, 1482, seven other Inquisitors were nominated, among them Thomás de Torquemada, the Queen's confessor, who had hitherto been content with being the power behind the scene. Other appointments followed at frequent intervals, and further tribunals were set up at Córdova, Jaen, Ciudad Real, and possibly also at Segovia. One of the earliest victims at the first-named city was the lovely mistress of the Treasurer of the Cathedral, who was himself burned in the following year. The tribunal of Ciudad Real was intended for the province of Toledo. Four persons only figured in its first *auto*, which was held on February 6th, 1484; but at the second, which followed on the 23rd and 24th of the same month, thirty men and women were burnt alive, as well as the bones or effigies of forty more who had anticipated proceedings by death or flight. In the two years of its existence, this Tribunal burnt fifty-two heretics and condemned 220 fugitives, as well as sentencing 183 persons to perform public penance.

In 1485, the seat of the Tribunal was transferred to Toledo. The *conversos* of this city, who were both wealthy and numerous, followed the example of those of Seville, and formed a plot to prevent the Holy Office from entering upon its functions. They planned to raise a tumult while the procession of Corpus Christi was going through the streets on June 2nd, with the intention of despatching the Inquisitors during the disorder. Subsequently they proposed to seize the city gates and the tower of the Cathedral, and hold the town even against the crown if it should be necessary. But, as at Seville, they proved singularly incapable of reaping any benefit from their wealth and influence, and the plot was betrayed. If it had any effect, it was only to make the proceedings more determined.

Seven hundred and fifty persons figured in the first *auto*, which was held on February 12th, 1486. Carrying unlighted tapers and surrounded by a howling mob, which had streamed in from the countryside for miles around to enjoy the spectacle, they were compelled to march bareheaded and barefoot through the city to the door of the Cathedral, where they were marked on the forehead with the symbol of the Christian faith, with the words: "Receive the sign of the Cross which ye have denied and lost." They were fined one-fifth of their property, the proceeds being assigned towards the cost of the war against the Moors; they were subjected to a perpetual incapacity to hold honourable office or to wear any but the coarsest clothes; and they were required to go in procession on six successive Fridays, flagellating themselves with hempen cords. In addition, it was decreed (a deadly corollary) that any disobedience to these injunctions would be treated and punished as a relapse into heresy. Nine hundred penitents appeared at the second *auto* and a further 750 at the third. Before the year had elapsed, the total of those thus treated with relative humanity had approached five thousand. In addition, large numbers were burned—as many as fifty persons sometimes in one day. Among the victims were several friars and ecclesiastical dignitaries, who had hitherto enjoyed a reputation of unblemished sanctity. At this interval of time, it is impossible to tell whether they were martyrs to a concealed faith, or victims of personal or (as seems most likely) racial spite.

To perfect the organisation, Thomás de Torquemada was placed at the head of a supreme council established in order to co-ordinate the work of the local tribunals of Castile and of Leon. The Papal brief making this appointment has never been found, but it must have been before October 17th, 1483, when his authority was extended also over the kingdom of Aragon, with Catalonia and Valencia. This, it may be said, was the first institution of united Spain. Thus the Spanish Inquisition was unified under one central control, and its head had the unenviable distinction of becoming the first Grand Inquisitor.

How he acquitted himself is notorious. Under his direction, the Inquisition rapidly took shape, and extended its activity throughout the country. It was owing to his personal zeal, it is said, that verdicts of acquittal were so infrequent in these early days. It is not altogether a compliment, perhaps, that in 1496 the infamous Borgia, Pope Alexander VI., wrote assuring him that he cherished him " in the very bowels of affection " for his immense labours in the exaltation of the Faith.

Torquemada was himself an ascetic. None the less, in order to maintain the dignity of his office, he resided in palaces, and surrounded himself with a princely retinue. He maintained a bodyguard of fifty mounted Familiars and two hundred infantry: his subordinates were allowed ten horsemen and fifty archers apiece. Where this train of death appeared, city gates were flung open, the resources of flourishing districts were placed at their disposal, and magistrates swore fealty. He accumulated vast wealth, but lived in perpetual fear of assassination. So mighty did he become that the Roman *curia* itself took alarm, and there were frequent quarrels between him and the Papal nominees. But the victory rested invariably, or nearly so, in the hands of the sunken-eyed ascetic.

The acme of Torquemada's activities in Castile was reached when he took proceedings against two prelates, of high character and great learning, who happened to be of Jewish descent. One was Pedro de Aranda, Bishop of Calahorra and President of the Council of Castile; the other was the venerable Juan Arias Dávila, Bishop of Segovia, who had given proof of his zeal for the faith by the ferocity with which he had persecuted the Jews of his diocese, this being the only indication of Jewish interest which he showed. One of the charges brought against him was the improbable one that, on the introduction of the Holy Office into his diocese, he had the remains of his forebears exhumed, in order to destroy proof of the fact that they had been interred in accordance with Jewish rites. Both these ecclesiastics were sent to Rome for trial. Dávila had the good fortune to pass away before sentence was promulgated; Aranda was deposed and degraded from Holy Orders, dying a prisoner in the Castle of S. Angelo. It is obvious that in both cases the accusations were based on nothing but spite or prejudice.

In the Kingdom of Aragon, notwithstanding the fact that the Papal Inquisition was already an established institution, there was great resistance to the introduction of tribunals on the Castilian model. At last, after violent debates, the Cortes assembled at Tarazona gave its assent on April 14th, 1484. Activities began almost immediately, tribunals being set up in Valencia and Saragossa in the course of the same year. The *conversos* of Aragon, however, were wealthy, influential, and well organised, and determined not to give way without resistance. Shortly after the first *auto* had taken place at Saragossa, on May 10th, 1484, the Inquisitor Gaspar Juglar was found dead. It was confidently asserted that he had been poisoned; but so unostentatious a method of expressing their opposition does not seem in accordance with the militant spirit of the *conversos*, and the evidence is far from convincing.

The moving spirit of the Tribunal was Pedro Arbués, Canon of the Cathedral of Saragossa, and on him the attention of the *conversos* was now concentrated. The conspiracy formed against him involved several of the most prominent persons in Aragon, including some whose sympathy with Judaism can have been at the best very feeble, but who realised the danger which the Inquisition threatened to all those of Jewish blood, especially if they were possessed of any wealth. They included Sancho de Paternoy, the Master of the Royal Household; Gabriel

Sánches, the High Treasurer of the kingdom; and Francisco de Santa Fé, assessor to the Governor of Aragon and son of the notorious conversionist, Gerónimo de Santa Fé. This talented band of conspirators raised a fund for action and engaged a couple of bravos to assist in carrying out the desperate deed. On the night of September 15th, 1485, while Arbués was kneeling in prayer in the Cathedral, between the choir and the High Altar, he was attacked. Notwithstanding the armour which he wore in anticipation of some such attempt, he was mortally wounded, and died two days later. He was of course revered as a martyr. Miracles were said to be effected by his relics: a splendid tomb was erected over his remains: and he was formally canonised by the Holy See in 1867.

When the news of the assassination became known in the city, excited crowds gathered together, swearing violent revenge. It was with the utmost difficulty that the Archbishop averted a murderous attack on the Jews and *conversos*. The latter, clumsy conspirators, had apparently planned no further step after the crime, and were unable to protect themselves from the bloody vengeance exacted by the Inquisition. Hundreds of persons were arrested and thrown into the dungeons of the Aljafería, the old Moorish fortress, while the Holy Office procrastinated over their fate—as many as forty persons, sometimes, in a single cell devoid of the most elementary amenities. The actual assassins were put to death with a refinement of cruelty, while their accomplices figured in a succession of public Acts of Faith. The total number of persons who suffered the capital penalty has been reckoned at as many as two hundred, though the figure is possibly exaggerated. Luís de Santángel, the Secretary of the Household, escaped, thanks to his influence at

Court; but his cousin and namesake, who had been one of the principal conspirators, was beheaded in the market-place, his head being set on a pole and his body burned; he had stood high in the royal favour, having been knighted by the last king for outstanding services in battle. Sancho de Paternoy, after long and excruciating torture, was condemned to perpetual imprisonment, though in the end he was able to purchase his release and was reinstated in office. Francisco de Santa Fé antici-pated his sentence by suicide. Numerous others fled to France, and were burned in effigy—a theatrical formality which, as has been seen, automatically permitted the con-fiscation of their property. Alfonso de la Caballeria, Vice-Chancellor of the Kingdom, appealed to Rome, and had his orthodoxy confirmed, but even he was unable to prevent the exhumation and burning of his grandmother's bones, or the appearance of his wife as a penitent in an *auto de fé*. Thus, when his son subsequently married King Ferdinand's granddaughter, the blood of the royal house of Aragon mingled with that of condemned heretics.

A large number of the *conversos* were now practically in the hands of the Tribunal of Saragossa, to condemn whensoever it pleased the Inquisitors. The names of the great families of Santángel and Sanchez appear with monotonous regularity in its records. Even the court his-torian, Micer Gonzalo de Santa Maria, fell into its clutches, and died in prison after three trials. Within fifteen years, over fifty *autos* had been held in the city, and there were few New Christian families who did not have to deplore some victims. In 1488, in spite of the general opposi-tion, activities began in Barcelona, where the tribunal for Catalonia had been set up at the close of the previous year; and among the earliest sufferers was another mem-ber of the family of Gerónimo de Santa Fé. In the following year, a tribunal for the Balearic Islands was set up in Majorca, where, in spite of the smallness of the population, a degree of suffering was inflicted which perhaps was equalled nowhere else in the whole land. Flight to foreign countries—particularly to the southern provinces of France—began to assume panic proportions. It was at this time for example that the ancestors of Michel de Montaigne's mother, one of whose family had been burned at Saragossa, emigrated to Bordeaux. The machinery of the Vatican was now set in motion, and Pope Innocent VIII. ordered all foreign potentates in whose countries fugitives had settled to hand them over forthwith to the Holy Office: and the Spanish sovereigns were prepared to enforce this (so far as small and inoffensive states were concerned) by force of arms.

Meanwhile, the labours for the faith were continuing in another direction. In 1492, Granada, the last relic of the Caliphate of the West, fell before the victorious armies of Christian Spain. The work of reconquest was thus at last completed, after seven centuries of battle and intrigue. The religious zeal which expressed the genius of the Spanish people (though sometimes, by a natural psychological phenomenon, converted into its opposite) was now at its zenith. In the flush of victory, there seemed to be no reason why the lesser alien element constituted by the professing Jews should any longer be tolerated. For the recent developments had not affected the latter to any great extent. It is true that they were only a miserable remnant of the flourishing communities of a century before, decimated by massacre and conversion and broken down by anti-Jewish legislation. So long as they did not meddle in matters of faith, however, the Inquisition was powerless against them; for they were not heretics within the Church, but infidels outside it, over whom no clerical

tribunal had jurisdiction. The position, logically considered, was preposterous. A Marrano, forced into baptism with a dagger at his throat, and Christian only in
name, would be burned alive for performing in secret
only a single detail of what his unconverted brethren were
doing every day in public with impunity. Moreover, so
long as Jews were present, to teach their kinsmen the
practices of their ancestral religion by precept and by
example, it was hopeless to expect to extirpate the Judaising heresy from the land, as every Churchman hoped and
prayed.

The fifteenth century had its methods for dealing with
such emergencies, no less than the twentieth. There
were indeed no Parliament buildings to burn: but a
trumped-up story of the ceremonial murder at Avila for
ritual purposes of an unnamed child from La Guardia,
by Jews and *conversos* acting in conjunction, was taken
by Torquemada as proof of the complicity between the
two elements. Recent research has established the fact
that the alleged victim never existed outside the frenzied
imagination of a few fanatical clerics, who may or may
not have believed in it themselves. Nevertheless, the
episode, utterly fictitious though its basis was, offered a
fresh weapon against both fractions of the hated minority.
The Inquisition was stimulated to fresh efforts, and within
eight years seventy persons suffered on this single preposterous charge. Simultaneously, there was taken the
last step (with one significant exception, which was to
engage the strength of the country and the energies of the
Holy Office for a century to come) to realise the religious
unity of Spain. On March 30th, 1492, in their council
chamber at the captured Alhambra of Granada, the
Spanish sovereigns signed the decree which drove into
exile two hundred thousand loyal Spaniards, whose

ancestors had lived in the country from time immemorial. Four months later, at the end of July, the last Jew had departed, and the great dream of Torquemada's life had been realised.

The history of the Marranos, thus left in isolation, entered now on a new phase, and with it that of the Holy Office as well. Cut off from all contact with Jewish thought, inevitably becoming less and less attached to the faith of their fathers, they were yet doomed to remain suspect for centuries by a majority which (as has happened again in our own day) was imperceptibly turning from religious to racial persecution. The task of the Inquisition, on the other hand, was simplified. There was now, at last, a clean-cut division between the two elements, the unconverted Jews and the converted. The former had gone into exile; the relatively simple task (as it seemed) remained, of forcing the latter into conformity.

CHAPTER III

INQUISITIONAL NOONTIDE

THOMÁS DE TORQUEMADA died in 1498 in an odour of sanctity, hardly distinguishable in this case from the reek of scorching human flesh. He was succeeded as Grand Inquisitor by the scholarly Diego Deza, the friend and patron of Columbus and one of the outstanding representatives of the Spanish Renaissance. It is symbolical that under his auspices the activities of the Holy Tribunal reached their zenith.

Shortly after the beginning of his period of office, in 1500, an hysterical Marrano woman who claimed to be a prophetess, was arrested at Herrera. She was a typical product of an age of tribulation, and her followers were numbered by the hundred. She and her disciples used to recount to their enraptured adherents how they were taken up to heaven, and there had a vision of those who had been martyred, installed on thrones of gold; and how all would be well with them before long, for the promised Redeemer (not He whom the Catholic Church adored) would speedily come to lead them back to the Promised Land. This provided the Holy Office with a unique opportunity for action, and proceedings were opened at once. On February 22nd, 1501, and the following day, two great *autos* were held at Toledo, at which the prophetess and over one hundred of her followers—principally women—were burned.

The greatest excesses, at this period, were in the diocese of Córdova. Here Diego Rodrigues Lucero (known as "El Tenebroso") was Inquisitor, and distinguished himself even then by the maniacal ferocity with which he

carried out the duties of his office. He seems to have sin-
cerely convinced himself that a conspiracy was on foot
among the Marranos to substitute Judaism for Christianity throughout Spain, and he was driven to hysterical
extremities in his efforts to forestall it. Accusations were
made wholesale, and the severity displayed was hardly
credible. The grounds for prosecution were of the flim-
siest nature, and ruthless employment of torture generally
sufficed to extract from the victims some sort of confession which justified condemnation. No other reason
was necessary for a man to be condemned to the stake
than that he was of Jewish blood. A reign of terror began
throughout Andalusia. The Archdeacon de Castro, one
of the most respected figures in local life, though he was
only in part of Jewish extraction, was sentenced and
made to perform public penance, his enormous fortune
being confiscated: and men began to wonder whether a
man's worldly wealth, as well as his descent, was now
become an incriminating circumstance. The persecution
reached its climax when 107 persons were burned alive
on the charge of having listened (not necessarily with approval) to the addresses of a certain Bachelor of Divinity
named Membreque, who was accused of attempting to
propagate the teachings of Judaism.

Complaints against the blood-intoxicated Inquisitor
now became rife, and in the most unexpected quarters.
He and his acolytes, complained the Captain of Córdova,
"were able to defame the whole kingdom, to destroy a
great part of it without God or Justice, slaying and rob-
bing and violating maids and wives, to the great dis-
honour of the Christian religion. . . ." On their side,
the New Christians applied to Rome, arming their representatives with the customary golden arguments, to induce
the Pope to take a merciful view of their plight and to

curb their oppressor. At length, the excesses became so
notorious that the rulers of Castile, Juana (daughter of
Isabella the Catholic, who had recently died) and her
husband the Archduke Philip, suspended all action
on the part of the Holy Office until they returned from
Flanders and were able to enquire into the matter in
person.

Before any definite steps could be taken in this direction, Philip died suddenly, under circumstances which
gave rise to the usual rumours of poison which, in the
sixteenth century, accompanied all deaths which were
not from recognised and recognisable disease: and his
widow was driven mad by the shock. Lucero seized the
opportunity to avenge himself for the check which he
had received, embarking into fresh extravagances. He
asserted categorically that most of the nobles and *cabal-
leros* of Córdova and of Andalusia as a whole were
Judaisers, and even maintained secret synagogues in their
houses. A batch of reckless accusations followed, no
rank or dignity being spared. The most illustrious of the
victims was the venerable Hernando de Talavera, Archbishop of Granada and formerly confessor to Isabella the
Catholic. He happened (though even this is not quite
certain) to have Jewish blood in his veins. There was
no more saintly figure in the whole of Spain, and no man
was working more zealously to propagate Christianity
amongst the Moslems of Granada. The charge was therefore ridiculous to a degree; but the old man died in consequence of the humiliation to which he was exposed.
The popular outcry now became so great that in 1507
Ferdinand the Catholic, who had at last achieved his
ambition and was ruling over Castile in his mad daughter's name, was compelled to take action. Deza, who
had condoned the outrages, was dismissed, and Cardinal

Ximenes, one of the most influential and learned figures in Spanish ecclesiastical life, was appointed to succeed him.

The latter, who continued to serve as Inquisitor General in Castile from 1507 to 1517, did his best to purge the Holy Office of the abuses which had developed in it, though he did nothing to mitigate its severity or its scope. The inhuman Lucero was of course at once dismissed; and proceedings (which however were ultimately dropped —it seemed the most tactful course after what had been discovered) were instituted against him. Other unsatisfactory Inquisitors were removed from office in subsequent years. But popular opinion was by no means reconciled as yet to the institution, which was more menacing by far to the ordinary Spaniard in actuality than it had appeared in prospect (even during Ximenes' ten-year tenure of office 2,500 persons were given to the flames). The people of Aragon were especially jealous of the encroachments of the new tribunal on their traditional rights, and more than once voiced their apprehensions. In 1512, representatives of Aragon, Catalonia and Valencia held a conference at Monzon, at which they drew up a statement of their grievances. They complained of the unnecessary multiplication of officials of the Holy Tribunal, of its extravagant claims to jurisdiction, of its pretended exemption from local taxation. In consequence, a tripartite agreement was arrived at between the King, the Inquisitor General and the Cortes, restricting the jurisdiction of the Inquisition to cases of actual heresy and to crimes in which heresy was involved, to the exclusion of such matters as bigamy, usury and sorcery.

Notwithstanding the constant discovery of new abuses, Ferdinand the Catholic, true to the "pious cruelty" which Machiavelli considered the outstanding feature of his character, had remained convinced of the enormous importance of the Inquisition as an instrument for consolidating the loosely knit Spanish kingdom and maintaining the central authority of the Crown. By his testament, executed the day before his death in 1516, he enjoined his grandson and successor, Charles V., to labour with all his might to destroy and extirpate heresy, and to appoint God-fearing and conscientious ministers to conduct the Holy Tribunal.

The new king was a boy of seventeen at the time, and entirely in the hands of his Flemish favourites, notoriously not over-favourably inclined to Spanish institutions. Accordingly, even before he arrived to assume the rule of his new dominions, the Council of State anticipated difficulties, and wrote to him that the peace of the realm and the maintenance of the royal authority depended on the maintenance of the Inquisition in its full powers. On the other hand, the deputies of the first Cortes which he held after his arrival, in 1518, at Valladolid, petitioned him on the same subject, complaining of the severity of the Inquisition and demonstrating that the people considered it to be an engine of oppression for the furtherance of private ends, without regard for precedent, law or justice. The *conversos* on their side were not idle, and promised the new King an enormous subsidy if he would restrict the power of the Holy Office, above all by abolishing the system of secret accusations which was its greatest and most dreaded weapon. Meanwhile, similar steps were taken at Rome, where Pope Leo X., faithful to the humanistic tradition of the Medici, prepared a Bull by which the desired concessions were granted.

Charles, however, after momentary vacillation, was ultimately convinced, as his grandfather had been, of the great political utility of the Tribunals. In his case, this conviction was reinforced by that narrow obscurantism which continued to characterise him through life. Not only did he refuse to accede to the request made of him, but he even went so far as to prohibit the publication of the Bull. Similarly, recurrent complaints from the Cortes of Aragon, which maintained that the agreement of 1512 was not being observed and that the Holy Office was departing from all precedent in the rigour of its procedure, were of no avail whatsoever. No more effective were those of the representatives of Castile, who alleged that the severity of operations far surpassed what was needed. The beginnings of the Lutheran movement in Germany were threatening the foundations of the Catholic faith: and, henceforth, the Spanish monarchy identified its interests with those of the Church of Rome. Far from being curbed, the authority of the Inquisition was extended. The Moorish population was soon to come within the scope of its operations, as will be seen later; from the middle of the century, it began to occupy itself more and more with Protestant heretics: its authority over lesser offenders was ultimately unquestioned.

Some slight measure of reform seemed indeed at one period to be in the air. The Cardinal Adrian of Utrecht (who had succeeded Ximenes as Inquisitor General five years before) became Pope in 1522. In his letter of congratulation, Charles went so far as to suggest that he should be careful in his appointments, and make provision to prevent the Inquisition from punishing the innocent, and its officials from thinking more about the property of the condemned than the salvation of their souls. This appeal had no result—mainly, no doubt, because it was not intended to have any. In the subsequent period, various new attempts were made by the New Christians and their fellow-sufferers to bribe Charles to abolish the secret procedure and to pay the Inquisitors fixed salaries, instead of permitting them to recoup themselves by results. All these efforts, however, proved futile, and the work of the Holy Office continued to be shrouded in impenetrable darkness. Once or twice in the subsequent generation, political embroilments or conflicts of jurisdiction caused awkward crises. Nevertheless, broadly speaking, after 1517 there was never any serious threat to the authority of the Inquisition in Spain for nearly three centuries.

A circumstance which added to the power of the Inquisition was the total collapse of local autonomy which followed the deadly class-war between nobles and bourgeoisie in Aragon in 1520-1522, known as the *Germania*, and above all the suppression of the Revolt of the *Comuneros* in Castile in 1521. In the previous year Toledo had set the example, by rising against the royal authority and forming a Government constituted by a " *comunidad* " of deputies from its various parishes—the earliest post-mediæval Commune. The revolt spread throughout Castile, and a loose union of the municipalities was formed under a revolutionary *junta*. Had not the nobility overlooked its jealousy of the Crown (a rare phenomenon) and declared against the rebels, it is highly probable that Spanish absolutism would have collapsed, and the overwhelming power of the Inquisition with it. But history shews that the traditional tendency of a people cannot be crushed or diverted by force of arms: and today the Spanish form of Anarchism—which is in fact local autonomy reduced to its most elementary form —is reviving, after four centuries, the very spirit and idea which inspired the *Comuneros* under Charles V.

The Holy Office could count implicitly throughout upon the sovereign's favour and protection. Very often, he graced with his presence an *auto de fé* arranged in his honour and solemnly swore to uphold its privileges. When the Imperial hermit lay on his death-bed at S. Juste in 1558, the outstanding duty which he enjoined on his successor, Philip II., as key to success in this world and felicity in the next, was to support the Inquisition to his utmost ability.

This advice was implicitly obeyed: and the institution remained strong in the unwavering support of the Crown. (Not without good reason were the two linked together in a significant Spanish proverb, *Con el Rey y con la Inquisición, chiton*—"With King and Inquisition, silence!") Philip was particularly zealous in its interests, and in his reign even foreign ambassadors were enjoined to obey its orders. On one occasion, when report of its abuses had reached Rome, the Pope (whose personal claims were incidentally entrenched upon by this ambitious organisation) was prevailed upon to remonstrate. The King is reported to have answered that, with his scruples, His Holiness would destroy religion.

So the great age of Spain arrived. Miguel de Cervantes was a boy at Saavedra, and El Greco was growing up in Crete. The Kings of Spain and their Hapsburg cousins ruled over half of Europe, and all that mattered of America. The Netherlands were as yet loyal, and there were hopes that England might once again become Papist. The treasure-fleets returned year by year from Lima and Vera Cruz, and upset the economy of the western world by pouring bullion on the market. A zealot now sat upon the throne of St. Peter, and a bigot wore the crown of Ferdinand the Catholic. Spain became a land of public processions, of stately religious services, of spectacular blood-sports. All these tastes combined in one thing—after America, Spain's most significant contribution to mankind: the *auto de fé*. For, though the Spanish Inquisition perpetrated its greatest devastation in the half-century which succeeded its establishment, and was most notorious abroad in the century which preceded its fall, it was in the sixteenth and seventeenth centuries that it achieved its greatest power and played its most prominent rôle in Spanish life.

Foreign observers made a point of attending the Acts of Faith, and of reporting the proceedings to their eager correspondents at home. Thus on one occasion in the middle of the sixteenth century we find the Venetian Ambassador at Madrid sending a slightly confused account to his Doge:

A fortnight ago last Sunday, an act was performed at Murcia which is called at Toledo an act of the Inquisition, whereat twenty-nine individuals were burned as Jews. Among them were some chief personages, so that the confiscation of their property will yield the King upwards of 4,000,000 ducats. I have already informed your Serenity that a Jew, whilst a prisoner in that city, corrupted a great part of the population, and how the deed was discovered: so punishment of the culprits is not yet ended. The twenty-nine persons who were lately burned were all impenitents; but, if they had recanted and demanded mercy even at the last, their lives would have been spared, though with loss of their property and freedom, by virtue of a privilege to this effect which is enjoyed by the Kingdoms of Murcia, Granada, Aragon, Catalonia and Valencia, but which is not conceded to those of Castile, where, unless recantation is made within a certain period, the individual who omits to make it is necessarily put to death.

The correspondent of the Fuggers at Seville was more conscientious, and he sent them a detailed account of the names and misdeeds of all those who appeared in that city at the *auto* of May 3rd, 1579. There was a Flemish book-binder who had burned pictures of the Saints and put his faith entirely on the teachings of Luther: a negro slave, who reviled the name of the Virgin and despised her miracles: an English master-gunner, captured with Sir John Hawkins: a Morisco who had fled into Barbary: a virgin who had visions of the Evil One, though apparently remaining none the less virgin: several persons who had married twice: an incautious individual, who had frivolously averred that it is no sin if a woman goes to a man and they copulate, as well as a Portuguese wench who stated that it was no sin to sleep with a strange man: a number of blasphemers: a baccalaureate, priest of San Salvador in Seville, who had been guilty of various misdemeanours, including necromancy and invocation of the devil: three citizens who had stated, no doubt with ulterior motives, that they were relations of the Inquisitors: as well as several Judaisers, making thirty-eight persons in all. Only one of them, the Lutheran book-binder, was condemned to the flames. However, it was a depressing roll. "Vale! I rejoice that this is at an end," wrote the scribe, as he concluded.

At rare intervals, the sky of the Inquisition clouded: but the period of danger generally left the institution stronger than it had been before. The reforming minister of Philip III., the Duke of Olivares, endeavoured to do something to restrict its overwhelming authority: but the attempt ended in failure, and in the end it was the minister who fell. There was a further episode of the sort during the course of the reign of Philip IV., when the Secretary of State for Aragon, Villanueva, became implicated

with the Holy Office, for his patronage of a convent where
the nuns went into transports ("demoniacal possession,"
it was called by their opponents), declaring that their
institution would be the means of the regeneration of the
Church. That, of course, implied that the Church needed
regeneration: and the wily Secretary thought it safest to
make voluntary confession to the Holy Office and to
obtain a certificate that his conduct in the matter had
been blameless. Eleven years later, however, to the
general amazement, he was denounced, arrested, imprisoned, and condemned to reconciliation and banishment from the capital. This meant the end of his political career, and he appealed to the Pope for redress. The
Holy See instructed that the case should be reviewed on
its behalf by certain Spanish bishops. At this, the Inquisitor General, Diego de Arce y Reynoso, took umbrage,
and ordered the bishops not to receive the brief. A
second brief was then despatched to another member of
the episcopate: but the Inquisitor persuaded the King to
seize it. The case was now summoned to Rome, Arce and
his associates being menaced with loss of authority in
case of recalcitrance. However, before the *curia* could
reach a decision, the unfortunate Villanueva, who had
been in the prime of life when the affair had opened,
thirty-two years earlier, died, an old and broken man.
The Inquisition had received a tactical defeat: but it was
left in occupation of the field.

This reign was memorable in Inquisitional record for
the inauguration of a new Tribunal—that of Madrid.
The steady growth of the new capital had attracted thither
in increasing numbers New Christians and other suspects.
Moreover, it seemed a pity that the metropolis should be
deprived of the privilege, as well as the salutary example,
of witnessing the punishment of delinquents. The good

people of Toledo were naturally vexed at the idea that the attractions of their ancient city should be shorn in this way, and this was one reason for the constant delays and set-backs. At last, about 1650, an independent tribunal was definitely established, and henceforth it was one of the most active in the Peninsula, both for the number of the victims and the splendour of the spectacles. Even before its formal foundation, in fact, an *auto* had been held here—on July 4th, 1632—one of particular pomp and importance, celebrating as it did (could fanatical unimaginativeness go further?) the safe delivery of the Queen. The entire Royal Family was present, as well as the Ambassadorial corps: and, of the fifty-three persons sentenced, seven were burned in person and four more in effigy. The same month witnessed the death of the Infant Carlos, in honour of whose sister's birth the celebration had been held; and observers were not slow to notice the coincidence, which they considered a judgement from heaven.

Greatest of all the spectacles staged by the Inquisition in Spain was the renowned *auto* held on June 30th, 1680, on the Plaza Mayor at Madrid. It was graced by the presence of the young Charles II. and his young bride, Louise Marie of Orleans, newly arrived from France to cement Franco-Spanish friendship and stimulate the King's prematurely jaded manhood with her fresh loveliness. The spectacle began at six o'clock in the morning and lasted for fourteen hours, until evening had begun to fall: and all the greatest and proudest of the Castilian nobility were happy to receive some minor function to perform. One hundred and eighteen heretics in all figured on this occasion, to make a Spanish holiday for the fifty thousand spectators. Fifty-one were relaxed, either in person or in effigy; and sixty-seven penitents were reconciled. The Court Painter, Francisco Rizi, immortalised the scene with his brush, and a familiar of the Holy Office, Joseph del Olmo, described it in minutest detail in turgid prose. He omitted, however, one detail. Among those sentenced to be burned was one strikingly lovely girl, of about seventeen. As she passed the royal stand, it is recounted, she addressed a last cry of despair to the young Marie Louise. "Noble Queen! Cannot your royal presence save me from this? I sucked in my religion with my mother's milk; why must I now die for it?"

Notwithstanding this heart-rending appeal, the semi-imbecile King himself set fire to the brand which kindled the *quemadero*. Olmo described the last scene with gusto. The Marquise de Villars, one of the Queen's gentlewomen, showed more humanity. "I did not have the courage to be present at this horrible execution of the Jews," she wrote, a few days after. "It was a hideous spectacle, from what I have heard. During the period of judgement, however, it was necessary to put in an appearance from beginning to end, unless one had a medical certificate; for otherwise one would have been considered a heretic. Indeed, people thought very ill of me that I did not seem to enjoy everything that was happening. The cruelties which were witnessed at the death of these poor wretches it is impossible for me to describe."

Such sentiments were natural only to a foreigner. The Spaniard was brought up to the idea that the Inquisition was indispensable for the preservation of the country, and that its rigours were not only necessary, but natural. It is desirable to examine in greater detail the channels through which they were exercised, and the objects upon which they were directed.

CHAPTER IV

THE UNHOLY OFFICE

WITHIN a comparatively few years of its establishment, the Inquisition had developed into one of the
greatest of all institutions in the Iberian Peninsula; with
all that panoply of pomp and circumstance which charac-
terised everything Spanish of the period. There was a
stately structure of ceremonial, an intricate hierarchy of
officers and functionaries, an elaborate maze of procedure, special formulas and a special vocabulary, the
inevitable struggles for precedence between rival dignitaries, a universal Bumbledom in minor officials, a whole
literature for the guidance of the principal performers.
Every action—even dying—had to be performed according to precedent. It is impossible to have an adequate
idea of the Holy Tribunal and its workings without first
obtaining some outline of this elaborate ecclesiastical setting, which distinguished the Spanish Inquisition from
other similar bodies and rendered it notorious in the outside world.

The root of the difference between the Spanish Inquisition and its mediæval precursor, or the Papal Inquisition
which existed contemporaneously with it (and still sur-
vives for certain purposes) lay in one seemingly unimportant fact. In the latter instance, the Inquisitors were appointed by the Holy See: in the former, by the Sovereign.
In the one case, therefore, the Tribunal was essentially
an ecclesiastical one, amenable to the authority of Rome.
In the other, though dealing with religious matters, it was
in effect a branch of the civil power, independent of all
external authority and sometimes going so far as to

oppose the dictates of the Papal *curia* itself. It was therefore a primary instrument of Spanish absolutism. To this fact, too, is to be traced its vast range of activity, far outdoing that of its precursor, and its unbridled ferocity. It evolved moreover its own rules of procedure; though they were based on those of the mediæval Inquisition, they sometimes made a completely new departure, or else developed existing institutions to such an extent that they became unrecognisable. Moreover, its independent status enabled it to amass wealth, heaped up by repeated confiscations, and this in itself rendered it a force to be reckoned with in the affairs of the country.

The number of Tribunals of the Holy Office in Spain ultimately totalled fifteen. They existed, with full panoply of officials and equipment, at Barcelona, Córdova, Cuenca, Granada, Llerena, Logroño, Madrid, Murcia, Santiago, Seville, Toledo, Valencia, Valladolid and Saragossa, with another for the Balearic islands situated at Palma, Majorca. The names of all these places are writ large in the history of human suffering. Some of them, however—Madrid, Seville, Toledo—were more active by far than the others, mainly by reason of the presence in their neighbourhood of larger numbers of New Christians. On the whole, activity was greatest in Old Castile and Andalusia; it was least, after the first frenzied outburst, in Catalonia.

As the co-ordinating authority over the various local tribunals there came into existence, towards the close of the fifteenth century, a central council, officially termed *El Consejo de la Suprema y General Inquisición*, but usually referred to with merciful brevity as *La Suprema*. At the beginning, its authority was confined to Castile only. Later (though there was an intermission between

1507 and 1518), it extended also over Aragon. From the beginning, its importance was immense. Ferdinand and Isabella had created four great Councils as the instruments for the exercise of their authority and the centralisation of the Spanish monarchy—the Council of State, the Council of Finance, the Council of Castile and the Council of Aragon. The Council of the Inquisition took its place by the side of these important State departments, among which it was by no means the least important. It met daily in the Palace for the despatch of business: it gave instructions to, and received requests for guidance from, the local tribunals: it extended its authority over the offshoots which were set up overseas: it nominated fresh inquisitors; it urged the local authorities into renewed activity when they showed signs of idleness. Later on, the President of the Suprema was invariably the Inquisitor General: but this was not the case during the first century, or a little more, of its existence, when the two offices were quite distinct.

With the passage of time, the authority of the Suprema increased almost constantly, and its claims to jurisdiction became greater and greater. In 1647, it was ordered that all sentences passed by the local tribunals were to be submitted to it for confirmation (to be just, it must be conceded that its influence, contrary to what might be imagined, was generally on the side of leniency). As confiscations spread and the property of the Inquisition increased, a good deal of its activity was concerned with purely financial and business formalities. It was also responsible for the *Instrucciónes* or Handbooks for Inquisitors, giving full details of procedure in all emergencies, which were published in successive editions from the time of Torquemada onwards.

As soon as a new tribunal had been established in any

place, it was customary to publish an "Edict of Grace" (as it was called), inviting those persons conscious of having committed heretical actions in the past to come forward spontaneously and confess their transgressions, on the understanding that they would receive merciful treatment. A "Term of Grace"—that is, a time limit, generally of thirty or forty days—was assigned for this purpose. After the expiration of this period, guilty persons who had not confessed their crimes were liable to be proceeded against with the full rigour of the Inquisition. Those who presented themselves under the "Edict of Grace" were required to denounce all those with whom they associated, or whom they believed to be guilty of similar offences, thus setting the Holy Office on the track of a first nucleus of wrongdoers, subsequently to be enlarged as those implicated were put to the question. At later stages, an "Edict of Faith" was periodically issued, summoning all the faithful, under pain of excommunication, to denounce to the authorities any person whom they knew (or imagined) to be guilty of certain specified heretical offences. By this means the Holy Office was provided with a vast mass of information which kept it busy for some time before the actual arrest of the suspect.

As one now peruses the information thus procured it is difficult to refrain from admiration of the detective methods employed. A chance indication discovered at a trial at one end of the country would lead to wholesale arrests and burnings at the other end. The disclosures made in one insignificant instance might ultimately involve entire families, or even communities, which would methodically and mercilessly be tracked down in their turn. The quantity of information obtained by these means is the more remarkable in view of the fact that persons confessing their own backslidings or denouncing the sins of others were by no means certain of securing their own safety, since to make an incomplete confession was considered an extremely grave offence which completely nullified the good effect of any admissions already made.   Nevertheless, the institution of the "Edict of Faith" succeeded in inculcating a general habit of what was in effect little less than espionage, so that the whole population became associated with the Holy Office in the task of detecting and extirpating heresy.

These Edicts specified certain practices, the denunciation of which was particularly desired.   Since, as we have seen, the Spanish Inquisition was, for a large part of its existence, directed principally against the "New Christians," the customs mentioned comprise all those popularly associated with Judaism and Islam.   Chief among them are over-scrupulous attention to personal cleanliness and hygiene, a predilection for or aversion from certain foods, observing various fasts and festivals, laying out the dead according to the Eastern method, etc.   All these practices were considered equally heinous, so that the denunciation of some trivial personal habit was frequently sufficient to bring a man to the stake.   In the following, a typical "Edict of Faith," issued at Valencia in 1519, the prominence given to unimportant customs and mere superstitions is noteworthy.

EDICT OF FAITH

"We Doctor Andres de Palacio, Inquisitor against the heresy and apostolic perversity in the city and kingdom of Valencia, etc.

"To all faithful Christians, both men and women, chaplains, friars and priests of every condition, quality

and degree; whose attention to this will result in salvation
in our Lord Jesus Christ, the true salvation; who are
aware that, by means of other edicts and sentences of the
Reverend inquisitors, our predecessors, they were warned
to appear before them, within a given period, and declare
and manifest the things which they had seen, known, and
heard tell of any person or persons, either alive or dead,
who had said or done anything against the Holy Catholic
Faith; cultivated and observed the law of Moses or the
Mohammedan sect, or the rites and ceremonies of the
same; or perpetrated diverse crimes of heresy; observing
Friday evenings and Saturdays; changing into clean
personal linen on Saturdays and wearing better clothes
than on other days; preparing on Fridays the food for
Saturdays, in stewing pans on a small fire; who do not
work on Friday evenings and Saturdays as on other days;
who kindle lights in clean lamps with new wicks, on Friday
evenings; place clean linen on the beds and clean napkins
on the table; celebrate the festival of unleavened bread,
eat unleavened bread and celery and bitter herbs; observe
the fast of pardon (Day of Atonement) when they do not
eat all day until the evening after star-rise, when they
pardon one another and break their fast; and in the same
manner observe the fasts of Queen Esther, of tissabav, and
rosessena; who say prayers according to the law of Moses,
standing up before the wall, swaying back and forth, and
taking a few steps backwards; who give money for oil for
the Jewish temple or other secret place of worship; who
slaughter poultry according to the Judaic law, and refrain
from eating sheep or any other animal which is trefa; who
do not wish to eat salt pork, hares, rabbits, snails, or fish
that have not scales; who bathe the bodies of their dead
and bury them in virgin soil according to the Jewish
custom; who, in the house of mourning do not eat meat

but fish and hard-boiled eggs, seated at low tables; who separate a morsel of dough when baking and throw it on the fire; who become, or know of others who become circumcised; who invoke demons, and give to them the honour that is due to God; who say that the law of Moses is good and can bring about their salvation; who perform many other rites and ceremonies of the same; who say that our Lord Jesus Christ was not the true Messiah promised in Scripture, nor the true God nor son of God; who deny that he died to save the human race; deny the resurrection and his ascension to heaven; and say that our Lady the Virgin Mary was not the mother of God or a virgin before the nativity and after; who say and affirm many other heretical errors; who state that what they had confessed before the inquisitors was not the truth; who remove their penitential robes and neither remain in the prison nor observe the penance imposed upon them; who say scandalous things against our holy Catholic Faith and against the officials of the Inquisition; or who influence any infidel who might have been drawn towards Catholicism to refrain from converting; who assert that the Holy Sacrament of the altar is not the true body and blood of Jesus Christ our Redeemer, and that God cannot be omnipresent; or any priest holding this damnable opinion, who recites and celebrates the mass, not saying the holy words of the consecration; saying and believing that the law of Mahomet and its rites and ceremonies are good and can bring about their salvation; who affirm that life is but birth and death, and that there is no paradise and no hell; and state that to practise usury is not a sin; if any man whose wife still lives, marries again, or any woman remarries in the lifetime of her first husband; if any know of those who keep Jewish customs, and name their children on the seventh night after their birth and with silver and

gold upon a table, pleasurably observe the Jewish
ceremony; and if any know that when somebody dies,
they place a cup of water and a lighted candle and some
napkins where the deceased died, and for some days, do
not enter there; if any know of the effort of a Jew or
convert, secretly to preach the law of Moses and convert
others to this creed, teaching the ceremonies belonging to
the same, giving information as to the dates of festivals and
fasts, teaching Jewish prayers; if any know of anyone who
attempts to become a Jew, or being Christian walks abroad
in the costume of a Jew; if any know of anyone, converted
or otherwise, who orders that his dress shall be made of
canvas and not of linen, as the good Jews do; if any know
of those who, when their children kiss their hands, place
their hands on the children's heads without making the
Sign (of the Cross); or who, after dinner or supper, bless
the wine and pass it to everyone at the table, which bless-
ing is called the veraha; if any know that in any house,
people congregate for the purpose of carrying on religious
services, or read out of bibles of the vernacular or perform
other Judaic ceremonies, and if any know that when
someone is about to set out on a journey, certain words
of the law of Moses are spoken to him, and a hand placed
on his head without making the Sign (of the Cross). And
if any know of anyone who has professed the Mosaic creed,
or awaited the coming of the Messiah, saying that our
Redeemer and Saviour Jesus Christ was not come and
that now Elijah was to come and take them to the promised
land; and if any know that any person had pretended to
go into a trance and wandered in heaven and that an angel
had conducted him over green fields and told him that was
the promised land which was being saved for all converts
whom Elijah was to redeem from the captivity in which
they lived; and if any know that any person or persons

be children or grandchildren of the condemned, and being disqualified, should make use of public office, or bear arms or wear silk and fine cloth, or ornament their costumes with gold, silver, pearls or other precious stones or coral, or make use of any other thing which they are forbidden and disqualified to have; and if any know that any persons have or possessed any confiscated goods, furniture, money, gold, silver, or other jewels belonging to those condemned for heresy, which should be brought before the receiver of goods confiscated for the crime of heresy.—All these things, having been seen, heard or known, you, the above-mentioned faithful Christians, have, with obstinate hearts, refused to declare and manifest, greatly to the burden and prejudice of your souls; thinking that you were absolved by the bulls and indulgences issued by our holy father, and by promises and donations which you had made, for which you have incurred the sentence of excommunication and other grave penalties under statutory law; and thus you may be proceeded against as those who have suffered excommunication and as abettors of heretics, in various ways; but, wishing to act with benevolence, and in order that your souls may not be lost, since our Lord does not wish the death of the sinner but his reformation and life; by these presents, we remove and suspend the censure promulgated by the said former inquisitors against you, so long as you observe and comply with the terms of this our edict, by which we require, exhort and order you, in virtue of the holy obedience, and under penalty of complete excommunication, within nine days from the time that the present edict shall have been read to you, or made known to you in whatsoever manner, to state all that you know, have seen, heard, or heard tell in any manner whatsoever, of the things and ceremonies above-mentioned, and to appear before us personally to declare and manifest what you have seen, heard, or heard tell secretly, without having spoken previously with any other person, or borne false witness against anyone. Otherwise, the period having passed, the canonical admonitions having been repeated in accordance with the law, steps will be taken to give out and promulgate sentence of excommunication against you, in and by these documents; and through such excommunication, we order that you be publicly denounced; and if, after a further period of nine days, you should persist in your rebellion and excommunication, you shall be excommunicated, anathematised, cursed, segregated, and separated as an associate of the devil, from union with and inclusion in the holy Mother-Church, and the sacraments of the same. And we order the vicars, rectors, chaplains, and sacristans and any other religious or ecclesiastical persons to regard and treat the above-mentioned as excommunicated and accursed for having incurred the wrath and indignation of Almighty God, and of the glorious Virgin Mary, His Mother, and of the beatified apostles Saint Peter and Saint Paul, and all the saints of the celestial Court; and upon such rebels and disobedient ones who would hide the truth regarding the above-mentioned things, be all the plagues and maledictions which befell and descended upon King Pharaoh and his host for not having obeyed the divine commandments; and the same sentence of divine excommunication encompass them as it encompassed the people of Sodom and Gomorrah who all perished in flames; and of Athan and Abiron who were swallowed up into the earth for the great delinquencies and sins which they committed in disobedience and rebellion against our Lord God; and may they be accursed in eating and drinking, in waking and sleeping, in coming and going. Accursed be they in living and dying, and may they ever be hardened to their sins, and the devil be at their right hand always; may their vocation be sinful, and their days be few and evil; may their substance be enjoyed by others, and their children be orphans, and their wives widows. May their children ever be in need, and may none help them; may they be turned out of their homes and their goods taken by usurers; and may they find nobody to have compassion on them; may their children be ruined and outcast, and their names also; and their wickedness be ever present in the divine memory. May their enemies vanquish them and despoil them of all they possess in the world; and may they wander from door to door without relief. May their prayers be turned to maledictions; and accursed be the bread and wine, the meat and fish, the fruit and other food that they eat; likewise the houses they inhabit and the raiment they wear, the beasts upon which they ride and the beds upon which they sleep, and the tables and napkins upon which they eat. Accursed be they to Satan and to Lucifer and to all the devils in hell, and these be their lords, and accompany them by night and by day. Amen. And if any persons incurring the said excommunications and maledictions, should persist therein for the space of a year, they should be regarded as heretics themselves, and shall be prosecuted by the same process as against heretics or suspects of the crime of heresy. Given on the   March, in the year of our Lord God, one thousand five hundred and twelve.''

Nullus amoveat sub pena excommunicationis.

(Item: Of no avail is the confession made to the confessor for procuring absolution from the sentence of excommunication to which the heretic might be subject, from the time the crime is committed.)

(Item: All who know anything of the things mentioned

in this present edict, or of other heresies, and do not come
forward to denounce and declare the same, are hereby
excommunicated and may not be absolved by their
confessors.)

El doctor   *De Mandato sue*
Palacio, inquisidor.   *Reverende paternitatis,*
                                 Petrus Sorell, notarius.

The opening stage of the proceedings before the Inquisition was based upon the fiction that the bishop or his
delegate was judge in an action between plaintiff and
defendant. The plaintiff was a special official styled the
Promotor Fiscal, a kind of Public Prosecutor whose
ostensible function was that of adviser to the Inquisitors
rather than accuser in the ordinary sense. Before the
case came up for consideration, the charges were examined
by "qualifiers" (*calificadores*) in order to determine
whether they presented *calidad de oficio*—that is, whether
they came within the jurisdiction of the Holy Office. This
"qualification" provided some safeguard, though but a
slight one, in those cases in which it was applied. There
were however numerous classes of charges—precisely, in
fact, those which needed protection most urgently—for
which this procedure was not admitted: for neither
Judaisers, Moriscos, renegades, nor persons accused of
certain types of immorality, could lay claim to this
restraining influence.

After the *Promotor Fiscal* had presented his formal
demand for the opening of proceedings, termed his "complaint" (*clamosa*), the next step was the arrest of the
accused and their transference to the prisons of the Inquisitions—generally annexed to the Palaces which in the
course of time they were able to construct out of their
accumulated funds. Some of the Inquisitional Prison-

Palaces still stand for the delectation of the tourist. That of Evora is now a hotel, that of Barcelona an antiquary's shop, that of Coimbra a stable, that of Toledo, until recently, the *Posada de la Hermandad*. The site of the notorious edifice at Lisbon is now occupied by the Opera House. A description printed in the *Annual Register* in 1821, when the building was at last opened for public inspection, gives an idea of what it had been like at the height of its power:

On the 8th inst., the palace of the Holy Office was opened to the people. The number which crowded to see it during the first four days, rendered it extremely difficult and even dangerous to attempt an entrance. The edifice is extensive and has the form of an oblong square, with a garden in the centre. It is three stories high, and has several vaulted galleries, along which are situated a number of dungeons, of six, seven, eight, and nine feet square. Those on the ground floor and in the first story have no windows, and are deprived of both air and light when the door is shut. The dungeons on the next story have a kind of breathing-hole in the form of a chimney through which the sky may be seen. These apartments were allotted to prisoners, who, it was supposed, might be set at liberty. In the vaulted wall of each dungeon there is a hole of about an inch in diameter, which communicates with a secret corridor running along by each tier of dungeons. By these means, the agents of the Inquisition could at any moment observe the conduct of the prisoners without being seen by them: and when two persons were confined in the same dungeon, could hear their conversation. In these corridors were seats so placed,

that a spy could observe what was passing in two
dungeons, by merely turning his eyes from right to
left, in order to look into either of the holes between
which he might be stationed.   Human skulls and
other bones were found in the dungeons.   On the
walls of these frightful holes are carved the names of
some of the unfortunate victims buried in them,
accompanied with lines or notches, indicating the
number of days of their captivity.   One name had
beside it the date of 1809.   The doors of certain
dungeons, which had not been used for some years,
still remained shut, but the people soon forced them
open.   In nearly all of them, human bones were found,
and among these melancholy remains, were, in one
dungeon, fragments of the garments of a monk, and
his girdle.   In some of these dungeons, the chimney-
shaped air-hole was walled up, which is a certain sign
of the murder of the prisoner.   In such cases, the
unfortunate victim was compelled to go into the air-
hole, the lower extremity of which was immediately
closed by masonry.   Quicklime was afterwards thrown
down on him, which extinguished life and destroyed
the body.   In several of these dens of misery,
mattresses were found, some of them old, others
almost new—a circumstance which proves, whatever
may be said to the contrary, that the Inquisition in
these latter times was something more than a scare-
crow.

Not all in this gruesome account is perhaps to be taken
literally—one should remember that it emanates from a
period, and a country, when anything connected with the
Holy Office was presented in the worst possible light.   The
possibility is not to be excluded, even, that some of the

bones discovered had originally belonged to some of the lower vertebrates. In the main, nevertheless, the picture is probably as reliable as it is vivid.

From the moment that the arrests were carried out and down to the conclusion of the whole affair, the accused persons vanished from the public eye. Strictly segregated even while on their way to prison, and of course even more strictly guarded in the secret dungeons, it was impossible for the prisoners to communicate with one another, with the outside world, or with those of their friends and relatives who had not yet fallen into the hands of the Holy Office: and, if by some miracle they succeeded in doing so, it was regarded as an extremely grave offence. Every step in the subsequent proceedings was surrounded with similar precautions, and all the parties concerned— the accused person, as well as witnesses, accusers, and officials, were sworn to secrecy. Breaches of this oath could be, and were, punished with the utmost severity. Even if a suspect obtained information of his approaching arrest and tried to escape, he was regarded as guilty of an offence on this score and suffered for it. This profound night of mystery and silence was perhaps the most terrifying weapon of the Spanish Inquisition.

A very considerable period—on one occasion which is on record, as long as fourteen years—sometimes intervened between the arrest of a person and the promulgation of sentence; while an interval of three or four years was commonplace. During this time, the captive had ample leisure to brood over the treatment he had received and the exact degree of his guilt. That very large numbers never survived to learn the results of their trial was inevitable: and, at every *auto*, there figured the effigies and bones of various persons who had died in the dungeons of the Holy Office.

That there were abuses was inevitable. Prisoners were kept in chains for years, in dark and insanitary cells, at the mercy of gaolers who were not always models of deportment: and it not infrequently happened that a woman was dragged pregnant to the stake. In 1512, the redoubtable Cardinal Ximenes issued an order threatening with death any official who was found carrying on an intrigue with one of his prisoners. This, however, was not sufficient to put an end to the abuse; and the case of the amorous André de Castro, *alcaide* of the Inquisitional prisoners at Valencia in 1590, accused of seducing one female prisoner and kissing or soliciting all the others who appealed to his taste, is enough to put the most hardened realistic novelist of today to the blush. It must nevertheless be realised, in common fairness, that the prisons of the Holy Office were no worse than those of any other authority at this period, and that its functionaries were not necessarily more lustful or more cruel.

The expenses of the imprisonment, however long its duration might be, were borne by the accused. In Sicily, those incurred during the detention of a nun acquitted and released in 1703 after a four years' incarceration were still being paid off by the unfortunate woman's heirs as late as 1872! There were, moreover, many classes of crime (including all of the more serious) the punishment of which might (and usually did) include confiscation. In these cases, it was the rule to seize all the possessions of the accused at the moment of arrest, in order to circumvent evasion. At a later period, permission might be given for the family of the prisoner to administer some slight portion of the property while proceedings were pending; but even so, prison expenses had the first claim, and in the case of a poor man these exhausted everything. Moreover, it was not only the families who suffered as a result of this sequestration, for the sudden disappearance of prominent men of affairs sometimes had very serious effects on the economic life of a whole town, or even province. Thus, when in 1647 the Marrano merchant-prince, Duarte da Silva, was arrested, the exchange on Lisbon slumped by 5 per cent. on the Amsterdam bourse, and it was bruited abroad that the Inquisitors had acted as they did on secret instructions from the Spanish court in order to undermine Portuguese credit. If the verdict was unfavourable, of course, all the sequestered property devolved on the Holy Office, which thus had every inducement to condemn the accused.

The rules of evidence varied considerably, according to the use made of the depositions. The prisoner was not under any circumstances permitted to call any witness who was likely to be of service to him; for example, kinsmen, servants, Moriscos and New Christians were all excluded on the grounds that their testimony would be unreliable. On the other hand, no such disability applied to the witnesses brought forward by the prosecution except what was termed "mortal enmity towards the accused." There seemed to the Inquisitorial mind nothing illogical or incongruous in the fact that the names of the witnesses were carefully concealed from the prisoner. This provision was originally introduced in the thirteenth century to meet the case of "powerful persons" who might be expected to intimidate witnesses unless the latter were protected by the secrecy of the proceedings. Later, however, Judaisers and heretics, although themselves in direr need of protection than anyone else, were denied the opportunity of learning the source of the accusations brought against them. Hence, while a man was being tried upon

a charge which might lead him to the stake, he was forced
to search his memory for the name of every person who
might conceivably bear him a personal grudge and perhaps have accused him without cause, and to demonstrate
that evidence derived from him ought not to be accepted.
It is pertinent to recall, in this connexion, that even in
enlightened England it is only since 1836 that persons
accused of felony have been able to avail themselves of
the assistance of Counsel, or see copies of the depositions
made against them.   The Spanish Inquisition, however,
carried this system to the last degree of absurdity, in a
manner which would be laughable were it not that so
much was at stake.

When the famour scholar and poet Fray Luis de Leon
was arrested in 1572, he succeeded in identifying some of
his accusers by the simple means of naming most of his
colleagues at the University of Salamanca as possible
personal enemies: but most prisoners did not have the
obvious advantage (from this point of view) of University
status.   He also denounced as untrustworthy the whole
order of the Dominicans and of the Geronimites, as being
generally prejudiced against that of the Augustinians, to
which he himself belonged, and even the professors of
the University of Alcalá, because they were rivals of those
of Salamanca!   The most serious of the many heretical
propositions attributed to Luis de Leon was his alleged
attack on the text of the Vulgate.   He was said to have
taught that the Vulgate text of the Old Testament was not
perfect, and that the Hebrew text had more authority.
Unfortunately for himself, Luis de Leon was of remote
New Christian descent; his great-grandmother, Leonor
de Villanueva, being connected with the Pacheco family.
Moreover, he was very friendly with the scholar Garjal,
also of New Christian origin, who was arrested at the

same time as Luis de Leon. "Garjal and Fray Luis, being notoriously New Christians, must be intent on obscuring our Catholic faith and returning to their own law," was the comment of the Inquisitor Diego Gonsalez when he recommended the arrest of one of Spain's greatest writers, undoubtedly a sincere Catholic. The story is well-known how, when after imprisonment he resumed his lectures at the University of Salamanca, he took up the thread just where he had left off, four and a half years before, with the words, "As we were saying the other day." One of the students asked why he was speaking in such a low tone. "I am hoarse," he replied. "Besides, it is better to speak softly, so that the gentlemen of the Inquisition may not hear." As a matter of fact they did, a little later on: and only his personal friendship with the Inquisitor General himself, Quiroga, saved him from serious consequences.

A charge which was in any case considered a heinous one thus became deadly if the accused was so unfortunate as to have the smallest proportion of infidel blood in his veins. Very little indeed was needed to make the Holy Office suspect that an individual of New Christian origin was knowingly heretical. Thus, the mere regard for personal cleanliness or unusual culinary tastes was often enough to convict a person of practising Judaism or Islam, and thus cost him his life. Under such circumstances, exculpation was enormously difficult. One is reminded of the despairing cry of the suspect charged before the Inquisition in the south of France in the thirteenth century. "Hear me, my lords! I am no heretic: for I have a wife and cohabit with her and have children; and I eat flesh and lie and swear and am a faithful Christian."

At every stage in the trial, a notary was present, who

took down every word and every detail in a detached, impersonal fashion. To this *procès verbal* were appended all relevant documents, an inventory of the prisoner's household effects and other property, copies of depositions, and (of course) full genealogical minutiæ. Notwithstanding the orgy of destruction which raged at the time of the abolition of the Holy Office in the nineteenth century, large numbers of these records are still extant—particularly as regards the activities of the Tribunal of Toledo, and those of the Portuguese Inquisition, the archives of which are virtually complete. In some *causes célèbres*, the record fills volume upon volume. Even in some cases of minor importance, it is not uncommon to find up to a thousand closely-written folio pages—a real mine of information for social and economic life, as well as a gruesome monument of human martyrdom.

Not the least formidable of the weapons of the Holy Office was the network of espionage with which it was surrounded. Not only was the whole population implicated in this, through the medium of the Edicts of Faith which invited denunciation, and the Confessional system which enforced it. In addition, there were professional spies, whose activities extended far beyond the bounds of the Peninsula, to North Sea ports where Spanish merchants imagined that they were beyond the reach of attentive ears and prying eyes. Moreover, as is the case in one European country at least in our own day, travellers returning from abroad were expected, and encouraged, to present themselves before the local Tribunal to report upon the behaviour of the *emigrés*. In 1609, a Portuguese returned from the south of France informed the Inquisition of Toledo of nearly two hundred persons who were misconducting themselves there, and whose relatives in the Peninsula were all thus put under suspicion. In 1617, a youth desirous of insinuating himself into favour denounced by name no less than 117 fugitives (including one ex-familiar of the Holy Office) who were then judaising in Amsterdam alone, as well as scores more in Venice, Hamburg, and Florence. Similar denunciations were received on more than one occasion regarding fugitives in England, and even in the New World. There is a certain macabre fascination in seeing how the Holy Office grimly collected evidence—sometimes for years—until it was ready to pounce, and how the Tribunals would despatch from one to the other scraps of information extracted under torture which might help in implicating some unfortunate victim, then going about his business without any idea of the web which was being spun around him.

The system lent itself, of course, to the most shocking abuses. In 1647, in the hope of securing release, a gaol-bird, in prison in Valladolid, gave information concering a secret congregation which (he alleged) existed at Ciudad Real. The principal member was the Paymaster of the army on the Portuguese frontier, in whose house various persons met each Friday for the purpose of ceremonially scourging images of Christ and the Virgin Mary! In consequence of this ridiculous story, a large number of arrests was carried out. Lavish application of torture secured, as it always did, ample confirmatory evidence, parents testifying against their children and sisters against their brothers in order to put an end to their awful sufferings. For four years, the trials dragged on, until it was established that the essential part of the story was simply a spiteful invention. Nevertheless, there were several convictions: and the Inquisition grew fat on the enormous fines which were imposed. On an earlier occasion, in Córdova, a single witness, who was a perjurer, drunkard, gambler, forger, and coin-clipper, was credited sufficiently to crowd the tribunal with some two hundred victims.

A curious vignette comes from Valladolid, in 1630. A student of that famous seat of learning appeared before the Tribunal and, in horror-stricken tones, denounced a certain Portuguese resident at Zamora for having endeavoured to convert him to Judaism. This was a case after the Inquisition's own heart. The receiver of the Tribunal was sent to Zamora, accompanied by an alguazil, to carry out the necessary arrests. However, they failed to find any trace of the persons accused, or even of the street in which they were supposed to be residing. When the matter was reported at Valladolid, the denunciant was sent for and accused of fraud and mockery of the Holy Office. He admitted his offence with engaging naiveté, explaining that he had been thrown into gaol for acquiring a mare by questionable means, and had hit upon this expedient so as to be temporarily released, in the hope of escaping to the asylum of a church. He was formally tried, reprimanded, and exiled from the city for a period of six years. In addition, a fine of two hundred ducats was imposed upon him which he was to pay if he should ever be able to afford it—a highly unlikely contingency, as it appears.

Again, in the early years of the eighteenth century, a Portuguese physician denounced a number of persons who, he alleged, had come together to practise Jewish rites, sixty-six on one occasion, and ninety-two on another. They were arrested, and several of them died in prison, but it was ultimately found that the accusation was entirely without foundation. Jacob de Castro Sarmento, Fellow of the Royal Society of Physicians, who was settled in London as a fugitive, was suspected by his

co-religionists of being responsible for these denunciations, but was able to clear his name, as the British
public was informed in a printed broadside. The true
culprit was severely punished by the Inquisition, being
executed at Lisbon on October 10th, 1723. But such instances of severity were uncommon, and those guilty of
the crime of bearing false witness usually escaped with a
far lighter punishment on those rare occasions when they
were detected.

The function of the Inquisition was a double one; it
existed not only to detect and punish crime, but also (one
should perhaps say primarily) to save the soul of the
criminal. In order to achieve the latter end, it was
essential that the accused should confess his guilt, profess
repentance and entreat pardon. If the prisoner refused
to confess voluntarily, steps must be taken to persuade
him to do so. The art of torture, spasmodically practised
in civil courts throughout the Middle Ages, was perfected
by the officials of the Inquisition. But it is wrong to
imagine that the Holy Office's position was unique in this
respect, as is generally imagined. It is true that, in the
fifteenth century, Sir John Fortescue in his *De Laudibus
Legum Angliæ* spoke of the absence of torture in England as one of the most precious national assets: but the
mere name of the Star Chamber and the allied tribunals
is a sufficient reminder that this principle was not con-
sistently adhered to. Compared with the Papal Inquisition, moreover, that of Spain (notorious though it was
for its cruelty) was in some respects mild: for at Rome
it was considered permissible to continue torture even
after a confession had been obtained, in order to extract
the names of accomplices and associates. But the difference in fact existed only in name: for even in Spain,
when a confession did not cover other persons who were

implicated in the same charge, the torture might be, and frequently was, continued *in caput alienum* (as it was termed) in order to elicit fresh evidence against them. On occasion, too, torture could be applied to a witness whose evidence appeared inconsistent or unreliable.

The methods of torment employed by the Spanish Inquisition were on the whole (contrary to what is imagined) conservative and unoriginal: the novelty lying rather in the assiduity and the recklessness with which they were applied. The commonest modes were the pulley or *strappado*, and the water-torment or *aselli*. In the former, the victim's wrists were tied behind his back and attached to a pulley, by means of which he was hoisted from the floor. If this did not prove sufficient to make him speak, weights were attached to the feet and, after being held suspended for a little while, the sufferer was let down suddenly, with a jerk which wrenched every part of the body. This process was repeated time after time, the weights being increased on each occasion. Refinements of this method were the *cordeles* and *garottes*, introduced at a later date as experimental research progressed. The water-torture was more ingenious, and more fiendish. The prisoner was fastened almost naked on a sort of trestle with sharp-edged rungs and kept in position with an iron band, his head lower than his feet, and his limbs bound to the side-pieces with agonising tightness. The mouth was then forced open and a strip of linen inserted into the gullet. Through this, water was poured from a jar (*jarra*), obstructing the throat and nostrils and producing a state of semi-suffocation. This process was repeated time after time, as many as eight *jarras* sometimes being applied. Meanwhile, the cords round the sufferer's limbs were continually tightened until it seemed as though every vein in his body was at bursting-point.

Richard Hasleton, an Englishman arraigned by the Holy Tribunal at Majorca in 1588, has left a heart-rending account of his sufferings on the rack. After undergoing the water-torment, he writes, he "could have no feeling of any limb or joint " but " lay in a most lamentable and pitiful manner for four ·or five days having a continual issue of blood and water forth of my mouth all that space, and being so feeble and weak, by reason of my torments, that I could take no sustenance."

The following eighteenth-century account of the procedure (which, it may be admitted, can be relied on not to under-emphasise) will make it unnecessary to go into any further detail regarding this particularly unpleasant subject:

AN ACCOUNT OF THE PROCESS OF THE INQUISITION AND ITS MANAGEMENT BY TORTURE

" When the prisoner has been examined three times and still persists in the negative, it often happens that he is detained a whole year or longer before he is admitted to another audience, that being wearied with his imprisonment, he may more readily confess what is desired; but if he still persists in the negative his accusation is at length delivered to him intermixt with a number of pretended crimes of a heinous nature, which composition of truth and falsehood is a snare for the unhappy wretch; for as he seldom fails to exclaim against the feigned crimes, his judges thence conclude the others of which he makes less complaint are true. When his trial comes on in good earnest, the witnesses are examined afresh, a copy of the depositions is delivered to him with those circumstances supprest as might discover the evidence; he replies to each particular, and gives interrogatories to which he would have the witnesses examined and the names of others that he would have examined in his behalf; an advocate is appointed for him, which tho' it has the appearance of Justice is really of no use to the prisoner—for the advocate is under an oath to the office, is not admitted to speak to his client but in the presence of the inquisitor, nor to alledge anything in his favour but what he thinks proper. After the process has been carried on in this manner for a considerable time, the judges with their assessors examine the proofs and determine the fate of the Prisoner; if his answers and exceptions are not satisfactory, nor the proofs against him sufficient for conviction, he is condemned to the TORTURE. The scene of the diabolical cruelty is a dark underground vault, the prisoner upon his arrival there is immediately seized by a torturer, who forthwith strips him. Whilst he is stripping, and while under the torture, the inquisitor strongly exhorts him to confess his guilt, yet neither to bear false witness against himself or others. The first TORTURE is that of ye ROPE which is performed in this manner. The prisoner's hands are bound behind him, and by means of a rope fastened to them and running through a pulley, he is raised up to the ceiling, where having hung for some time with weights tyed to his feet, he is let down almost to the ground with such sudden jerks as disjoint his arms and legs, whereby he is put to the most exquisite pain, and is forced to cry out in a terrible manner. If the prisoner's strength holds out, they usually torture him in this manner about an hour, and if it does not force a confession from him to their liking, they have recourse to the next torture, viz.: WATER. The prisoner is now laid upon his back in a wooden trough which has a barr running through ye midst of it upon which his back lies, and upon occasion his back bone is hereby broke and puts him to incredible pain. The torture of water is sometimes performed by forcing the prisoner to swallow a quantity of water and then pressing his body by screwing ye sides of ye trough closer; at other times a wet cloth is laid over the prisoner's mouth and nostrils, and a small stream of water constantly descending upon it he sucks ye cloth into his throat, which being suddenly removed draws away with it water and blood and puts ye unhappy wretch into the AGONIES OF DEATH. The next torture, viz.: that of FIRE, is thus performed, the prisoner being placed on the ground his feet are held towards a fire and rubbed with unctious and combustible matter, by which means, the heat penetrating into those parts, HE SUFFERS PAINS WORSE THAN DEATH ITSELF."

It is not remarkable that death under torture was by no means uncommon, though in most instances the physician present enforced sufficient moderation to avoid a fatal conclusion. The presiding Inquisitor safeguarded his conscience, however, from such a contingency: for before the process began he made a formal declaration that, if the victim should die or suffer grievous bodily harm under torture, this must be imputed not to the Holy Office but to the culprit himself, who had failed to take the opportunity to tell the truth spontaneously. Neither age, nor sex, nor even pregnancy, could save a prisoner on these occasions. Although he was delicate and much wasted by a fever contracted in prison, Luis de Leon was sentenced to be examined on the rack, and this "notwithstanding the fact that the theologians now profess themselves satisfied with the answers which he has given to the propositions condemned as heretical." The Inquisitors added that "as the accused is of delicate health, the torture shall be applied moderately." Owing to special circumstances, the poet escaped altogether: but in this he was particularly fortunate.

Now and again, one obtains gruesome sidelights on the application of the torture and its consequences, which serve to demonstrate that the nominal regulations and safeguards were not always observed. On one occasion, the notary of the Inquisition at Cordova locked a girl of fifteen in a room, stripped her naked, and scourged her until she consented to bear testimony against her own mother. On another, a prisoner was carried in a chair to the *auto*, with his feet burned to the bone. It is only fair to state, however, that both these instances belong to the period of recognised abuse at the beginning of the sixteenth century.

It is not surprising that the mere threat of torture was sufficient to put a prisoner in an agony of fear. Elvira del Campo, wife of the scrivener Alonso de Moya, was tried by the Inquisition of Toledo in 1567-9 on a charge of not eating pork and of putting on clean linen on Saturdays. She admitted having committed these criminal acts, but denied that she had had any heretical intentions. This did not satisfy the inquisitors, who condemned her to the torture. When the sentence was read out to her formally, she fell upon her knees, and begged to know what they wanted her to say. This candid request did not satisfy the inquisitors, who proceeded with their work.

"She was carried to the torture chamber, and told to tell the truth, when she said she had nothing to say. She was ordered to be stripped and again admonished, but was silent. When stripped she said, 'Señores, I have done all that is said of me and I bear false-witness against myself, for I do not want to see myself in such trouble; please God, I have done nothing.' She was told not to bring false testimony against herself but to tell the truth. The tying of the arms commenced; she said, 'I have told the truth; what have I to tell?' She was told to tell the truth and replied, 'I have told the truth and have nothing to tell.' One cord was applied to the arms and twisted and she was admonished to tell the truth but said she had nothing to tell. Then she screamed and said, 'Tell me what you want for I don't know what to say.' She was told to tell what she had done, for she was tortured because she had not done so, and another turn of the cord was ordered. She cried, 'Loosen me, Señores, and tell me what I have to say: I do not know what I have done, O Lord have mercy on me, a sinner!' Another turn was given and she said, 'Loosen me a little that I may remember what I have to tell; I don't know what I have done; I did not eat pork for it made me sick; I have done everything; loosen me and I will tell the truth.' Another turn of the cord was ordered, when she said, 'Loosen me and I will tell the truth; I don't know what I have to tell— loosen me for the sake of God—tell me what I have to say —I did it, I did it—they hurt me, Señor—loosen me, loosen me and I will tell it.' She was told to tell it and said, 'I don't know what I have to tell—Señor, I did it— I have nothing to tell—O my arms! Release me and I will tell it.' She was asked to tell what she did and said, 'I don't know, I did not eat because I did not wish to.' She was asked why she did not wish to and replied, 'Ay! loosen me, loosen me—take me from here and I will tell it when I am taken away—I say that I did not eat it.' She was told to speak and said, 'I did not eat it, I don't know why.' Another turn was ordered and she said, 'Señor, I did not eat it because I did not wish to—release me and I will tell it.' She was told to tell what she had done contrary to our holy Catholic faith. She said, 'Take me from here and tell me what I have to say—they hurt me—Oh my arms, my arms!' which she repeated many times and went on, 'I don't remember—tell me what I have to say—O wretched me! I will tell all that is wanted, Señores—they are breaking my arms—loosen me a little—I did everything that is said of me.' She was told to tell in detail truly what she did. She said, 'What am I wanted to tell? I did everything—loosen me, for I don't remember what I have to tell—don't you see what a weak woman I am? Oh! Oh! my arms are breaking.' More turns were ordered and as they were given she cried, 'Oh, oh, loosen me for I don't know what I have to say—if I did I would tell it.' The cords were ordered to be tightened when she said, 'Señores, have you no pity on a sinful woman?' She was told, yes, if she would tell the truth. She said, 'Señor, tell me, tell me it.' The cords were tightened again, and she said, 'I have already said that I did it.' She was ordered to tell in detail, to which she said, 'I don't know how to tell it, señor, I don't know.' The cords were separated and counted, and there were sixteen turns, and in giving the last turn the cord broke.

"She was then ordered to be placed on the potro (frame). She said, 'Señores, why will you not tell me what I have to say? Señor, put me on the ground—have I not said that I did it all?' She was told to tell it. She said, 'I don't remember—take me away—I did what the witnesses say.' She was told to tell in detail what the witnesses said. She said, 'Señor, as I have told you, I do not know for certain. I have said that I did all that the witnesses say. Señores, release me, for I do not remember it.' She was told to tell it. She said, 'I do not know it. Oh, oh, they are tearing me to pieces—I have said I did it—let me go.' She was told to tell it. She said, 'Señores, it does not help me to say that I did it, and I have admitted that what I have done has brought me to this suffering—Señor, you know the truth—Señores, for

God's sake have mercy on me. Oh, Señor, take these things from my arms—Señor, release me, they are killing me.' She was tied on the potro with the cords, she was admonished to tell the truth and the garrotes were ordered to be tightened. She said, 'Señor, do you not see how these people are killing me? Señor, I did it—for God's sake let me go.' She was told to tell it. She said, 'Señor, remind me of what I did not know—Señores, have mercy upon me—let me go for God's sake—they have no pity on me—I did it—take me from here and I will remember what I cannot here.' She was told to tell the truth or the cords would be tightened. She said, 'Remind me of what I have to say for I don't know it—I said that I did not want to eat it—I know only that I did not want to eat it,' and this she repeated many times. She was told to tell why she did not want to eat it. She said, 'For the reason that the witnesses say—I don't know how to tell it—miserable that I am that I don't know how to tell it. I say I did it and my God how can I tell it?' Then she said that, as she did not do it, how could she tell it—'They will not listen to me—these people want to kill me—release me and I will tell the truth.' She was again admonished to tell the truth. She said, 'I did it, I don't know how I did it—I did it for what the witnesses say—let me go—I have lost my senses and I don't know how to tell it—loosen me and I will tell the truth.' Then she said, 'Señor, I did it, I don't know how I have to tell it, but I tell it as the witnesses say—I wish to tell it—take me from here. Señor, as the witnesses say, so I say and confess it.' She was told to declare it. She said, 'I don't know how to say it—I have no memory—Lord, you are witness that if I knew how to say anything else I would say it. I have nothing more to say than that I did it and God knows it.' She said many times, 'Señores, Señores, nothing helps me. You, Lord, hear that I tell the truth and can say no more—they are tearing out my soul—order them to loosen me.' Then she said, 'I do not say that I did it—I said no more.' Then she said, 'Señor, I did it to observe that Law.' She was asked what Law. She said, 'The Law that the witnesses say—I declare it all, Señor, and don't remember what Law it was—O, wretched was the mother that bore me.' She was asked what was the Law she meant and what was the Law she said the witnesses say. This was asked repeatedly, but she was silent and at last said that she did not know. She was told to tell the truth or the garrotes would be tightened but she did not answer. Another turn was ordered on the garrotes and she was admonished to say what Law it was. She said, 'If I knew what to say I would say it. Oh, Señor, I don't know what I have to say—Oh, oh, they are killing me—if they would tell me what—Oh, Señores! Oh, my heart!' Then she asked why they wished her to tell what she could not tell and cried repeatedly, 'O, miserable me!' Then she said, 'Lord, bear witness that they are killing me without my being able to confess.' She was told that if she wished to tell the truth before the water was poured she should do so and discharge her conscience. She said that she could not speak and that she was a sinner. Then the linen *toca* (funnel) was placed (in her throat) and she said, 'Take it away, I am strangling and am sick in the stomach.' A jar of water was then poured down, after which she was told to tell the truth. She clamoured for confession, saying that she was dying. She was told that the torture would be continued till she told the truth and was admonished to tell it, but though she was questioned repeatedly she remained silent. Then the inquisitor, seeing her exhausted by the torture, ordered it to be suspended.''

The torture thus ordered to be "suspended" (not ended, for though as we have seen it was forbidden to apply torture more than once, unless new evidence supervened, it could be continued after a break) was particularly mild, since only one *jarra* of water was applied. This prisoner, too, appears to have been sparing in her screams and tears, all such details being meticulously noted by the secretary who recorded in a cold, unmoved style whatever took place in the torture-chamber. (This indeed appears to the modern mind one of the most revolting aspects of the whole system.) But the sufferings of Elvira del Campo were by no means at an end. The Inquisitors did not grant her request to be prompted what to confess; indeed, since their object was to save her immortal soul, they could not very well do so. After a lapse of four days (an interval during which, as experience had shown, the limbs would have time to stiffen, so that the repetition became all the more painful) she was again brought to the torture-chamber. On this occasion she broke down entirely when she was stripped, and piteously begged to have her nakedness covered. The torture and interrogation were nevertheless resumed. Her replies were at first even less coherent than before, but ultimately the Inquisitors were able to obtain the desired result: she confessed to Judaism, expressed repentance and begged for mercy, and was ultimately reconciled to the Holy Catholic Church at a public *auto de fé*.[1]

By a somewhat nauseating legal fiction, it was held that

[1] This account—the most detailed of the sort accessible in English—is cited here from Lea, *The Inquisition in Spain*, iii. 23-6, after the original from the records of the Toledo Inquisition (now in Madrid).

It is right to add that the Portuguese Inquisition was in this respect less ferocious than the Spanish, the methods of torture being restricted.

a confession obtained by the use, or even threat, of torture
was invalid. Hence, after an interval of at least twenty-
four hours, the prisoner was taken to a place removed from
the torture-chamber, where his confession was read out to
him. He was then requested to declare, upon oath, that
it was correct in every detail, and that he ratified it
not through fear of torture, but from mere love of veracity.
If the confession were not ratified, the "suspended"
torture might be continued.

Torture was potentially a double-edged weapon: and
it may be imagined that had the same methods been
applied to the Inquisitors as the latter applied to their
victims, the results would have been very similar. On
one occasion, indeed (if we are to believe a contemporary
account) the experiment was tried. The physician of
a certain powerful Portuguese noble was arrested by the
Holy Office on the charge of being a Judaiser. His employer wrote to the Inquisitor, giving his personal assurance that the accused was as good a Christian as himself.
The reply came that the prisoner had confessed his crime
under torture, and that sentence was about to be pronounced. The noble, greatly incensed, invited the Inquisitor to dinner. Afterwards, he had his guest seized
by his servants, and amused himself by practising on him
the preliminaries of a few favourite Inquisitional torments. The victim was able to escape only after signing
with his own hand a declaration that he, too, was a secret
Jew, like his victim. . . . One is to imagine, presumably,
an exchange of confessions, followed by the acquittal of
the accused; but it is not altogether impossible that
the Inquisitor's admissions were actually founded on
truth.

For it is obvious that the evidence extracted under
torture shews a depressing tendency to reveal precisely

what the judges desire and expect, whether true or false. It was under torture, for example, that in the thirteenth century (the only occasion when the Inquisition was formally active in England, and then only for a few months) the Templars confessed that, on their admission to this crusading Order, they were compelled to adore an idol with the unconvincing name Baphomet: yet no two descriptions of it coincided, and in spite of all the searches made in the Templars' houses no such object was ever found. Similarly, it was under torture that mediæval heretics in Italy revealed in revolting detail an improbable abomination called "barilotto," consisting of the roasting of a new-born child and the drinking of its ashes from a sacramental cup at secret conventicles, when nameless and promiscuous lust was ritually practised.

It should however be recognised that in most instances torture was imposed only to induce the prisoner to confess what the Inquisitors already knew: for (as we have seen) unless he confessed fully, penitence was impossible, and the result was damnation to the soul as well as death to the body. A study of the records shews that the Inquisition generally proceeded only after having collected ample evidence of crime, and the cases in which a condemnation did not result were thus extremely few. In the Toledo tribunal, for instance, the acquittals between 1484 and 1531 averaged less than two yearly. The number of those condemned by the Portuguese Inquisition comes to well over three-quarters of the total number of cases tried. On the other hand, even when the Inquisitors were ultimately convinced that the silence of the accused under torture was based on innocence, a certain measure of culpability was nevertheless assumed: for the accused had been guilty of behaving in a suspicious manner, and this in itself was an offence for which penance was required. Indeed, in most cases, the formula of acquittal intimated, not that the accused was innocent, but that the accuser had not been unable to prove his case. A man might leave the Inquisition without being burned, the proverb ran, but he was certain to be singed.

CHAPTER V

QUEMADERO

THE conquerors of Spain have all left behind some contribution to her public life and amenities. In the eighth
century, the Arabs introduced to Andalusia their sport
of baiting animals, which developed into the Bull-Fight.
In the fifteenth, the Christians, combining the legacies of
Imperial and of Papal Rome, and infusing something of
their own morbid bitterness, evolved the *Act of Faith*, or
Auto de Fé. The more common form, *Auto da Fé*, is
Portuguese, and illustrates the unenviable notoriety
which the smaller country enjoyed in this respect in
Northern Europe. There was, however, no difference,
excepting perhaps in accentuation, between the institution as it existed in the two countries.

The spectacle was not always a public one. Sometimes, when less serious penalties were involved (abjura-
tions *de levi*, as they were termed), it was held with a
minimum of publicity in a church. This ceremony was
called an *auto particular*, or Private Auto; though the
Spaniards, with their love of diminutives, invented a new
word for it, *autillo*. But in most cases the ceremony was
public. This was partly in order to stress the serious
nature of the crime, partly to spread the glories and
terrors of the Holy Catholic Faith, partly to provide
the famished populace with a spectacle (it is one of the
handicaps of a democratic monarchy that jubilees or
coronations cannot be staged at more frequent intervals)
and partly because it was considered improper to pro-
nounce a sentence involving capital punishment within
the precincts of a consecrated building. The Public Auto

(*Auto Publico General*, as it was technically termed) ultimately became the centre of an elaborate ceremonial.

It would have been announced two or three weeks
before, spiritual benefits being promised to all who were
present. For days, the peasantry would stream in from
all the surrounding countryside to witness this great
spectacle. That night, no accommodation would be available for money (though perhaps it was for love) in the
whole city, and thousands might be sleeping out of doors,
under the star-spangled Andalusian sky. Early in the
morning, they were aroused by a general clanging of
bells. This was the signal for the beginning of a great
procession, in which all the clergy of the city took part,
headed by the official standard of the Inquisition. In
this pageant appeared all condemned to make public
penance. Those abjuring *de vehementi* carried lighted
tapers in their hands and wore the *sambenito* or *saco
bendito* ("sacred sack"), which was termed the *abito* in
the official sentence. This was an innovation of the
Spanish Inquisition. It consisted of a long yellow robe,
transversed by a black St. Andrew's cross (in the case of
those convicted only of formal heresy, only one of the
diagonal arms was necessary). Where the heretic had
escaped the stake by confession, flames pointing downwards (*fuego revuelto*) were painted on the garment,
which in these instances was sometimes of black. Those
condemned to be burned bore in addition a representa-
tion of devils thrusting heretics into the fires of hell. All
wore, moreover, a tall mitre (*coraza*) similarly adorned.
As a supplementary punishment the *sambenito* had to be
worn, in certain cases, in public, particularly on Sundays
and festivals, even after the release of the prisoner, for
months or even for years, exposing him to universal scorn
and derision. After its immediate utility had passed, it

was generally hung up in the parish church of the delin-
quent, accompanied by a suitable inscription, the family
of the wearer being thus marked out as objects of lasting
humiliation and suspicion.   These memorials of shame
were destroyed only with the abolition of the Inquisition
in the early years of the nineteenth century.

The horror which the *sambenito* inspired was extreme.
An amusing story is recorded by Ribeiro Sanchez, the
famous Marrano physician and reformer.   In Lisbon,
those who had been penanced at an *auto* had to present
themselves at church in this hideous garb every Sunday
to learn orthodox Christian doctrine.   On one occasion,
the press of people who were waiting to see the performers was so great that they were unable to leave the
building.   One of them therefore took off his *sambenito*
and advanced, waving it about him.   So great was the
popular fear of being contaminated by its touch that there
was a general stampede, and the path was completely
and immediately cleared.

Passing through the town, the procession arrived at the
place where the *auto* was to be celebrated, generally the
principal square of the city.   Two stagings were erected
here, at considerable expense, for the principal actors—
one for those convicted and for their spiritual attendants,
the other for the civil and ecclesiastical authorities.   Pulpits and a temporary altar, draped in black, were set up
between them.   On their arrival, the penitents and dignitaries took their place on these scaffoldings.   At this
stage, the notary of the Holy Office held up a cross and
made the people raise their hands and swear solemnly to
defend the Catholic faith and to support the Inquisition.
(When the sovereign was present, he had to take a special
oath besides the general one.)   A distinguished ecclesiastic
then delivered a sermon, the subject of which was not so

much the edification of the audience as the discomfiture
of the condemned, upon whose heads a torrent of insults,
revoltingly cruel in the circumstances, was poured. The
penitents then appeared one by one before the pulpit to
hear their fate, which had hitherto been kept a profound
secret except in the case of those condemned to death,
who were informed of it on the previous night. The
reading of the sentences took some time, for every detail
of the charges was enumerated, and hence the proceedings were sometimes spread over more than one day.
The formal acts of abjuration were sometimes performed
in batches (much like the conferring of degrees at a
modern University on busy occasions), half a dozen
prisoners or more appearing before the altar at a time.

The sentences were nominally decided on, not by the
Inquisitors alone, but by a body termed the *Consulta de
Fé*, or Council of Faith; this contained, besides the Inquisitors, a representative of the Bishop of the prisoner's
diocese, whose presence was required by Canon Law, and
a number of distinguished lawyers and theologians who
were invited to act as "consulters." Any convicted
person who professed repentance, whether spontaneously
or as a result of torture, was "reconciled" to the bosom
of Holy Church. He was made to swear before a crucifix, publicly, that he adhered to the Catholic faith in
every detail; that he detested every form of heresy, particularly that to which he had confessed; and that he
accepted fully the punishment which had been imposed
upon him by way of penance. There were two forms of
"abjuration," as it was termed; light (*de levi*), and
vehement (*de vehementi*). In the former case the person
convicted added that if he failed to comply with the
sentence he should be held impenitent; in the latter, that
should he fail to perform his penance, he desired to be

treated as a relapsed heretic. Since the penalty for relapse was death at the stake, reconciliation of this sort could properly be performed only once, and an abjuration *de vehementi* was a very serious matter.

Every form of reconciliation was accompanied by an appropriate punishment. Although the offences committed by the culprits were of a spiritual nature, the spiritual penances (such as fasting on Fridays for a certain length of time or reciting a number of Ave Marias or Paternosters) were the most infrequent. For "serious" crimes, harsher penalties existed. Scourging was very frequent indeed in the earlier period, but sank into disuse as time went on in Spain, though it persisted in Portugal. It was executed publicly, with every circumstance of humiliation; and as many as two hundred strokes were a commonplace. The *verguenza* ("shaming") was a similar penalty, with the omission of the lashes. The guilty, both men and women, were paraded through the town stripped to the waist and bearing the insignia of their offence, while a crier proclaimed the sentence and details of the crime before them. Sometimes a gag was applied, this being regarded as an additional humiliation. Such was the abhorrence with which this public shaming was regarded that many considered death a merciful alternative.

A completely new penalty, introduced with a view to his own advantage by the economical Ferdinand the Catholic, was that of the galleys, by means of which the state was able to benefit even from heresy. In 1573, and again in 1591, the Supreme Council of the Inquisition ordered that all convicted New Christians, even if they confessed their crime freely, should be sent to row in the royal ships of war; and it remained a punishment which was frequently meted out. The sentences ranged from three years to life; but these terms frequently approximated, as the sufferings involved often had fatal results. In the course of the eighteenth century, other types of penal servitude were substituted. For women, the most frequent alternative was forced service in hospitals or houses of correction. Another common punishment was perpetual imprisonment. The prison was known by the euphemistic title of *casa de la penitencia* or *de la misericordia* ('' House of Penitence '' or '' House of Mercy '') and appears to have been less rigorous than the secret prisons (*cárceles secretas*) in which the accused were incarcerated while awaiting sentence. In later years, although the official term '' perpetual punishment '' was retained, the duration of imprisonment was generally reduced to eight years or even less. In Portugal, the term was fixed in 1640 at three to five years. Other penalties included exile (frequently to the colonies), exclusion from certain cities, and the rasing to the ground of the house of any peculiarly heinous offender, or one in which heretical services had been held.

One of the most serious consequences of a conviction for heresy, or for other grave offences, was the disability which fell not only on those penanced, but upon their children and descendants for some generations to come. They were perpetually excluded from any public dignity, and were not allowed to enter Holy Orders. Among the professions closed to them were those of physician, apothecary, tutor of the young, advocate, scrivener, and farmer of revenue. They were forbidden to wear cloth of gold or silver, or to bedeck themselves with jewelry, or to ride on horseback—a mule, or donkey, was the utmost to which they could aspire. If they possessed only the slightest tincture of New Christian blood, those guilty of any misdemeanour (however trifling) were henceforth considered to belong to that category in the fullest degree, and suffered from all the theological and social prejudice which resulted from that fact: and this, too, passed on to their children. Neglect of these provisions, even after the lapse of several generations, might bring the offender once more into the clutches of the Tribunal. Often, however, infractions were punished only by fine, and rehabilitations, in return for a financial consideration, ultimately became very common and constituted an additional source of revenue for the Holy Office.

The most terrible weapon of the Inquisition, other than the power of inflicting the death sentence, was the right it enjoyed of confiscating the property of those whom it convicted. At first, the proceeds were handed over to the sovereign, and general compositions on the part of the New Christians, in order to save themselves from the possibility of arbitrary confiscation, were not uncommon. Later, however, the proceeds of confiscation devolved upon the Holy Office, only a very small proportion reaching the public treasury. It now became impossible for communities to purchase immunity. We have already described the desperate struggle of the *conversos* and their descendants against this right, which they considered to be a perpetual incitement to proceedings against them, however unimpeachable their orthodoxy might be. It was through this means that the Spanish Inquisition was raised into a corporation of such vast influence and wealth. Moreover, it became overwhelmingly to its interest to procure the conviction of all who were brought before it, especially when they were persons of means. By the use of this weapon a man's whole family might be reduced at one blow from affluence to beggary, and the economic life of the whole country disorganised. There was only one certain way of avoiding this—migration. No other single factor, perhaps, was so instrumental in draining the Peninsula of its accumulated wealth during the course of the sixteenth, seventeenth, and eighteenth centuries.

The final, and greatest, sanction in the power of the Holy Office was euphemistically termed "relaxation." No ecclesiastical person was supposed to be a direct party to the shedding of blood. (It will be recalled how for this reason prelates went into battle in the Middle Ages armed with maces instead of swords.) Hence the Holy Office handed over, or "relaxed," to the secular arm persons guilty of the gravest offences, for which there was no expiation other than death. This procedure was accompanied by a formal recommendation to mercy, with the proviso that, if it were found absolutely necessary to proceed to the extreme penalty, it should be effected "without effusion of blood"—that is, by burning. It was understood that the secular authorities would immediately condemn those "relaxed" to the stake, and the sentence of "relaxation" was thus equivalent to a death-sentence. This was an ancient legal fiction of the Church, dating back to the eleventh or twelfth century, and the actual mode of punishment was justified by a text from the Gospels (John xv. 6): "If a man abide not in me, he is cast forth as a branch and is withered: and men gather them and cast them into the fire, *and they are burned*."

The sentence of relaxation was inflicted upon four classes of culprits, who were, generally speaking, those who had rejected the opportunity to repent. These comprised the "contumacious," who gloried in their crime, and died true martyrs to their convictions; the "relapsed," who had been reconciled *de vehementi* on some previous occasion, whose backsliding proved their insincerity, and from whom no further profession of repentance could possibly be accepted; the "*diminutos*," whose confession was incomplete, or who shielded their accomplices; and the "*negativos*," who refused to confess to the charges brought against them, or who, while admitting that they had performed the actions of which they were accused, denied having had any heretical intention. Among the cases of "*diminutos*" several are recorded who, in spite of the fact that in their confessions they had implicated hundreds of other persons, including the whole of their own families, were nevertheless condemned to the flames on the ground that their admissions were incomplete. Finally, those relaxed occasionally, though infrequently, included "dogmatisers," or those who propagated heretical views. Such persons might be unbaptised as well as baptised, and in the earlier Inquisitional period some professing Jews (and later, Moslems, as well as Protestants) suffered under this head.

It should be noted that by no means all those persons upon whom a capital sentence had been pronounced were burnt alive, as is generally imagined; this is indeed a traditional Protestant fallacy, which has no basis in fact. Even after the culprit had been condemned, a profession of repentance was usually sufficient to secure the preliminary mercy of garotting, only the corpse being concremated at the stake. This is what occurred probably in a majority of the cases after the Inquisition had emerged from its ferocious infancy. Even so, of course, mistakes might sometimes occur. At one *auto* held in Mexico, the executioner began to garrot one of his victims in error, under the impression that he had been accorded this preliminary grace by reason of a last-moment profession of repentance. The mistake was however discovered in time, and the unfortunate victim was dragged half-dead to the pyre, thus (as the contemporary chronicler complacently phrases it) tasting the agony of both deaths.

The effigies and bones of those who had escaped the stake by death (sometimes in prison, or under torture), together (*faute de mieux*) with effigies of fugitives, were also committed to the flames. In these cases, reconciliation was clearly impossible, while the entire property of the condemned was confiscated by the Holy Office, no matter how long a time had elapsed since the offence had been committed. The passing of such sentences upon the dead was therefore far from being a mere formality.

It is obviously incorrect to consider all the victims of the Inquisition as martyrs to their faith. Those who went to the stake proudly confessing their heretical views were a comparatively insignificant minority. On the occasion of the great persecution of New Christians in Majorca in 1691, only three persons out of a total of some forty were burned alive: the rest had saved themselves from the worst agonies by a timely profession of repentance, and only their dead bodies were committed to the flames. The proportion was not peculiarly high. It was not to be expected that persons who for years had sedulously practised a system of subterfuge would suddenly acquire the spirit of martyrdom in their last moments, though that did occasionally occur. Among those who were burnt alive were a certain number of *diminutos* or *relapsados*, whose profession of repentance was now insufficient to procure mercy, while others were *negativos*, some of whom were undoubtedly innocent. These victims perished professing the Catholic faith up to their last moment upon earth. It is on record on the other hand that suspects sometimes decided to deny all the charges brought against them, because they would thus have some slight chance of escaping sentence, and might be able to avoid implicating their friends. It is this which explains the silence of some persons, indubitably guilty, who by their negative attitude deprived themselves not only of the final mercy of garrotting but also of the satisfaction of martyrdom.

It is necessary to remember that the idea of death by burning was not the unmentionable horror to our ancestors that it is to us. England, too, burned her religious dissenters, Protestant or Catholic according to the religious system which prevailed at the time, down to the reign of James I. The punishment remained on the statute-book (not for witches only, as is commonly believed) well after that date. Thus, as late as 1786, the body of a woman condemned and executed for the crime of coining was burned at the Old Bailey in London. Precisely a quarter of a century earlier, in enlightened France, two persons were burned after strangulation for an alleged offence against the Sacrament. Even so, the penalty was not so hideous as that of the *peine forte et dure*, consisting of pressing to death in the most excruciating manner, which was inflicted in England down to the end of the eighteenth century on persons arraigned for felony who had refused to plead.

On the evening preceding the Act of Faith, those who were to be "relaxed" to the secular arm were brought to the Palace of the Inquisition to hear their fate. From that moment, a couple of eloquent Confessors were attached to the person of each one, in the hopes of persuading him to save his soul by a last-minute repentance. At the *auto*, these sentences were left to the last. Those "relaxed" were then formally condemned by the civil magistrate and conducted to the *quemadero* or place of burning (also known as the *brasero*, or brazier). The prisoners were accompanied by a detachment of soldiers, whose presence was sometimes necessary to protect them from the fury of the mob. The function of mounting guard at the *autos* and of furnishing wood for the pyre was relegated in some cities to a special body known as the *compañia de la Zarza*. With them were borne the effigies of those who had anticipated their fate by flight or death, as well as the exhumed remains of the latter, all of which were committed to the flames.

John Addington Symonds has described this aspect of the spectacle in terms which, though they may not exaggerate, certainly leave nothing to be imagined. It is hardly possible to improve upon them: " To make these holocausts of human beings more ghastly, the pageant was enhanced by processions of exhumed corpses and heretics in effigy. Artificial dolls and decomposed bodies, with grinning lips and mouldy foreheads, were hauled to the huge bonfire, side by side with living men, women and children. All of them alike—*fantoccini*, skeletons, and quick folk—were enveloped in the same grotesquely ghastly San Benito, with the same hideous yellow mitres on their paste-board, worm-eaten or palpitating foreheads. The procession presented an artistically loathsome dissonance of red and yellow hues, as it defiled, to the infernal music of growled psalms and screams and moanings, beneath the torrid blaze of Spanish sunlight."

The pious duty, or honour, of lighting the brand with which the pyre was kindled was usually allotted as a special compliment to some distinguished visitor—often to visiting royalty. It should be noted that the execution of sentence did not form an integral part of the ceremony of the *auto de fé*, as is generally imagined, being carried out at a different place (generally outside the city walls) and some time later. It was however witnessed by many spectators, who paid high prices for windows with a good view. Sometimes, even, a special staging would be erected for the convenience of honoured guests.

An eager crowd awaited the last appearance of the heretics: and it was the fiendish custom of the populace to set fire to the beards of the condemned, so as to give them a preliminary taste of their suffering (this was termed " Shaving the New Christians "). In some towns, such as Toledo, the *Plaza de Quemadero* still retains its name or did until very recently. At Lisbon, the place of burning was at the great square on the sea-front, where tourists now land (at present called the *Praça do Municipio*, but formerly the *Terreiro do Paço*) adjacent to the former Royal Palace. At Madrid, the site is now occupied by the Glorieta de San Bernardo: at Seville, more aptly, by the Bull Ring. The ashes of the victims were supposed to be scattered to the four winds, but masses of bones have been more than once found during the course of recent excavations (notably at Madrid and Saragossa) shewing that the fire did not always complete its work.

From the very beginning, the *auto* was reckoned a great public spectacle, vying in popular appeal with bull-fights. Tens of thousands of persons of all sorts and degree would stream in from the surrounding countryside or from the adjacent towns in order to be present and to combine with a pleasant outing the advantage of the spiritual benefits conferred by the forethought of the Inquisitors. At Córdova, at one great *auto* held in 1665, nearly 400,000 maravedis were expended on the entertainment of the Inquisitors, their retinues, and the numerous guests. The proceedings lasted from seven o'clock in the morning to nine o'clock at night; and fifty-seven Judaisers were relaxed either in person or in effigy, three who held out to the last being roasted alive. As was the practice in this city, it is to be presumed that the Holy Office, " realising the general inconvenience and danger to morals which would have resulted if the final scene took place at night," was so considerate as to arrange for the recital of the sentences, in the case of those condemned to death, to conclude at four in the afternoon. (The latter's convenience was, after all, so circumscribed that it was unnecessary to take it into account). They were then escorted to the *quemadero* on the Campo del Marrubial (now the Plaza de la Corredera), outside the Puerta de Plasencia, where all preparations had been made the day before. Such was the press of spectators who had come from far and near to witness this degrading spectacle that the vast expanse of the Campo was one dense mass of coaches, horses and human beings, none of whom could move until the whole affair was over.

Another especially noteworthy *auto* took place at Seville in 1660. It lasted for three days, and was according to all accounts one of the greatest ever known, a throng of no less than 100,000 being reported to witness it. Forty-seven Judaisers figured (mostly Portuguese), of whom seven were burned—three of them alive. Besides these, thirty fugitives were burned in effigy, including a Professor at the University of Seville and one of the most popular playwrights in Madrid.

Special celebrations were often arranged in honour of royalty. Thus the visit to Toledo in February, 1570, of Philip II. and his bride Isabella of Valois (who had succeeded to the couch of Mary of England) was marked by an *auto* spread over two days. (Some other examples are noted elsewhere in these pages in a different connexion.) This attitude of mind lasted for a long while; and it is said that in the eighteenth century, when an English Prince of the blood-royal was about to leave Lisbon after a short visit, he was waited upon by the Inquisitor General, who humbly requested His Royal Highness to stay a few days longer in order to be present at the *auto* which was being arranged in his honour.

To suggest that nothing more than Catholic zeal brought these vast concourses of people together is out of the question. It was the same base, ghoulish curiosity which was responsible for the enormous attendances at public executions held in England until a generation ago; with a far greater approach to humanity, it is true, and certainly with more justification, than was the case with the wretched martyrdoms in Spain. That this is so is demonstrated by a note affixed at the close of the official account of the Seville *auto* of March 29th, 1648. One individual only was relaxed in person—a young Marrano merchant named Simon Rodrigues Nuñez, who had relapsed into his offence. On the following day, the scourging of those sentenced was carried out, and in the afternoon twenty-one effigies of the dead and fugitives, as well as the living culprit, were taken to the pyre. Enormous numbers of people had assembled, we are informed, a rumour having spread that Nuñez was inconstant in the faith, and would in consequence be burned alive. To the general disappointment, however, he professed repentance, and was first garotted. Similarly, on an occasion at Valladolid in 1609, great popular discontent was caused because the one person condemned to relaxation finally escaped the stake.

The same attitude of mind is demonstrated in the literature of the *autos*, which is abundant. The sermons preached on these occasions were often printed—seventy-five are extant in Portuguese alone—in order to familiarise the faithful throughout the country with the precise terms in which the martyrs were assailed at their last moment. *Listas* of the persons who appeared were hawked about the streets to satisfy the ghoulish tastes of the populace—much like race-cards at more convivial gatherings of today. A French visitor of the eighteenth century informs us how the only manner of avoiding some of the more gruesome sights he had to witness was to bury his face in his *Lista*: otherwise, he would have been suspected of sympathising with the sufferers, which was only one degree removed from heresy itself. Subsequently "Relations" of the *autos* containing full details of the proceedings—occasionally, solid volumes of some hundreds of pages—were published and republished, to spread the good news far and near of the new triumph for the Holy Catholic Faith.

With regard to the number of victims who suffered at the hands of the Inquisition, estimates vary enormously. Llorente, the ex-Secretary of the Holy Office who wrote a bitterly antagonistic account of it at the beginning of the nineteenth century, based on manuscript material which is no longer extant, states that all told, from its foundation down to 1808, the total number of heretics burned in person in Spain alone totalled 31,912, those burned in effigy 17,659, and those reconciled *de vehementi* 291,450. These figures are so enormous as to seem highly suspicious. It must be recalled, however, that at the outset, the activity and the violence of the Holy Office was boundless: and to suggest that during the first century of its existence, ten tribunals burned on an average thirty heretics each yearly—a hypothesis which would amply justify this high estimate—certainly does not appear to be out of the question. This reckoning is borne out by the intensely Catholic historian Amador de los Rios, usually most moderate in his views, who estimates that between 1484 and 1525, the number of those burned in person came to 28,540, those in effigy to 16,520, and those penanced to 303,847. On the other hand, Rodrigo, the apologist of the Inquisition, puts forward the impossible assertion that less than 400 persons were burned during the whole history of the Inquisition in Spain. Even if this refers to those who remained steadfast to the last, and so were burned alive, it is a manifest under-statement: indeed, it should be possible without much difficulty to draw up a nominal roll far in excess of this number.

As far as Portugal and its dependencies go, the figures can be provided with a much greater approach to precision. There are extant the records of approximately 40,000 cases tried before the three tribunals of that country from the middle of the sixteenth to the middle of the eighteenth century. Of these, upwards of 30,000 resulted in condemnations. The sentences were carried out at recorded *autos de fé* totalling approximately 750. In these, 1,808 persons were burned at the stake (1,175 in person and 633 in effigy) and 29,590 were reconciled. Another account places the number burned in person at 1,012; but the larger figure is certainly to be preferred, as during the period of decline, between 1651 and 1760, there were 419 recorded victims. Lists have been compiled of little less than 2,000 *autos* which took place in the Inquisition and its dependencies from 1480 down to 1826. But the precise figures and proportions are after all of no great significance. The institution was an abomination on the face of the earth, whether its victims were reckoned in hundreds or in thousands.

Nothing perhaps impresses the modern reader in the record of the Inquisition quite so much as the unnecessary inhumanity which was shewn to the victims—particularly to those about to die. The Sermons which were delivered at the *autos de fé* never omitted any opportunity to revile the condemned. Their sufferings were increased by the incessant objurgations of the attendant friars. There seems a strange lack of proportion in the tribute paid to the self-sacrificing monks and friars of all orders, who, we are told in one account of the Córdova *auto* of March 3rd, 1655, were "made insensible to the baking heat of the sun by their ardent zeal for the welfare of these souls"; nor can the modern mind see much to admire in the conduct of the Marquis de los Veles, who, on the same occasion, pressed forward to a particularly obdurate heretic "with a crucifix in his hand and much Christian zeal in his breast," imploring him "by the bowels of that Lord to become converted to the Holy Catholic Faith." The steadfastness of the victims seldom evoked the grudging tribute of admiration: it was ascribed to the prompting of the Evil One: "such was the possession of the Devil upon his body and his soul," we are told, at the close of one account. We are informed moreover that these victims died with a terrible expression on their faces and the utmost fury in their eyes—not like Catholic martyrs, who went to their death calm and serene, with their eyes mirroring the assurance and justice of their cause.

Yet an objective study of the Inquisition and its methods on the basis of the original records, and not second-hand abridgements, is sufficient to convince even an unfavourable critic of the care (and it is not unfair to add, zeal) with which it worked. It seldom made an arrest unless it was fairly certain of its case: and torture was generally employed to obtain confirmation of what it already knew, or fresh details to implicate others. To be sure, even contemporaneously adverse critics refused to admit this. They considered that a considerable proportion of those who suffered at the hands of the Inquisition were condemned unjustly. Above all, they denied that the *negativos* (those, that is, who refused to make any admission of guilt, and so were burned alive) could possibly be guilty, excepting in an insignificant minority of cases. They adduced for example the tragic story of two elderly nuns, who were burned alive at Evora in 1673, and who died with the name of Jesus on their lips, after having lived an unblemished life in their convents for as long, in one case, as forty years. In the same category, they claimed, was a distinguished soldier, João Alvarez de Barbuda, who took with him into prison a book of hours and a little image of Saint Anthony, but nevertheless was burned alive. During the course of the *auto* held at Lisbon on May 10th, 1682, eight persons who had died a more or less natural death in prison because of their sufferings were pronounced innocent. In the following year, the Tribunal of Coimbra acquitted a woman who had died after seventeen years of incarceration, and was now pronounced to be an Old Christian of unblemished family and reputation. Such instances however cannot have been very common.

It will have been observed that of the victims of the Inquisition, a large proportion were women. Sometimes, indeed, they far outnumbered the men. In its earliest days, an admiring observer noted that of those who held out heroically to the end the majority belonged to what was generally considered the weaker sex. The tradition thus set continued. Thus for example, at the celebration held at Coimbra on May 23rd, 1660, no less than thirteen of the eighteen persons condemned to the stake were women. There was, of course, no limitation as to age. The record is perhaps held by the venerable Ana Rodriguez, of Chaves, who figured as a penitent at the Lisbon *auto* of May 10th, 1682, at the hoary age of ninety-seven: but she is run close by Maria Barbara Carillo, who was burned alive at Madrid in 1721, in her ninety-sixth year. Maria Alejandra Rodriguez, a woman of ninety, was similarly "relaxed" at Granada at about the same time. On the occasion when Ana Rodriguez was punished a woman of seventy was sentenced to deportation to Brazil. At the other end of the scale we frequently find children of either sex, of twelve or thirteen, similarly condemned, and forced to implicate entire families in their confessions. In 1659, two girls of only ten years of age were "reconciled" by the tribunal of Toledo.

Beauty, apparently, made no more impression on the Inquisitors than did age. Garcia d'Alarcon, tried before the Inquisition at Granada in 1593, was described in the official record as the most lovely woman in the whole kingdom; but this did not save her from condemnation to the indignities of reconciliation, followed by condign punishment.

Nor did one condemnation save the victim from further persecution. A certain Isabella, wife of Francisco Dalos of Ciudad Real, was tried by the Valladolid tribunal in 1608, when only twenty-two years of age. Subsequently she was again arraigned five more times—twice at Llerena, twice at Cuenca, and finally at Toledo. Altogether about eighteen years of her life were passed in the Inquisitional dungeons. The last trial began in 1665, when she was in her eightieth year and lasted until 1670. During its course, notwithstanding her advanced age, she was tortured three times, ultimately succumbing (as was not remarkable) to her sufferings. Nevertheless, the Tribunal would not be baulked of its revenge, and her body was burned, together with her effigy, as that of one who had died in sin.

Among the most interesting Inquisitional victims was Dona Ana de Castro, one of the last of those who suffered martyrdom in the New World. She was a leader of society in Lima, of high social standing though of dubious reputation. Her love affairs were notorious throughout the province; and she was rumoured to have ceded (the malicious said sold) her favours to the Viceroy himself, as well as to many of the proudest colonial hidalgos. In 1731 she was accused before the Inquisition as a Judaiser. Notwithstanding her persistent denials, she was put on trial, tortured and ultimately condemned to the stake. In the solemn *auto* of December 23rd, 1736, she was burned alive, notwithstanding the agonised weeping which aroused the sympathy of all who saw her on the way to the *quemadero*. But, not long after, persons began to whisper that she had been the victim of a judicial murder; and, looking back on the whole episode from a distance of two centuries, it seems almost certain that she was in fact brought to her death in consequence of an intrigue on the part either of her enemies or—what is more probable— her rivals and competitors.

Only one occasion is on record when a prisoner managed to be avenged on his arch-persecutor. This was in Sicily, in 1657. A certain renegade Augustin Friar, Diego Lamattina, was in custody on the charge of being a heretical blasphemer, despiser of the Sacraments and insulter of the sacred images. While he was in prison, a newly appointed Inquisitor General, unusually conscientious, made the rounds of the secret dungeons. When he entered Fra Diego's cell, the latter snapped his manacles and dashed them again and again against the other's head, causing wounds which ultimately proved fatal. The final outcome was only what might have been anticipated. An enormous crowd assembled on March 17th, 1658, on the Piano di S. Erasmo at Palermo, to witness the execution of the sentence. At the last moment, the errant friar thought of a fresh argument, and summoned the attendant priest back to the *quemadero*: had not God announced that He did not desire the death of sinners, but only that they should repent from their illdoing (as he was prepared to do) and live (which no one had seriously suggested in his case)? The priest tactfully pointed out that it was spiritual life which the prophet had in mind. "Then God is unfair," retorted the heretic—an outrageous leave-taking to this world, which induced the new Inquisitor to give orders for his ashes to be scattered after burning, for greater certainty.

On one occasion, an incorrigible humorist brought an element of comic relief even to the last grim scene. Balthazar Lopez was a native of Valladolid, who had amassed a considerable fortune as Court Saddler. In 1645, after a trip abroad, he was arrested, put on trial, and condemned. With fifty-six other persons, he figured in the great *auto* held at Cuenca on June 29th, 1654, he himself with nine others being condemned to be burned at the stake. The confessor, who remained in attendance on him from the moment that sentence was promulgated, persuaded him to avoid the worst agonies by a profession of repentance. He did so: and, as they approached the *quemadero*, the priest exhorted him to rejoice, since as a result of his contrition the gates of Paradise were opening for him freely. "Freely! do you say, Father?" retorted Lopez. "The confiscation of my property has cost me two hundred thousand ducats. Do you infer that I have been swindled?"

At the *brasero*, he looked on critically, while the executioner, Pedro de Alcalá, clumsily garotted a couple of his fellow-victims. "Pedro," he said, mildly, "if you can strangle me no better than you are doing those poor souls, I had rather be burned alive."

When his turn came at last, the executioner began to fasten his feet. Lopez struggled against this indignity. "*Por Dios!*" he cried. "If you bind me, I won't be-lieve in your Jesus. Take this crucifix away!" Suiting action to the word, he threw it from him. His attendant priest, horrified, succeeded after some little trouble in persuading him to accept it back again and to ask for-giveness.

The end now approached. As the executioner began to do his work, the priest asked whether he was truly repentant. The dying man looked at him in mild re-proach. "Father," said he, "do you think that this is a time to joke?"

CHAPTER VI

THE MARRANOS

It is frequently stated, and generally believed, that the principal object of the existence of the Inquisition was to burn Jews. Strictly speaking, this is completely untrue. It is almost possible (though not quite) to go to the other extreme, and to say that the Inquisition never burned a Jew. For the object of the Inquisition was to deal with heretics *within* the Church—that is to say, persons who had been baptised, or who asserted that they were Christians, but departed from the practice and teaching of Roman Catholicism. Normally, then, professing Jews did not come into the scope of its activities, unless they had been guilty of interfering with the faith of some baptised person and thus "favouring" heresy, or were "dogmatisers" who preached it. Accordingly (as has been seen), at the outset the Holy Office proceeded against a few Rabbis and others on a charge of proselytisation among their baptised kinsmen or conniving in their return to the Jewish fold. Normally, however, the Inquisition had no power over Jews as such: and occasionally an accused person put up as his defence the plea that he was a Jew, who had never been baptised and never pretended to be anything else. If this claim could be established, he was safe from any Inquisitional punishment: though what the civil power would do is another matter.

Notwithstanding this fact, that the Inquisition normally had no power over Jews, it is true that Judaism constituted from beginning to end one of its greatest problems, if not the greatest of all. It was not however a question of declared Jews, but of those Marranos or New Chris-

tians who, left behind in Spain after the expulsion of
1492, were baptised at birth, brought up as Christians,
and observed the outward ceremonials of the Catholic
faith, while at heart remaining Jewish and secretly practising whatever Hebraic rites they could. For the first
half-century of its existence, this was almost the solitary
preoccupation of the Inquisition. After that period, it
remained among its principal cares. Moreover, once the
menace of Protestantism had been suppressed, in the
second half of the sixteenth century, Judaising was again
considered the greatest of the crimes within its scope.
Its minor activities were largely concerned with trivial
offenders: its major were with the Judaisers, who to
the end furnished a disproportionately large number, not
perhaps of those who appeared at the *autos*, but certainly
of those condemned to death.

On the other hand, after the expulsion of the Jews from
Spain, the knowledge of Judaism—so largely a religion
of ceremonial and tradition—dwindled tragically among
the New Christians. They retained indeed a firm and
unyielding belief in the stern monotheism of their fathers.
Other than this, and an equally determined rejection of
image-worship, there was little but a diminishing family
tradition, reinforced by surreptitious study of the Old
Testament. It is on record, indeed, that sometimes the
Marranos sought guidance in the published accounts of
the crimes of the Inquisitional victims, so that, by dis-
covering what they were supposed to avoid, they might
know what to do.

The Holy Office, on its side, drew up detailed lists of
the most absurd and unimportant practices, which, it was
persuaded, were the marks of a convinced Judaiser. As
we have seen, an over-zealous regard for personal cleanliness at inconvenient times, or changing linen on Satur-

day, or a distaste for pork, was often sufficient to bring
about a person's arrest: and, with recourse to torture,
the worst might follow. The reader will recall Lawrence
Sterne's story of Corporal Trim's brother Tom, who
wooed and wed the widow of a prosperous sausage maker.
After the wedding, they were both dragged out of bed
and hauled before the Inquisition. It would never have
happened, according to the Corporal, if " they had but
put pork into their sausages."

The ruthlessness with which the Marranos were persecuted by the Holy Office actually fulfilled its object to a
very considerable extent. By the middle of the sixteenth
century, the native Spanish Judaisers had either been
exterminated or else cowed into subjection: and it should
now have been possible to say that the problem, to cope
with which the Inquisition had been called into existence,
had at last been solved. But at this stage, the native
Judaisers were reinforced by an influx of similar mis-
believers from Portugal, and it was these who engrossed
the attention of the Spanish Inquisition to a very large
extent from the sixteenth century to the close of the
eighteenth.

These immigrants were not, in fact, strangers: they
were in the main natives, returning after a short absence
to the land in which their fathers had lived. On the expulsion of the Jews from Spain in 1492, a very large proportion—a majority, perhaps—had crossed the frontier
into Portugal. Their reception here had been uncordial.
It was however tolerable—though no more—until, with
the accession of King Manoel the Fortunate, romance
and high policy entered the question. The soured
Isabella, Infanta of Spain, to whose hand he aspired,
refused to set foot in Portugal until its King followed the
pious example set by her parents, Ferdinand and Isabella,

and purged his realm of disbelief as drastically as they had done. It was a great match: a match which might have resulted in uniting the whole of the Peninsula under the rule of Manoel's children. The vistas which opened out were too enticing to be neglected: and it was the Jews who paid the price. In December, 1496, less than a week after the royal marriage-treaty had been signed, there was issued a decree banishing all Jews and other unbelievers from the country within ten months.

Hardly was the ink dry on his signature when Manoel began to consider the other side of the question. He was unwilling, even now, to deprive his realm of the most industrious and profitable section of his subjects. As Jews, indeed, their days in it were numbered. But, were they converted to Christianity, the edict of banishment would no longer apply. Their souls would be saved, his humane instincts mollified, and his kingdom benefited, in one simultaneous process. For the next few months, accordingly, he turned all his energies to a feverish attempt to impose conversion on the Jews, as the one possible alternative to their exile. No means were left untried: blandishments, bribes, craft, and force. The Jewish children were all seized throughout the country, on a single day, and forcibly baptised, in the expectation that their parents would follow their example and thus avoid the agonies of separation. Many adults were treated in the same manner. In Lisbon, where the Jews were ordered to embark, they were herded up without food or drink, in an unbelievably narrow space, in the hope that their deprivations would open their eyes at last to the verities of the religion of mercy: while eager proselytisers moved among them and made despairing efforts to save their souls. Those who persisted in refusal were kept immured until the time limit set for their expulsion from the country had elapsed, when they were informed that through their failure to comply with the terms of the edict of expulsion they had forfeited their liberty, which could be regained only at the price of baptism. This menace broke down the resistance of a majority of the survivors, and they permitted themselves to be escorted in droves to the churches. Others, who were more obstinate, were dragged to the font by brute force, or tortured until they gave their consent.

The remnant of Portuguese Jewry, which was ultimately set ashore in Africa, did not number more than seven or eight broken men. All the rest—rich and poor, ignorant and learned, Rabbis and laymen—were henceforth, officially, Christians.

It could not be expected that conversions carried out by such means could have been very effective or sincere. In reality, conditions in Portugal remained very much as they had been before 1497, excepting that thousands who had previously termed themselves Jews were now, officially, Christians. At heart they were unchanged. Their beliefs were entirely unaffected—and they were not too careful to disguise the fact. They continued to observe as far as possible all the practices of Judaism, if only from force of habit. Though young and old, fathers and children, were driven periodically to church to learn the elements of the faith to which they now nominally belonged, they were lamentably ignorant even of its fundamental beliefs and practices. They bore for the most part high-sounding Portuguese patronymics, conferred upon them by those who had stood their sponsors at baptism, and under these appellations (like the Marranos of Spain) they made phenomenal progress in business life and in the learned professions. But, among themselves, they continued to be known by their old Jewish names, which they transmitted sedulously from generation to generation.

For some years, the Portuguese people awaited, with considerable forbearance, the break-down of the resistance of the ex-Jews and their full assimilation into the general mass of the population.   At last—though not before the popular detestation had expressed itself in a series of gruesome massacres—their patience came to an end.   Neglecting all the pledges which King Manoel had given at the time of the General Conversion and afterwards, his successor, João III., determined to enforce conformity by the most drastic means which lay in his power, and applied to the Vatican for the introduction of an Inquisition similar to that which had existed in Spain since 1478.   Pope Clement VII., that true son of Renaissance humanism, was unwilling to comply, but he had no alternative.   After prolonged negotiations, a Bull was issued, on December 17th, 1531, establishing the Inquisition in Portugal and appointing Frei Diogo da Silva, the royal confessor, first Inquisitor General.

The news leaked out: and the Portuguese New Christians put up a determined resistance.   They bought over to their side the Papal Nuncio at Lisbon: they sent to Rome as their representative an old soldier named Duarte de Paz (who, though of Jewish extraction, finally found refuge at the court of the Grand Signor, where he espoused Islam): and they procured from the easy-going Pope a Bull of Pardon, which in effect suspended the action of the Holy Office.   It was round this instrument that the struggle was henceforth centred.   But they were fighting a losing battle.   In 1536, the Emperor Charles V., King of Spain, arrived in Rome, fresh from his triumph over the Moslems at Tunis, and threw the weight of his authority into the scale against them: and on May 23rd,

THE PRISON OF THE INQUISITION
By Goya (by permission of the Trustees of the Bowes Museum,
Barnard Castle).

ISABELLA THE CATHOLIC
The Prado, Madrid.

THE EMPEROR CHARLES V.
By Titian. The Prado, Madrid.

CONCORDIAS

HECHAS, Y FIRMA-
das entre la jurifdicion Real, y
el Santo Oficio de la
Inquificion.

AGREEMENT CONCERNING THE FAMILIARS OF THE INQUISITION
Valencia, 1568 (collection of the Author).

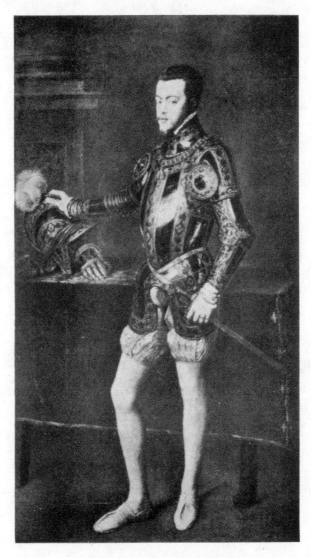

PHILIP II., KING OF SPAIN
By Titian. The Prado, Madrid.

AN AUTO DE FÉ AT LISBON

From the engraving by Picart (collection of the Author).

RELACION

DEL AUTO PARTICULAR DE FE, QUE
celebrò el Tribunal del Santo Oficio de la Inquisicion de
Granada, en el Real Monasterio de San Geronimo de
dicha Ciudad, el Sabado 30. de Mayo de
este año de 1722.

Se hallarà en la Plazuela de la Calle de la Sarten, en casa
de Isidro Joseph Serrete, Librero, y Portero de la
Ilustre Congregacion de San Pedro Martyr
de Madrid.

"RELATION" OF AN AUTO DE FÉ
Granada, 1722 (collection of the Author).

THE TORTURE-CHAMBER OF THE INQUISITION
From the engraving by Picart (collection of the Author).

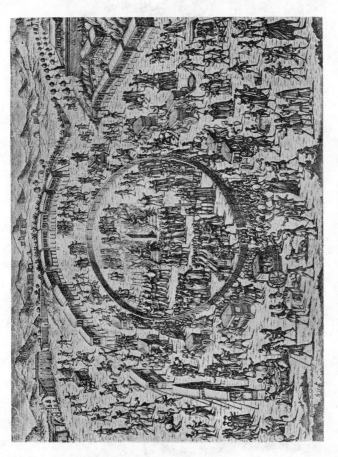

THE GREAT AUTO DE FE AT PALERMO, 6TH APRIL, 1724
From a contemporary engraving (collection of the Author).

THE INQUISITIONAL PALACE AT CARTAGENA
From a photograph.

LISTA

DAS

PESSOAS,

QUE SAHIRAÕ, CONDENAC.ÕES, QUE TIVERAÕ,
e sentenças, que se lêraõ no Auto publico da Fé, que se celebrou na
Igreja do Convento de S. Domingos desta Cidade de Lisboa
em 16. de Outubro de 1746.

SENDO INQUISIDOR GERAL

O EMINENTISSIMO, E REVERENDISSIMO

SENHOR

NUNO DA CUNHA,

PRESBYTERO CARDEAL DA SANTA IGREJA DE ROMA
do titulo de Santa Anastasia, do Conselho de Estado.

HOMENS.

Num. Idades.

PESSOA, QUE NAM ABJURA,
nem leva habito.

Penas.

1   28   Ernando José da Guerra, Bacharel formado, solteiro, filho de
Lourenço Tiçaõ Moreira, que foy Capitaõ Mór da Villa do
Rosmaninhal, natural da mesma Villa, e morador na de Monsanto, Bispado da Guarda; por prender certa pessoa da parte-
do Santo Officio, sem ter ordem; mandando fazer sequestro
em seus bens, e tomando-lhe os que levava.

Degradado por 5. an-
nos para Castro-Ma-
rim, e restituido á parte o
que lhe tomou, ficando
esta com o direito sal-
vo, para haver perdas,
e damnos pelos meyos
competentes.

PESSOAS, QUE ABJURAM, E NAM LEVAM HABITO.
ABJURAÇ,AM DE LEVE.

33   Felis da Silva, Barqueiro, natural, e morador do Lugar de Arrentela, termo da
Villa de Almada, deste Patriarcado; por dar favor, e ajuda aos XX. NN. que
fugiaõ deste Reino com o temor de serem prezos pelo Santo Officio.

40   José Vieira Tavares, official de Selleiro, natural, e morador da Villa do Itú, Bispado
de S. Paulo; por casar segunda vez, sendo viva sua primeira, e legitima mulher.

41   Manoel de Andrade, Caminheiro, natural da freguezia de Santa Catharina do Cabo de
Praya, na Ilha Terceira, e morador nesta Cidade; pelas mesmas culpas.

27   Antonio da Silva Gayo, aliás Antonio da Silva Barroca, Barqueiro, solteiro, filho de
Francisco da Silva Gayo, Pescador, natural, e morador do Lugar de Arrentela, termo da Villa de Almada; por favor, e ajuda ao XX. NN. que fugiaõ deste Reino com o temor de serem prezos pelo Santo Officio; e por perturbar o seu recto
procedimento.

Açoutes, e 4. annos
para galés.

O mesmo, e 5. an-
nos para galés.

O mesmo, e 6. an-
nos para galés.

O mesmo, 6. annos
para galé, e restitua
á quem de direito per-
tencer o que injusta-
mente levou ás partes.

PESSOAS, QUE ABJURAM, E LEVAM HABITO.

PRIMEIRA ABJURAC,AM EM FÓRMA POR JUDAISMO.

23   Francisco Nunes de Lara, X. N. Tratante, solteiro, filho de Braz Nunes, Mercador, natural da Cidade da Guarda, e morador na Villa de Linhares, Bispado de
Coimbra.

45   Gabriel Tavares X. N. Mercador, natural, e morador do Lugar do Fundaõ, Bispado
da Guarda.

Carcere a arbitrio,
e habito, que se tirará
no Auto.

O mesmo.

José

PROGRAMME OF AN AUTO DE FÉ
Lisbon, 1746 (collection of the Author).

"THE CURSE OF SPAIN"

Original American caricature of 1818 (collection of the Author).

1536, a Brief was issued, repealing the previous Bulls and confirming the establishment in Portugal of an Inquisition on the Spanish model. On September 20th, 1540, an Act of Faith was held at Lisbon—the first of a long and gruesome series, which was to continue until the second half of the eighteenth century. Henceforth, in Portugal as in Spain, the pure skies were defiled at frequent intervals by the smoke which went up amid the popular jubilation from the *quemaderos*. The smell of roasting human flesh became familiar; and the shrieks of dying heretics sounded as sweet music in the ears of blameless adherents of the Church, who celebrated the immolation with a public holiday.

In view of the nature of the Forced Conversion in Portugal, it was natural that the Portuguese Marranos shewed a greater tenacity than the analogous class in Spain. The conversions had taken place not only among the weaker elements in the population, but embraced all, including many who would far rather have submitted to death. Moreover, they had nearly half a century to adapt themselves to the new conditions, before the Inquisition was introduced into the country. Hence, notwithstanding the efforts of the Holy Office, Portuguese crypto-Judaism proved invincible. It gave the local tribunals the overwhelming proportion of their victims down to the close of their existence. In the end, it survived the Inquisition itself: and one of the most romantic episodes of our days has been the discovery in Northern Portugal of an entire community of Marranos, numbering many thousand souls, still preserving a subterranean form of Judaism among themselves and sublimely ignorant of the existence in the greater world of Jews who could afford, even in the twentieth century, to practise their religion in public.

At the outset, six tribunals of the Inquisition were set up in Portugal—at Lisbon, Evora, Coimbra, Thomar, Lamego and Oporto. The three last-named were, however, discontinued before long as being superfluous: though a contributory reason was the discovery of particularly gross irregularities and abuses (partly of a sexual nature) in their administration. Activities were henceforth concentrated in the other three cities. Lisbon naturally far outdistanced the other two, and it was through it that the activities of the Holy Office were best known abroad. It was, too, the city of the Grand Inquisitor and of the Supreme Council of the Portuguese Inquisition, which, notwithstanding all efforts to the contrary, succeeded in maintaining its independence of the Spanish tribunal even during the period when Portugal was subjected politically to Spain.

Portuguese New Christians who fell under the suspicions of the Inquisition would naturally flee, if the opportunity offered, into Spain, where they would settle down and commence life afresh in some place where they and their antecedents were unknown. In any case, the larger and wealthier country always exercised a powerful attraction on the smaller—especially on the mercantile classes, to which the New Christians in the main belonged. This was the case above all during the period, from 1580 to 1648, when the Spanish sovereigns usurped the throne of their kinsmen across the border and a formal political union existed between the two countries. Hence, from the middle of the sixteenth century, when Spain appeared to be on the point of solving the problem of its native Marranos, they were reinforced by their brothers in disbelief from across the border, impelled to emigrate on the one hand because of the danger behind them, on the other by the material attractions which lay ahead. To be a Portuguese in Spain at this period (as indeed, to a large extent, elsewhere in Europe) was itself a somewhat suspicious circumstance: for it was generally assumed that a very good proportion of the Portuguese were Jews at heart, and that they had good grounds for emigrating. (The same, though they did not like to be reminded of the fact, applied to the Spaniards themselves. "A Happy Easter to your Excellency," once said Gondomar, the Spanish Ambassador in London, to Sir Francis Bacon. "A Happy Passover to you," retorted the latter.)

Hence after the middle of the sixteenth century, so far as the Spanish Inquisition busied itself with Judaisers, immigrants from Portugal or their immediate descendants were generally in question. It became rarer and rarer to find a member of a native family among the victims: and from the details given it is generally obvious that, if he were not himself born in Portugal, he was of Portuguese descent. From time to time, little settlements of Portuguese Judaisers would be discovered in various parts of the country and harried down with all the ruthlessness of which the Holy Office was capable. In 1630, there was unearthed in Madrid a secret community which held services at a house in the Calle de las Infantas: and its members figured in the great *auto* of July 4th, 1632, which initiated the labours of the Holy Office in the capital. The house in which the services were alleged to have taken place was ceremoniously destroyed, a Capuchin convent being erected on the site. In 1635, a further group of Portuguese was tracked down in the city of Badajoz, not far from the frontier and a natural place of refuge. One hundred and fifty of the persons implicated managed to avoid arrest, whether by flight or otherwise: but the tribunal of Llerena was kept busy in trying the remainder for some years after. At

the little town of Beas, a small colony of refugees from
Portugal had established themselves, and for some time
managed to live without disturbance. Ultimately, the
attention of the Cuenca tribunal was attracted to them.
Thirteen were arrested and put on trial, and finally
appeared at an *auto de fé*. Nine others fled just in time,
leaving their property behind. This was of course confiscated, and their effigies were burned in the great Seville
auto of 1660, when there figured eighty-one Judaisers
(nearly all of Portuguese birth) and seven perished at the
stake.

Two or three of the Beas fugitives, who had settled at
Malaga and considered themselves out of harm's way,
were tried by the Inquisition at Toledo in 1667. Two
more, who had taken the additional precaution of
changing their names, were arrested after long adventures at Daimiel in 1677, and, after two and a half years'
trial, were condemned to perpetual imprisonment. It
was nearly twenty years since they had been burned in
effigy at Seville—a remarkable illustration of the fact that
the length of the memory of the Holy Office was no less
terrifying than that of its arm.

Similar little groups continued to be unearthed from
time to time up and down the country. At Córdova, in
1625, nearly one half of the fifty persons reconciled were
Portuguese from the little town of Baeza. Thirty years
later, the same city witnessed the punishment of the
members of a group who had been apprehended during
a raid on Ecija, many of whom were burned. At
Seville, in 1660, thirty-seven of those who figured—
nearly one-half of the total—had been Judaisers from the
little town of Osuna, while eight others were from Utrera.
During a trial at Toledo in 1679, the Holy Office received
details of twenty-two culprits residing in Pastrana, nearly

all of whom figured at an *auto* a little later on. Three years previously, a similar group was unearthed at Berin, in Orense, and over twenty of them received condign punishment. Even after the eighteenth century was well advanced, raids of the sort were not unknown and brought in fruitful results.

There was only one part of Spain in which the native Marrano tradition long proved ineradicable. In the Balearic Islands, the Jewish settlement dated back to Roman times, but it had come to an end in 1435, when a particularly absurd charge of ritual murder in Majorca brought about a judicial massacre, followed by a forced baptism. After this date, no declared Jews lived on the island. As on the mainland, the descendants of the converts remained true to their ancestral faith, providing the Inquisition (which was introduced to Palma in 1488) with its principal field of activity. The initial solemnity took place on August 18th, 1488, when no less than 338 persons were compelled to perform public penance. In the following year, seven Acts of Faith were staged, a considerable number of Judaisers being burned either in person or in effigy. By 1535, some 1,300 persons had been tried, of whom 750 were penanced, 460 relaxed in effigy, and 99 (all but five of whom were accused of adherence to Judaism) were burned in person—many of them alive.

This initial outburst of ferocity was, to all appearances, so effective that the work of extermination seemed to be completed, and there was some talk of allowing the vacant posts on the Tribunal to lapse. Such slight activity as still continued centred upon refugees (mainly Portuguese) from the mainland.

The temporary quiescence seems to have made the native Judaisers imagine that all danger was past, and to have emboldened them to throw off their caution. In consequence, their lack of circumspection caused attention to be drawn in 1678 to a meeting held in a garden outside the city, where a synagogue was rumoured to exist. The Inquisitors' notice was called to this, and an investigation was held. As a result, a very large number of New Christians were arrested forthwith, and put on trial. They were not, it seemed, the stuff of which martyrs are made, and all confessed their wrongdoing. A series of four public *autos* was held, at which 219 of them figured as penitents: but, to the disappointment of the public, there were no burnings. The penitents comprised in their number a large proportion of the wealthiest merchants on the island; and, out of the confiscations which resulted, the Inquisition constructed a magnificent new Palace, which was reputed to be the finest in Spain.

The treatment of those who had been convicted and their families was deplorable, and the slightest deviation from strict orthodoxy would now cost them their lives. A group of them accordingly formed a plot to leave the island, on an English boat, for some place where they might be able to worship God as their consciences dictated. Storms, however, delayed the sailing: their secret was betrayed: and, between the hours of two and three on the morning of Monday, March 8th, 1688, the entire group was thrown into prison. Their action, in endeavouring to leave the country without licence, was considered a sufficient proof of crime. Thus they were treated as heretics who had "relapsed" into guilt, and there could be no question of mercy. After a mere formality of trial, they were all condemned.

The sentences were carried out at a series of four *autos* which were held between March and July, 1691. An immense *quemadero*, eighty feet square and eight feet high, furnished with twenty-five stakes for the victims, was erected to serve as the stage for the last tragic scene. With a delicate consideration for the comfort of the ordinary population (it is this which strikes the modern observer as being so fantastically incongruous) the site chosen by the Inquisitors was on the sea-shore, a couple of miles from the city, in order that the stench should cause no public inconvenience!

There figured at this holocaust eighty-seven persons in all, of whom thirty-seven were burned. The majority professed repentance, as they had done before, and thus secured the preliminary grace of being garotted before their bodies were committed to the flames. Only three held out to the last—Raphael Valls, the leader of the little community (whose fate was till recently still commemorated in a local ballad) together with two of his pupils, a man and a woman. These all suffered, with some of their less heroic associates, in the principal *auto* of the series—the third, which was held on May 6th. The newly appointed Governor of Milan, on his way to take up his high office, was so impressed by the tears and apparent piety of one of the condemned persons that he petitioned for her life, but in vain.

The contemporary record of the martyrdom, written in an ecstasy of pious exultation by a Jesuit who participated in the ceremony, makes too gruesome reading even for the most callous modern taste. The girl, who had confessed proudly that she was a Jewess and desired to remain one, cried out from the middle of the flames in the most pathetic manner for mercy, but to no avail. Her brother, a stalwart youth of twenty-one, struggled hard to escape, and ultimately succeeded in snapping his bonds; but, as he broke loose, his strength gave out, and he fell back on the pyre. Raphael Valls, a simple soap-maker, who had succeeded in holding his own in argument against the most erudite theologians of the island, was old and weak, and he collapsed almost as soon as the fire was lighted. After a short time, we are informed, his entrails burst open, and, flaring like a torch, he died the death of Judas, to the great edification of the bystanders.

By this awful lesson, crypto-Judaism in Majorca was blotted out. Before long, the Holy Office lapsed into quiescence, from lack of human material on which to practise. Nevertheless, though their orthodoxy was henceforth unimpeachable, the descendants of the New Christians—to the number of some 300 families—continued to be made to suffer for the sins of their fathers, and were treated with every circumstance of degradation and contempt. They were generally designated as *Chuetas* (a contemptuous form, it seems, of *judío*, or Jew). They were not allowed to live outside the old Jewish quarter, in the Calle de Montesion. They were excluded from all public office and from all professions. They were compelled by the contempt of their neighbours to marry only among themselves. At public worship, they were forced to sit apart; in death, they were buried in a special section of the cemetery. They were treated in every respect as though they were still Jews, though their fidelity to Catholicism was never seriously questioned. The Church on the island did its best to keep the discrimination against them alive, publishing as late as 1755, and republishing in the following century, a list of those families who had suffered between 1678 and 1691, as a warning to their neighbours. Even the royal protection was powerless against this unanimous social discrimination.

This astonishing state of affairs continued until the

Spanish Revolution of 1931, when the emancipation of these down-trodden descendants of converts of five centuries before at last became effective. Yet, though discrimination may have ceased, unpopularity still continues: and to allege that a political opponent is a descendant of the *Chuetas* is still, in parts of Spain, the most resented of all taunts. Whether the despised island community does in fact still preserve any vestige of Judaism is a mystery: if they do, they guard their secret prodigiously well.

The New Christian martyrs of the Inquisition were found in every walk of life, from beggars to pastry-cooks, from university professors to children scarcely out of school. Sometimes, they comprised persons of the utmost influence and reputation—merchants, whose arrest unbalanced the exchanges, physicians who were in attendance on the highest in the land, aristocrats allied to some of the noblest families, writers of international reputation. One of the most illustrious was Manoel Fernandes Villareal, a prominent poet and politician, a friend of Richelieu's and Portuguese Consul-General in Paris, who was arrested by the Holy Office while on a visit to Lisbon in 1650 and was burned two years later. In 1624, a whole group of persons connected with the University of Coimbra, including the Reader in Mathematics and Professor of Canon Law, figured in an *auto* in the same city, several of them being put to death. More surprisingly still, quite a number of the secret Judaisers sought refuge in the bosom of the Church; and it was not uncommon to find priests, nuns and friars, or even Inquisitors—who were condemned to the flames on the charge of being secret Jews!

On the other hand, that same ferocity with which the Marranos were persecuted drew attention to their cause, and sometimes even secured them adherents. When Isaac de Castro Tartas was burned in Lisbon in 1647, the profession of faith that he was heard to cry from the midst of the flames created such an impression that it was repeated about the town by the populace until they were ordered to desist. On occasion, those condemned by the Inquisition for Judaising comprised persons in whom the proportion of Jewish blood was insignificant—sometimes, even, absent—who were attracted to Hebraic ideas by reason of the heroism of the martyrs. An outstanding case was that of Don Lope de Vera y Alarcon, burned at Valladolid in 1644, on a charge of Judaising—an Old Christian of gentle birth and aristocratic lineage, whom Spinosa regarded as a proof that the spirit of martyrdom had not yet died out among the Jews.

It would be natural to wonder why the New Christians, persecuted as they were, persisted in remaining in the Peninsula. The reason was that it was universally realised that their first step, once they escaped, would be to revert to Judaism: and in consequence, over a large part of the period under discussion, it was forbidden, or at least made extremely difficult, for the suspects to leave the country. But notwithstanding this there was in fact a constant stream of more or less surreptitious emigration; first to Italy, Turkey and the Mediterranean countries, a little later to Northern Europe—France, Germany, Holland, and across the North Sea to England. It was to Marrano fugitives, indeed, that some of the most important Jewish communities of the world owed their origin in the first instance—those for example of Amsterdam, Hamburg, even London and New York. In all these centres and in many others, there were in the seventeenth and eighteenth centuries settlements of Spanish and Portuguese Jews (whose descendants still in many cases retain their identity), speaking those languages among themselves, perpetuating in the fogs of Northern Europe something of the stately traditions of Lisbon or of Madrid, and from time to time holding special services to commemorate their kinsmen martyred in the latest *auto de fé*. In some ancient synagogues, indeed, with a touching conservatism, a prayer is still offered up, on the most solemn occasion of the year, on behalf of co-religionists in peril at the hands of the Inquisition.

Among the descendants of those Marranos who were driven to seek refuge abroad owing to the persecutions of the Inquisition, many romantic legends are still extant regarding their escape. The Gomez family, of Bordeaux and New York, told how they were descended from a *hidalgo* who stood high in the royal favour. One day, the King, hearing that the Holy Office was contemplating his favourite's arrest, warned him with the enigmatical words: "Gomez, the onions begin to smell." Another Anglo-American family recounts how its progenitor was smuggled out of his house when the familiars came to arrest him, in a large pannier under a pile of washing, which a family retainer of gigantic strength carried on his back on board an English ship. A famous Court Physician at Lisbon, hearing that orders had been issued for his arrest, gave a dinner-party to which he invited the élite of the capital. In the middle of it he slipped out and made his way to an English brigantine which happened to be in harbour. The arrival in England in 1726 of John da Costa Villareal, ancestor in the female line of Viscount Galway and the Marquess of Crewe, was announced in the contemporary Press with elation: "We are informed that Mr. John da Costa Villareal . . . being threatened by the Inquisition, made his escape lately from Lisbon with his family . . . during a great conflagration in the city.'' He was apparently accompanied by several of his associates. It would be interesting to know what exploit this dry newspaper report conceals.

The mental calibre of these fugitives may be gauged by the bare mention of the names of some of their descendants. Benjamin Disraeli, whose memory is still one of the most influential forces in British political life: Benedict Spinosa, father of modern philosophy: David Ricardo, founder of political economy, as well as his successor, William Nassau Senior: and Arthur Wing Pinero, one of the great figures in modern English drama, with David Belasco in America and Georges de Porto-Riche in France: Benjamin N. Cardozo, Justice of the Supreme Court of the United States and one of the most distinguished living jurists—all these and many, many more were descended from families forced to migrate from Spain because of the Inquisition. The measure of the loss which the Holy Office caused to Spanish life may be gauged from this distinguished roll.

CHAPTER VII

THE TRAGEDY OF THE MORISCOS

THE first objective of the Spanish Inquisition after the secret Jews, both logically and chronologically, was the secret Moslems. The followers of Islam had of course been numerous in the Peninsula, ever since Tarik's first incursion in 711 to the Rock which still bears his name. When the Christian principalities of the north-west had begun the work of reconquest, the Mohammedans had been butchered as a matter of course in every captured town and village. But before long this initial enthusiasm waned. It was realised above all that such a policy invited reprisals against the defenceless Christians of the South. Henceforth, the wars assumed more and more of a dynastic, and less and less of a religious, character. When the great cities of the centre and the south capitulated, it was generally on condition that the former inhabitants should be left to enjoy their property undisturbed: and throughout Spain, in every great city, by the side of the *judería* where the Jews lived and maintained their synagogue, there was the *morería* where the Moors lived and maintained their mosque. Political considerations protected the Moors from any wide-spread wave of massacres, such as that which broke the pride of Spanish Jewry in 1391. There was in consequence in Spain no considerable body of crypto-Mohammedans, to parallel the crypto-Jews: and, when the Inquisition was set up in 1478, it was with the latter exclusively that it occupied itself.

Thirteen years later, the crown was set on Spanish unity and orthodoxy alike by the conquest of the Kingdom of Granada. The terms granted to the vanquished were as liberal as precedent could teach, prudence allow, or a heroic resistance deserve. Above all full liberty in the exercise of their religion and the maintenance of their own laws was accorded to all of the former inhabitants who would peacefully submit to Christian rule. Nothing, it seemed, indeed, could be more liberal than the terms which were conceded: and Ferdinand and Isabella took a solemn oath, for themselves and their successors to the end of time, to protect the religion, property, and customs of their new subjects.

But the expulsion of the Jews from Spain in the following year whetted the appetite of the Christian religious zealots. A few years later, a campaign of proselytisation began in the new province, under the auspices of Cardinal Ximenes, later Inquisitor General. Persuasion was backed up by force: and, in the end, in 1501, after a succession of revolts and emigration *en masse* on the part of some of the hardier spirits, the population of Granada was apparently shepherded into the Catholic Church. So as to enable this fresh class of *conversos* ("New Christians out of Moors," as they were termed) to learn the rudiments of their new faith, it was stipulated at the same time that the Inquisition should have no authority over them for forty years.

This success emboldened Ximenes to make a similar experiment in Castile, where the native Moslems, or *mudéjares*, had hitherto been undisturbed. Here, after some success had been achieved by preliminary persuasions and threats, the Expulsion of the Jews of 1492 was copied in 1502 in an Edict of Expulsion for the Moslems. It was, in fact, a misnomer: for the measure was intended to enforce not exile, but baptism. All the children were detained and baptised, in the hope that this would encourage their parents also to see the light of faith;

expatriation was made so difficult that many even of the most zealous had to remain, in spite of themselves. They were permitted to take with them neither gold nor silver nor other prohibited articles: they were forbidden to take refuge in any Christian land, or in Turkey, or in Africa: and it was difficult to discover any other place of refuge within the normal man's reach. In fact, there was for the vast majority no possible alternative: and whole communities all over the kingdom formally embraced Christianity. In the kingdom of Aragon, there was no similar legislative measure: but the example of Granada was followed, and the Moorish population succumbed in the end to blandishments and threats. When in September, 1525, Charles V. proclaimed that no Mohammedan should remain in his kingdom, he merely gave formal sanction to what was already almost a fact.

Hence, after the close of the first quarter of the sixteenth century, the Christian religion was nominally supreme throughout Spain. But it was absurd to expect orthodoxy from persons converted in droves, in such circumstances as this. Some semblance of the baptismal ceremony had been performed over them, and their Mosques were closed: but this was all. Their case was even more preposterous than that of the Jews: for they were more numerous by far, formed compact geographical and sociological groups, still constituted a majority in certain parts of the country, and even spoke their own language.

From 1510, therefore, the Inquisition had begun to think increasingly in terms of "Moricos" (as they were termed) as well as of Jews. From time to time, Edicts of Faith were issued indicating that many had fallen into error for lack of adequate instruction, and inviting confessions from the delinquents, on the understanding that the usual serious consequences would not follow. Those who failed to take advantage of this opportunity were to be treated, on the other hand, with all the severity of which the Holy Office was capable: while any who confessed and then fell back again into error were to be treated as relapsed heretics. Spying and informing were encouraged: and abstinence from wine or pork, or the use of the traditional Moorish dances and songs at weddings, or above all the scrupulous regard for personal cleanliness which distinguished these unbelievers, henceforth figured, like the indications of observance of the Law of Moses, among the misdoings which might bring a man to his death.

In some of the extant accounts of this persecution pathos and absurdity are mingled. At Toledo, in 1538, a little group of Moorish slaves were penanced, on the charge of coming together at night to play musical instruments and perform *zambras* (or Moorish dances) and—most revealing sign of heterodoxy!—to eat that peculiar, and to European palates unpalatable, North African preparation known as *kuskus*. Ten years before, a tinker, aged seventy-one, was charged with abstaining from pork and wine, and using certain ablutions. He replied that, having been converted at the age of forty-five, he had no palate for the foods which had been specified, which he had never tasted before, and that his trade obliged him to wash himself frequently, in the interests of cleanliness. This defence was not sufficient to shield him entirely: and he was finally condemned to appear at an *auto* carrying a candle, and to pay four ducats to cover the expense of his trial. Most pathetic of all is the case of a slave-girl of Moorish birth, who was suspected of being a disguised infidel. A Moorish spy, turned loose on her, won his way into her affections and, having seduced her, reported to the Holy Office her habits in the matter of sexual hygiene, which were sufficiently discriminating to secure her conviction.

As a consequence of such activities, the Moriscos were reduced to outward conformity in most of the districts of Spain, especially in Castile: while in some areas they even gave up their characteristic dress and abandoned their use of the Arabic language.

This did not apply to Granada, where, thus far, the Inquisition had not been allowed to function. In 1526, however, when the Emperor Charles visited the city, he was besieged by the local authorities with complaints regarding the absurdly low state of Christianity that prevailed among the Moriscos, and the manner in which they neglected, or even maltreated, the priests sent to work among them. No more than seven true Christians, it was alleged, were to be found among the entire body! Only twenty-five years before, immunity against the Holy Office had been specifically granted in Granada for nearly twice that period. In spite of this, an edict was now issued setting up a new tribunal of the Holy Office. Henceforth, the practice of any Moslem rite in the ancient Moorish state was a crime, punishable by death.

At the outset, the new Tribunal behaved with studied moderation. The first *auto* was held only three years later, in 1529, and then but three Moriscos were sentenced, as against seventy-eight Judaisers, who were numerous in this part of the country as well. It was only after Philip II. came to the throne, in 1556, that the spirit of fanaticism at last triumphed. There was a certain excuse for the change of attitude. The Barbary Corsairs (stimulated by the no less piratical forays of the Knights of Malta on the African coast) were beginning to become the bane of the Mediterranean: and it was suspected—probably not without reason—that the Moriscos were in correspondence with their brethren in Northern Africa and encouraging their raids on Andalusia. It was determined accordingly to make a final effort to put down secret adherence to Islam. In 1566, a member of the Supreme Council of the Inquisition was appointed President of the Chancellery of Granada, and ordered to carry out a rigorous policy of suppression. An edict which Charles V. had been persuaded to withdraw in 1526, which aimed at all Arabic folk-ways and domestic customs as well as their religion proper, was reissued, and this time sternly enforced. The use of the Arabic language was forbidden: Moorish garments had to be laid aside: the baths, by which they approximated cleanliness to godliness, were to be closed down, thus preparing the way for orthodox Christian lice: Christian midwives were to be present at all births, so as to ensure baptism and to preclude Islamic "superstitions": all doors were to be left open on feast-days, Fridays, Saturdays, and during weddings, to prevent the practice of Moorish ceremonies: the use of henna for staining had to be abandoned: and so on, *ad infinitum*. With a needless callousness, moreover, this edict was published on January 1st, 1567—the anniversary of the surrender of Granada, when Ferdinand and Isabella had solemnly sworn to permit the practice of Islam in this new kingdom for all time. To show that it was meant seriously, all the baths which had been the pride of Moorish Granada were forthwith destroyed, beginning with those of the Alhambra itself.

A year later, orders were issued to abandon Moorish costume forthwith, and to surrender all children between the ages of three and fifteen to the priests, who would place them in schools where they might learn Christian doctrine. The result was to provoke an immediate rebellion. The Moriscos calculated that they could raise a hundred thousand fighting men, and they reckoned, too, on support from their brethren in Northern Africa. But a premature rising in December, 1568, in the Moorish quarter of Granada, led by a hot-headed young dyer, brought their carefully-laid plans to the ground. In the country-side, on the other hand, the response to the call to arms was whole-hearted. The semblance of Christianity was tossed aside like an empty bauble. The war assumed all the characteristics of a *Jehad*. Neither sex nor age nor cloth was spared in any of the Christian settlements: and, to replenish their empty armouries (for a consistent attempt had been made to disarm the newly-conquered districts), captives were sold to the Algerian corsairs for a musket apiece. Bobadilla, nominally the Last of the Moors, was succeeded by a reputed descendant of the royal house of the Ommayads, known in Christian circles as Don Hernando de Córdoba y de Valor. He had been a member of the Town Council of Granada, but was put on trial, the Cabildo carrying a dagger. Fleeing to the rebels, he was proclaimed their king and reverted to his Moslem name of Muley Mohammed ibn Humeya.

The area of the revolt nevertheless was limited. None of the large towns associated themselves with it. Moreover, the assistance which was confidently expected never materialised, as at the time the Grand Turk had all his energies absorbed in the War of Cyprus. The Spanish authorities, on their side, carried on the hostilities with all the ferocity which from time immemorial has been associated with internal conflicts in Spain. The command was entrusted to the Marquis de los Veles, an incompetent veteran of former wars whose ferocity earned him the title, "The Iron Headed Devil." No quarter was shewn in battle: the country-side was ravaged: even peaceful villages were sacked: and in Granada itself there took place a massacre of suspects which had no parallel even in Spain until the civil war of 1936.

Since this brutality only encouraged the insurgents to fight still more desperately, the plan of campaign was changed. In 1569, Don John of Austria, Philip's half-brother, was appointed to the supreme command, in place of De los Veles, whose incapacity had equalled his brutality. The new commander ordered all the Moorish inhabitants of Granada to leave the city which they had made famous, and to find new homes in the interior as best they could: and in October Philip, who had trans-ferred his court to Cordova in order to be nearer the seat of operations, issued an edict in which he gave instruc-tions that the war was to be conducted henceforth with "fire and blood."

On the other side, the operations were now under the direction of Muley Abdullah ibn Abu (formerly Diego López), the last Moorish king, who had been elected to lead the revolt when Ibn Humeya fell a victim to the vengeance of one of the women of his seraglio—the last typical drama of Moorish Spain. The initial successes of the "little King" (as he was called) were striking; for he obtained confirmation of his title from the Grand Signor and extended the area of revolt to the borders of Murcia. This made the Spanish authorities at last realise the seriousness of the situation. Don John of Austria was given a free hand, and now had the first opportunity to display the military genius which was to culminate at Lepanto. He took the field in January, 1570. By the following May, the Moriscos had been brought to their knees. They submitted almost unconditionally, on the understanding that, in return for their lives, they would submit to be removed from their native district and dis-tributed elsewhere about the country. At the last moment

Ibn Abu refused these humiliating terms, and attempted to raise the standard of revolt once more; but he was assassinated by one of his former adherents, bribed by the Spanish authorities.

The long-drawn agony now entered its last phase.   In the following October, an edict was issued ordering the deportation of every Morisco from the disturbed districts, no exception being made in favour even of those who had remained punctiliously loyal, and against whose orthodoxy there was no suspicion of doubt.   Their houses and lands were forfeited to the Crown.   The areas chosen for their new homes were scattered all over the country—from La Mancha in the south to Estremadura and even Galicia in the north, in which areas they were to be prevented from forming compact blocks.   Any Moor who dared to quit without leave the abode chosen for him was to be punished with flogging and sent to the galleys, and they were forbidden to approach within ten leagues of Granada, under pain of death.   Naturally, all the former measures against the observance of Moorish customs and folk-ways were to be rigorously enforced: and there was even a prohibition, under savage penalties, against keeping any Arabic book.   (It is well known how, not long after the capture of Granada, there had taken place under Torquemada's auspices a wholesale literary holocaust, which had no parallel in Europe until 1933).

That the deportation was carried out as humanely as possible, as the royal apologists claim, is beside the point. It was in itself a crime—a crime for which the whole land did expiation.   For, deprived of its children, of their skill and of their devotion, Andalusia became a desert. The old system of irrigation fell into disrepair; the terraced hill-sides were allowed to lose their soil: the population dwindled to a tithe of its former level: and what had once been the garden of Spain became a byword and a reproach. The land in which the former inhabitants had lovingly tended every inch of ground was now so depopulated that, centuries after, a man might travel through it for a day's journey without seeing more than a handful of half-ruined hovels and a company of half-starved charcoal burners.

The political power of the Moriscos was thus broken, once for all. But the spiritual reserves of their faith were unaffected: and in the new homes they proved as questionable Christians as they had been in the old. The same, of course, was the case in Old Castile and in Aragon, where, notwithstanding the promise of temporary immunity, the Holy Office had taken steps against some of the less cautious Crypto-Moslems. Its activities throughout the country continued without intermission, and on such a scale that it became obvious that neither force nor blandishments had had the slightest effect, and that Islam was nearly as powerful a force, despite the outward veneer of Christianity, as it had been a century before. So far was this the case that even the old Islamic dietary laws were observed, and Moriscos would eat only meat slaughtered by one of their own kinsfolk according to the traditional manner. This was countered by an edict forbidding any person belonging to the accursed race to act as butcher, or even to kill a chicken for a sick man. There were plottings with the Barbary Corsairs, with the Turk, even with Henry IV. of France, who counted upon a rising of the Moriscos in his favour when he decided to invade Spain.

At length, Catholic patience gave out. In 1599, an edict was issued by Philip III., giving the Moriscos of Valencia—now the most compact as well as notoriously the most infidel body remaining—a final chance of making their peace with Holy Church. This had no more effect than any of the other appeals, proclamations and menaces that had been so common in the past: and yet further evidence of plotting and intrigues shewed how serious the situation had become. The King and his advisers now determined to sweep away the problem which they had been unable to solve. Several plans had been proposed for this purpose. The most simple was that of the Marquis de Velada, the royal majordomo, who suggested a repetition of the Sicilian Vespers. A similar but more dignified plan, to be carried into effect under Inquisitorial auspices, was put forward by the Archbishop of Valencia, the Blessed Juan de Ribera. The Inquisitor of Valencia suggested an alternative which might have made a considerable difference to the growth of the British Empire—deportation to Newfoundland, as helots to a military settlement. The Bishop of Segorbe, who *ex professo* was uninterested in procreation, added a cheerful rider—that the problem would be solved more rapidly if the preliminary precaution were taken of castrating the males.

The solution which was finally adopted was more moderate. In April, 1609, it was determined by the Council of State to banish all the Moriscos from the country, beginning with Valencia. The decision was kept a profound secret until the following September, by which time troops had been brought back from Italy to suppress any opposition and a fleet had been assembled to cover the proceedings. The victims were treated (at the beginning, at least) more humanely than the Jews had been, one hundred and seventeen years earlier. They were allowed to take with them whatever could be transported of their worldly possessions, and shipping was provided—at the outset, free of charge—for their transport. Moreover, those against whose conduct in the matter of religion there was no breath of suspicion—who for two years had comported themselves as good Christians, and had been admitted regularly to Holy Communion—were allowed to remain, as were also those women who had found Old Christian husbands. But in the end it was discovered that the differentiation could not be easily maintained, and to save the trouble of deciding it was determined to banish even the "Old Moriscos"—descendants of the *mozarabes* who had been living in the northern kingdoms as professing Christians for many generations. Preparations were made by Henry IV. of France to establish a number of these, especially from Aragon, in his dominions, between the Garonne and the Dordogne: but his assassination threw his plan into confusion, and the sufferings of the exiles on the borders, or on the long road towards the Mediterranean ports, beggar description. The most fortunate were those of the first group, who sailed from Valencia direct to their new homes.

Many of those deported were good Catholics, who found themselves as uncomfortably situated in their new place of residence as any Moslem was in Europe, and who longed, as they listened to the interminable readings from the Koran, for the odour of the incense and peal of the organ and trilling of the choir and all the stately church ceremonial to which they had been accustomed from their youth upwards. Conversely, many *mudéjares,* whose fathers had lived undisturbed in Old Castile for generations, were as much Spaniards as any of their neighbours had been, speaking the same language and following the same customs, excepting that they had frequented their Mosques while the others went to Church. Now, notwithstanding the identity of religion, they were hopeless strangers in the midst of those with whom their lot was henceforth cast. For many generations to come, they continued to preserve something of their Spanish heritage in this hostile environment, to compose their Muslim religious works in Castilian, and, in a strange land, to sing their songs to Allah in the tongue of their fathers.

These, however, were the exceptions. The majority of the Moriscos were happy to be gone, happy to be able once more to worship the God of their ancestors without fear of death hanging constantly over their heads, happy to be able to tell their incredulous kinsfolk of their experiences of the religion of mercy and how it attempted to gain fresh adherents.

It was not until 1615 that the process of deportation was completed. The number of the exiles has been estimated variously between 300,000 and 3,000,000. It probably lies much nearer the first of those figures. But even so, the sum of the human suffering involved was appalling. Spain was rid at last of that section of her children who, in the ninth and tenth centuries, had raised Spanish culture to its greatest heights. The country even now bears traces of that suicidal fanaticism which deprived it of some of its most skilled craftsmen, its most industrious peasantry, its potentially keenest brains.

Here and there, indeed, the process was not quite complete. For some time longer, scattered cases of suspected adherence to Islam on the part of native Spaniards continued to occupy the attention of the Holy Office. As late as 1769, the existence of a secret Mosque (probably, however, frequented by more recent converts) was reported at Cartagena, and in 1728 the members of a Mohammedan conventicle were punished at Granada. Even today, there are some areas of the country where

Morisco characteristics are so marked that official Christianity seems little more than a veneer. There were, moreover, frequent instances of slaves, captured in the wars with the Moslem powers and baptised as a matter of course, whose fidelity to their new faith was not above question: of renegades who arrived at the Mediterranean ports and found Christianity a convenient method to establish a claim on public charity: of folk-customs which were regarded by the Inquisitors as indicative of recondite theological obloquy. Yet all these cases added together did not amount to much. By the drastic measure of 1609 to 1615, unity of faith had at last been established in Spain. Except for the Marranos scattered here and there about the country, and practising their mysterious rites in deepest secrecy, formal orthodoxy had finally triumphed in the country. Never again was the muezzin to summon the faithful publicly to prayer in Castile until, three centuries later or a little more, a Spanish general, reverting to the authentic tradition of his country, brought back descendants of these Moorish exiles into Spain to fight (as the bewildered world was informed) to save the Spanish Church.

CHAPTER VIII

THE PROTESTANT MARTYRS

THAT the Inquisition became a byword for horror in Northern Europe was not due to the activity which has been described in the foregoing pages, nor to the atrocities which accompanied its birth. No one in Europe, outside Spain and the Balkans, was particularly interested in the Moriscos: and, while the Jews were familiar in most countries, their fate was a matter of indifference. But, as the years went on, the scope of the Inquisition had widened until it involved a category of persons who evoked a special feeling of sympathy in England, in Holland, and in Germany. For sympathy is, as it were, a species of fear lest the spectator may (God forbid!) be involved in the same fate as the sufferer. The inhabitants of Northern Europe were not conspicuously tolerant, according to modern lights. But, in their own eyes, the difference between them and the Spanish papists was the same as between the dogmatism of Mr. Matthew Arnold and that of Mr. Thomas Carlyle—the one was dogmatic and right, while the other was dogmatic and wrong. It was therefore above all by reason of its treatment of Protestants and Protestantism that the Spanish Inquisition became the scandal and reproach which it remains to the present day.

Protestantism was however the last of the great problems which the Spanish Inquisition was called upon to face, and the first which it more or less adequately solved. It was moreover the only one of these problems in which its position, unlike the ferocity of its punishments, was logically not altogether indefensible. The Marranos and

163

the Moriscos had been dragooned into the Church, and then were proceeded against savagely because their orthodoxy was suspect. The Protestants, on the other hand, were at the outset born into the Holy Catholic Church, considered their brand of Christianity the true one, knowingly and deliberately rejected Catholic doctrine, and even, in that rushing spring-tide of the Reform Movement, did everything in their power to spread their disbelief and to imperil other immortal souls by their propaganda.

At the outset of the Reformation the Spanish soil did not appear altogether unfavourable for the spread of the humanistic spirit. The New Learning had its votaries in the Peninsula; a scholarly new text of the Scriptures had appeared in the original under the auspices of Cardinal Ximenes: and Erasmus (who was once invited to settle in Spain) himself had many Spanish friends and admirers, who included even the Inquisitor General Manrique. To be sure in April, 1521, an order had been issued for the confiscation of Lutheran books: but this was no more than was happening in England, and no Spanish sovereign had yet qualified for the title "Defender of the Faith."

With the passage of years, and the progress of the Lutheran movement abroad, the Holy Office began to be more suspicious. In 1533, a priest who had been dismissed from his employment for seducing a nun submitted to the authorities a list of seventy persons whom he accused of Lutheran heresy. The most important of them was Juan de Vergara, Professor of Philosophy in the University of Alcalá and a close friend of some of the most eminent Spanish churchmen of the time, against whom various minor charges had previously been preferred. He was arrested, and formally charged with possessing Lutheran works and adhering to various Lutheran doctrines, besides being an abettor and defender of heretics, a defamer of the Inquisition and corrupter of its officials. After a trial dragged out over two years, he was condemned to adjure *de vehementi*. At the same time, a Benedictine Abbot named Alfonso de Virues (subsequently to be Bishop of the Canaries, and a favourite of Charles V.) was arraigned on a similar charge, though the intervention of the Pope himself saved him from any serious consequences. These instances, and a few others like them, sounded the danger-signal, and gave a warning that no weakness in matters of faith, however academic, was to be tolerated.

Nothing more ominous than this took place for some time: and the few distinguished Spanish Protestants of this early period who are known to us by name lived abroad—men like Francisco de Enzinas (better known as Dryander), who translated the New Testament into Spanish and was subsequently Professor of Greek at Oxford: Juan de Valdés, a friend and associate of the Italian reformers, who settled in Naples: Antonio del Corro, preacher to the Spanish Protestant community in London: and above all Miguel Serveta or Servetus, who was burned in righteous indignation by Calvin at Geneva in 1553. The first native Protestant victim of the Spanish Inquisition was indeed brought back from abroad. This was Francisco de San Roman, of Burgos, who became so infected with Reformed doctrines during a visit to Germany and the Low Countries that he set out on an adventurous mission to Ratisbon, with the object of converting the Emperor himself. Not unnaturally, he was arrested and sent back to Spain, where, about the year 1540, he was burned at the stake. That in this case the Holy Office seemed to be interpreting the popular feeling is demonstrated by the fact that he was assaulted by the mob before he reached the *quemadero* and stabbed again and again. Excepting for one or two cases like this, the labours of the Inquisition in the suppression of Protestantism were mainly confined as yet to over-ardent foreign proselytisers, like the Burgundian legalist Hugo de Celso, who was so imprudent as to endeavour to preach the new gospel in the dominions of the Catholic Monarch.

It was not until the middle of the century that Protestantism began to raise its head seriously in the country. It centred throughout in two cities—Seville and Valladolid, with offshoots at Zamora and in the kingdom of Aragon. The founder of the movement was a certain Rodrigo de Valer, a man of substance and good family, who went about the streets of Seville inveighing against the abuses in the Church and teaching numerous heretical opinions. For the moment, the Catholic Church felt so secure of its position, so far as Old Christians were concerned, that the Inquisition was content to treat him as a madman, not responsible for his actions. He had been sane enough, nevertheless, to convert the learned Juan Gil, or Egidio, a popular preacher who was designed by Charles V. for a Bishopric. It was noticed that some of Egidio's sermons delivered in the Cathedral were shaky on certain points of doctrine, such as the invocation of saints and the existence of purgatory. After lengthy proceedings, he was compelled to recant and suffered various minor disabilities. Long afterwards, however, it was realised that the punishment had been too light, and his bones were exhumed and solemnly condemned to the flames.

The next incumbent of his vacant Canonry proved to be only too faithful a successor. This was Constantino Ponce de la Fuente, a former Royal Chaplain and Con-

fessor. A chance search in the house of a widow named
Isabella Martínez resulted in the discovery of several of
his manuscripts and of the existence of a complete
Lutheran organisation over which he presided. His principal coadjutor was one Juan Ponce de Leon, in whose
house services were regularly conducted. Another in-
trepid member was a certain Jualianillo Hernández, who
smuggled into the country in bales of merchandise Protestant works printed at Geneva or Antwerp. As for
Ponce de la Fuente himself, he was guilty of highly improper doctrines, the most objectionable of which was
that Purgatory was merely a bugbear invented by monks
to fill their bellies.

Meanwhile, a similar conventicle had been discovered
in Northern Spain. Here, the poisonous weed was
definitely an importation from abroad. An Italian Protestant, named Carlo de Seso, bent on spreading the new
doctrines, had been travelling about armed with heretical
literature and making converts over a wide area. His
greatest success was achieved in Valladolid, where he
gained over an eloquent preacher named Augustin de
Cazalla as his most distinguished adherent. (It is noteworthy, it may be mentioned, how Spanish Protestantism
found the most zealous of its adherents precisely among
that class which might have been expected to defend the
Catholic Church most devotedly.) Some unguarded talk
on the part of one of the little brotherhood—it did not
number, probably, more than sixty or a hundred all
told—led to a more detailed enquiry: and in the spring
of 1558 denunciations were made to the Holy Office
giving full details of the membership and practices of the
group.

On being informed of the existence of this nest of
heretics, Pope Paul IV. issued a brief instructing the In-

quisitor General to spare no efforts, but to exterminate the evil forthwith. Charles V., too, then on his deathbed, besought his son Philip II., who had taken over the reins of government from his tired hands, to listen to the exhortations of the Holy Father. Philip required no encouragement, and forthwith published an edict condemning to the stake all who bought, sold, or read prohibited books. This he fortified with a reminder that according to law the accuser was to receive one-fourth of the confiscated property of condemned persons. Meanwhile the Pope, fearful of losing the obedience of yet another kingdom, commanded confessors to urge on penitents the duty of informing against suspects, and ordered the Inquisition to deliver to the secular arm, for capital punishment, even those who abjured their errors, unless their sincerity was beyond question. He even went further: he made a grant from the ecclesiastical revenues of Spain to defray the expenses of the Inquisitorial establishment, confident that the expense would be reimbursed from the proceeds.

The Inquisition hardly needed these inducements to activity, more especially as the principal seat of the problem was at Seville, the diocese of the Grand Inquisitor, Archbishop Fernando Valdés. Here, on the very day when proceedings were opened, no less than 800 persons were arrested. On September 24th, 1559, the results were seen at an *auto de fé*, when Ponce de Leon (who had never credited that a man of his birth and position would be treated like a common Judaiser) was among the eighteen Lutherans relaxed to the secular arm. Twenty-one other persons were reconciled: and the crowd which thronged the city for the occasion was so vast that many persons had to pass the night in the fields outside the walls. At the end of the following year, the work was continued in another great *auto*, where, apart from other sufferers, fourteen Protestants were relaxed in person and three (among them De la Fuente, who had the good fortune to die in prison) in effigy. Two other Seville *autos* in 1562, with subsequent solemnities of like nature in 1564 and 1565, sufficed to obliterate the last traces of the Reformed doctrine in the southern part of the country. The last year saw also a similar holocaust at Toledo, where twenty-two Lutherans were burned, eleven of them alive (June 17th, 1565).

Meanwhile a similar process of extermination had been carried out at Valladolid. Here, proceedings had been more speedy, and the first Protestant *auto* had taken place six months earlier than at Seville, on May 21st, 1559. All the ringleaders were not prepared to maintain their opinions to the pitch of martyrdom. Augustin de Cazalla, for example, had recanted, and was horrified to learn that he was to be put to death. Nevertheless, he made an endeavour to convince the Inquisitors of his sincerity, professing his execration of Lutheran doctrine and trying to persuade his fellow-sufferers to repent. The only one of the latter who held out stubbornly to the end, and so was burned alive, was Antonio de Herrezuelo, one of the outstanding members of the little community. He was gagged on his way to the *brasero*, lest he might utter something that would shock the bystanders. The latter were so wrought up that they stoned him as he stood awaiting his end, while one of the soldiers stabbed him through the belly with his halberd. In spite of his sufferings Herrezuelo never flinched, and died a martyr's death. His young and beautiful wife, who had recanted and was condemned to perpetual imprisonment, withdrew her recantation after seven years and, in 1568, was burned alive, as a relapsed heretic. Cazalla's mother, in whose house the reformers had held their services, was dead; but her remains and effigy were burned, and the unwittingly offending building was rased to the ground.

Six months later, King Philip II. himself, just returned from Flanders, paid a visit to Valladolid in order to grace with his presence the second *auto*, at which the survivors of the dissenting conventicle were punished. In view of the especial solemnity of the occasion, the affluence of spectators was unusually great—a Flemish visitor estimated them at 200,000 persons. Of the thirty culprits who figured twenty-six were Protestants, all of whom were relaxed. The majority recanted, and so were spared the last agony—including even Domingo de Rojas, a Dominican friar who had proved an active proselytiser, but whose heart failed him at the last moment. Only two, therefore, were burned alive—Juan Sanchez, who had been sacristan to Cazalla's brother, and the Italian enthusiast, De Seso. Together with Fray Domingo, the latter had attempted to flee, and had been arrested at Pampeluna while on the point of crossing the Pyrenees into safety. He now maintained his calm to the end. As he passed the royal stand, on his way to the *brasero*, he asked the King, as one *Caballero* to another, how he could permit a gentleman to be treated with such indignity by a batch of friars. "I myself would bring the faggots to burn my own son were he as perverse as you," replied Philip: and he meant it.

The nervousness which prevailed at this period found its expression in one famous case. It has been pointed out above that a large number of those sentenced by the Inquisition for sympathising with Protestantism were clerics of various grades. The Holy Office, however, was no respecter of persons, and at least nine bishops in all were condemned by it to various acts of penance at one time or another. Its most illustrious victim by far was

Bartolomé de Carranza, Archbishop of Toledo. This learned prelate, who had taken an important part in the earlier sessions of the Council of Trent, and in whose arms Charles V. had died, had accompanied Philip II. on his journey to marry Mary of England, and prided himself on his share in persecuting the English Protestants. Notwithstanding this, when he returned to Spain, in August, 1559, he was arrested and arraigned for heterodox opinions. It is conceivable that, while persecuting the English heretics, he had unconsciously absorbed some of their views; it was certain that his writings were sometimes as incoherent as they were prolix, and that support could be found in them for many points of views which their author can hardly have entertained seriously. It was reported, for example, that the Reforming conventicle at Valladolid had found considerable comfort and support in the perusal of his Commentaries on the Christian Catechism.

All this need not necessarily have been decisive; but the enormous revenues of the diocese of Toledo were an unanswerable argument. The trial dragged on for many years, the documents in it filling some 40,000 pages in all. There was a squabble for jurisdiction between the Holy Office and the Holy See, which at one time threatened to bring the Inquisition toppling down in ruins. Finally, the case was transferred to Rome, where sentence was at last promulgated in 1576—seventeen years after it had been opened. In the end the Archbishop was convicted of holding doctrines akin to those of Luther, and was condemned to abjure sixteen propositions found in his writings, to perform certain acts of penance, to be suspended from his episcopal functions for another five years, and meanwhile to be confined in a convent. Some modern enquirers have held that the whole affair was based on nothing more than a characteristic display of ecclesiastical jealousy and intrigue. There seems in fact to have been rather more in it than that. In any case, it proved a warning to the Spanish hierarchy that a little learning was a dangerous thing, and that the Almighty had conferred the power of speech on man the better to dissemble injudicious opinions.

This *cause célèbre* seems to have been prompted by an exaggerated nervousness. For it may be questioned whether the peril was at any time so great as Philip and his advisers believed. The sentiment of religious unity in Spain had been cemented by the campaign against Jews and Moslems. Clerical immorality, which was one of the principal grievances of Reformers elsewhere, was not conspicuous in the Peninsula: and the Church, to do it justice, made every endeavour to put down those instances that came to light. Any sympathy which may have existed for Reform was hence finally and effectively crushed by the brief but ferocious campaign between 1558 and 1565. Thereafter, individuals who felt leanings in that direction emigrated to lands of greater freedom, such as England, where they could express their sentiments without fear. Those who remained behind were few in number: and they kept their secret well.

It was not, in fact, in Spain that the Spanish frenzy against Protestants and Protestantism reached its height, but in the Low Countries, then under Spanish rule. Philip II., in his zeal for the faith, here outdid himself. It was in 1560 that he introduced the Inquisition, though not in its Spanish form, into his Flemish dominions, to cope with the menacing growth of the Reform movement. The country was thereby thrown into a turmoil, and the problem of rebellion became inextricably involved henceforth with that of heresy. The process of repression reached its climax under the Duke of Alva and his Council of Blood, which comprised one member who is reported, whenever he woke up from his judicial nap, to have called out automatically, " To the gallows! to the gallows!" Ultimately, for economy of effort, a decree of the Inquisition (confirmed by Royal Proclamation) condemned all the inhabitants of the Netherlands to death as heretics, save for a few specially exempted persons—a total of some 3,000,000 souls: the men being generally burned and the women buried alive. Fortunately, no opportunity offered for carrying this unspeakable brutality into effect. But the final results in those parts of the country where the Spaniards re-established their control were appalling. Alva is said to have boasted that 18,600 persons were executed during his period of rule, and 60,000 more were driven into exile to England alone. So far as the persecution of Protestants is concerned, there is nothing in the history of the Spanish Inquisition to compare with this ghastly record.

In Spain, by now, the vast majority of those accused of sympathy with the doctrines of Luther and of Calvin were visitors from foreign parts. The Holy Office believed —and not without reason—that the foreign Protestants were engaged in a deliberate attempt to propagate their erroneous views in the Peninsula. Protestant works were printed in considerable numbers outside the kingdom in the Spanish language and sent to Spain *via* Flanders—at the outset by sea, and then, when surveillance became more strict, overland by way of Lyons, whence they were smuggled over the Pyrenees into Aragon and Navarre. Many of these works were published in London; but the principal centre of the traffic was Frankfort, where twice a year, during the fairs, enthusiastic propagandists came to replenish their stocks. There was one Antwerp bookseller who had agents at Medina del Campo and Seville, where Latin and Spanish translations of Protestant publications could be procured. It was even said that some enthusiasts sent money out of the country to finance the clandestine printing-presses where these works were produced. But not all this publishing activity was carried on outside the country: for Calvin's epoch-making *The Christian Institution* was actually printed in Saragossa. The parts of Spain where proselytisation was particularly active were Aragon and Andalusia, which were filled with New Christians, as yet unstable in their faith and ripe to receive the new gospel. Indeed, it is a fact that the Marrano refugees settled in the Low Countries took a lead in the establishment of the new form of Christianity and lent themselves whole-heartedly to the work of propagating it in Spain.

At the Seville *auto* of December, 1560, there figured for the first time a new category of victim, whose persecution was to do more than any other of its activities to spread the evil report of the Holy Office. Among the persons relaxed, by the side of Julianillo Hernández (who had maintained his defiant attitude to the very last moment) were two Englishmen, William Brooks and Nicholas Burton.[1] The latter was the supercargo on a ship which had put into the port, and made no secret of being an adherent of the Reformed faith, in which he had been born and educated. Subsequently one of the owners, anxious about his property, sent a young man named John Frampton to recover it. After much delay and travelling backwards and forwards, his luggage was searched and what was

[1] That these were the first English victims of the Spanish Inquisition, as is invariably stated, is not quite correct; for an Englishman named Anthony Basor had appeared as a penitent at Valladolid on May 21st, 1556.

presumed to be an heretical book was discovered in it—actually, an English translation of Cato. Arrested and tortured, he consented at last to embrace Roman Catholicism, and was rebaptised in great pomp.

These were the earliest instances of what was to develop into an intolerable abuse. Any English or Dutch sailor, brought up in the Reformed faith, was according to the Inquisitional system a heretic, deserving of nothing but death. But intercourse between Spain and Northern Europe could not very well be suspended on that account: and the question of treatment of Protestant sailors or merchants in Spanish ports remained for many generations a recurrent problem of European diplomacy. Meanwhile, pious ears in England were shocked from time to time at the report of the sufferings of some simple Devon or Wiltshire lad who had been apprehended by the bloody Papists for a careless action in the streets of Cadiz, Vigo, or Seville, and was made to expiate for it with his life. Such stories, seized upon by the fervent English and Dutch martyrologists, and not minimised in the telling, were responsible for the undying hatred of the Spaniard which continued until the eighteenth century was well advanced. In the single year 1565, according to a sorrowful note made by the great Lord Burleigh, not less than twenty-six English subjects were burned at the stake in different parts of Spain, while ten times as many were languishing in Spanish dungeons. It was to no avail that Sir John Smith was sent on a special mission to His Catholic Majesty concerning them: for in 1576 English merchants trafficking in Spain presented a petition complaining of the dangers which they ran at the hands of the Inquisition, and not long after, in 1596, a Scotsman named James Bolen was relaxed at Seville. English merchants resident in Spain, too, would sometimes be disturbed, as was the case in

1643 with George Penn, the uncle of the famous Quaker statesman and coloniser. This was not the case only in sea-ports. Even in inland towns, persons would be arraigned not infrequently for "Anglicanism." Thus at Toledo, Richard Bayle, an Oxford Master of Arts in the service of the English Ambassador, was put on trial in 1577: and a Thomas Wilcox, metamorphosed into Viluqoques, also in diplomatic employment, in 1621.

A typical cry of distress was heard in 1561 from an English merchant in the Canaries:

> I was taken by those of the Inquisition twenty months past, put into a little dark house two paces long, loaded with irons, without sight of sun or moon all that time. When I was arraigned I was charged that I should say our mass was as good as theirs; that I said I would rather give money to the poor than buy Bulls of Rome with it. I was charged with being a subject to the Queen's Grace, who, they said, was enemy to the Faith, Antichrist, and with other opprobrious names; and I stood to the defence of the Queen's Majesty, proving the infamies most untrue. Then I was put in Little Ease again, protesting very innocent blood to be demanded against the Judge before Christ.

We know in greater detail of the case of Richard Hasleton, of Braintree, who, being captured by a Barbary Corsair on his way to Turkey in 1582, rowed as a slave for some years in an Algerian galley. At last he had the good fortune to be shipwrecked, and was rescued by a Genoese vessel. The Captain, hearing that he was a Lutheran, handed him over to the tender mercies of the Tribunal of Majorca, which proceeded to break his spirit with all the inhuman pressure of the Inquisitional machinery. He seems to have been a lad of mettle, and, when a crucifix was offered to him, spat clear in the Inquisitor's face. It can hardly be regarded as a token of brutality that one of the Familiars gave him a buffet which nearly deprived him of his senses, so that (as he records) "for that day we had no more reasoning."

One audience succeeded another, until in the end the Inquisitors' patience gave out, and he was confined in the dungeon of the Castle. A year later, during a public feast, when the gaoler's son had taken his father's place, he managed to escape, but after wandering about for some time he was caught again, thrown back into prison and submitted to torture, ultimately being whipped through the city and brought back again to his dungeon. At last he managed to make good his escape to North Africa, and so, after a further period of slavery, back to England. His account of his ten years of suffering was published in London in 1595, and it may be imagined what sentiments it aroused in the breasts of his Rome- and Spain-hating fellow-countrymen.

A little later, in 1614, they were regaled to the "Totall Discourse of the Rare Adventures and Painful Peregrinations" of the euphuistic William Lithgow, containing (in addition to much misuse of the English language, one of the earliest accounts of the use of coffee, and a hearty denunciation of the over-popularity of currants) "an account of the tortures he suffered under the Spanish Inquisition, by racking, and other inhuman Usages, for his owning the Protestant Religion. Together with his Miraculous deliverance from the Cruelties of the Papists, which far exceeded any of the Heathen Countries, herein largely described."

It cannot be seriously suggested that the behaviour of the paladins of Protestantism was always tactful. When

English sailors made an unsuccessful attempt to singe the King of Spain's beard or to capture his silver galleons, and were so unfortunate as to be apprehended, an overwhelming temptation was offered to the other side: and the entire crews would sometimes be put on trial, not for piracy, but for heresy. This was especially the case in the branch-tribunals beyond the Atlantic. Before the end of the sixteenth century, the Council of the Indies had insisted on the necessity for measures to deal with the threat to the faith constituted by the heretical foreign sailors and sea-faring-men: and it was suggested (though nothing came of the proposal) that a special tribunal should be set up for this purpose at San Domingo, with jurisdiction over the West Indies. The fact that this was not carried into effect did not imply that the heretics were left undisturbed. John Drake, for example, a cousin of the great Sir Francis, was shipwrecked on the Pacific coast of South America, and, after spending a year among the natives, made his way across the Continent to Buenos Aires, whence he hoped to sail for Europe. He was apprehended, however, and figured in an *auto* as a penitent. In 1594, a son of Sir John Hawkins, Richard, was captured by the Spaniards after a brisk fight at San Matteo. Most of his crew were sent to the galleys, but he and a few others were conveyed to Lima for trial by the Inquisition. None were so outspoken in their Protestantism as to be sent to the stake: but it is interesting to note that the most zealous of the group, who was sentenced to perpetual imprisonment, bore the surname Leigh, which to everyone who remembers his *Westward Ho!* will always suggest the quintessence of Elizabethan daring.

In Mexico similarly, a score of English Lutherans were tried by the Inquisition between 1560 and the end of the century, and a few (such as George Ribley, of

"Xuambra," in 1574, and later John Min, barber, of Cork) were burned. When in 1568 a party of patriotic filibusters from Sir John Hawkins' slave-fleet was cornered after the disastrous fight at San Juan de Ulloa, persecution was a little deferred (for the Inquisition had not yet been set up formally in Mexico, as will be seen later on). After three years' tranquillity, however, the Inquisitors arrived, and the Englishmen were hunted down, thrown into dungeons, examined concerning their faith, lashed through the streets of the city amid a jeering mob, some burned in an *auto de fé*. The majority were sent back subsequently to Spain, where they were submitted to the solicitude of the Holy Office at Seville. One night, they broke prison, and seven managed to escape. The remainder however were recaptured, their prospects now worse than ever. At an *auto* in February, 1573, two of the party, Robert Barret, formerly master of the *Jesus*, and John Gilbert, were relaxed: a fate subsequently shared by others, including two of the musicians on Hawkins' flagship. Numerous others (among them John Hortop, who published an account of his experiences many years later, after he had returned to England) were condemned to the galleys—to remain a diplomatic pawn for some years. "Ginos Raros," a master-gunner with Hawkins ("Juan Alquino"), "who had comported himself by land and sea as is the custom among the Lutherans," recanted at the Seville *auto* of May 3rd, 1579, and was sent to join them.

All this was recounted at home, without any minimisation. The sufferers, even if they had recanted, were all regarded as martyrs: the provocation which they had offered was overlooked: their piracy was considered condonable, or even laudable. Thus the Protestant legend of the Inquisition was created: and it still endures.

Froude, in his *English Seamen in the Sixteenth Century*, puts forward this point of view in his nostalgic prose:

> "A new and infinitely dangerous element had been introduced by the change of religion into the relations of English sailors with the Catholic powers, and especially with Spain. In their zeal to keep out heresy, the Spanish government placed their harbours under the control of the Holy Office. Any vessel in which an heretical book was found was confiscated, and her crew carried to the Inquisitional prisons. It had begun in Henry's time. The Inquisitors attempted to treat schism as heresy and arrest Englishmen in their ports. But Henry spoke up stoutly to Charles V., and the Holy Office had been made to hold its hand. All was altered now. It was not necessary that a poor sailor should have been found teaching heresy. It was enough if he had an English Bible and Prayer Book with him in his kit; and stories would come into Dartmouth or Plymouth how some lad that everybody knew—Bill or Jack or Tom, who had wife or father or mother among them, perhaps—had been seized hold of for no other crime, been flung into a dungeon, tortured, starved, set to work in the galleys, or burned in a fool's coat, as they called it, at an *auto de fé* at Seville."

It was not, strictly speaking, true in every detail. But it represents what was believed at the time: and what is believed to have taken place often has a far greater historical importance than what actually occurred.

When, at the close of the reign of Elizabeth, English relations with Spain were put on a more normal footing, an attempt was made to solve this delicate problem by diplomatic means. Thus in the Treaty of London, of 1604, an article stipulated that the subjects of the King of England should not be molested by land or sea for matter of conscience, within the dominions of the King of Spain, provided that they did not give occasion of public scandal. But the last all-important phrase constituted a constant source of difficulty. It was officially defined as not alone failing to make obeisance towards the altar on entering a church—which, after all, was unnecessary, and could be avoided—but also failing to bow the knee while the Sacrament was being borne through the streets—which might at any time place the pious Puritan sailor in the awkward position of performing an action which was in his eyes tantamount to the recognition of the doctrine of the Real Presence. Moreover, this concession applied only to visitors: and foreign merchants resident in Spain remained as much liable to interference as before. This, nevertheless, was as much as the Spaniards would concede, either to English or to the Dutch: and when peace was again concluded with Spain, after the War of 1626-1630, the clause was reinserted without alteration.

Even Cromwell's Protestant zeal and trained infantry could not extract any more favourable concession. One of the privileges which he demanded in 1654, as the price of an Anglo-Spanish alliance against France, was liberty of conscience for Englishmen in Spain, so that they might worship God after their own lights in private houses, coupled with freedom of trade in the Spanish possessions in America. "You ask for my master's two eyes," cried the Spanish ambassador, surprised and shocked at the request. It was in consequence of this *impasse* that negotiations broke down. Philip IV. proudly informed the Supreme Council of the Inquisition what had happened, declaring that he would rather risk his kingdom, and spill the last drop of his blood, than do anything to prejudice the purity of faith of his dominions. The Suprema acknowledged his declaration with gratitude, declaring that his words deserved to be recorded for the benefit of remote posterity in imperishable bronze. They are indeed inscribed, for those who have eyes to read, on the map of the world: for the fact that Jamaica became a British possession was one immediate result of this display of stubbornness.

The old Spanish intolerance hence persisted. Even when the eighteenth century was well advanced, foreign Protestants of whatever nationality could obtain no greater protection or concessions in Spain than they had under her treaty with England in 1604. These slender privileges applied, even so, only to subjects of Protestant states, French Huguenots and the like thus remaining as much liable to persecution as the native-born Spaniards themselves. From time to time, some instance of a peculiarly tactless or brutal persecution would occasion a flood of excited literature, scandalise Protestants abroad, and confirm the current impressions of the "Inquisition Dogs and the Devildoms of Spain." It was noteworthy that few such difficulties arose with the Portuguese, a prudent trading nation. Though no less zealous in matters of faith, they had the tact to confine their attention to their own subjects; and, while the Inquisition was still in full power, a Protestant conventicle, and an English cemetery, were allowed to exist in Lisbon. The Spanish *hidalgo*, on the other hand, scorned trade and the mundane considerations bound up with it. He was content to know that his country, of all the world, was least contaminated with the taint of heresy. This fact justified in his mind, as it does in that of many of his descendants today, all the devastation that the Holy Office wrought in the life of the country. But the question remains whether, in any case, the Spanish soil was propitious for the spread of the new doctrines, and whether, in this most vaunted and most successful of its achievements, the Inquisition was not in fact tilting (in the classical tradition of La Mancha) at a non-existent windmill.

CHAPTER IX

ALARMS AND DIVERSIONS

PROTESTANTS, Moriscos and Judaisers constituted the major preoccupation of the Spanish Inquisition. But there was nothing too small, just as there was nothing too great, for its notice. There were so many pitfalls for the faithful: so much from which he needed protection: so many seemingly innocent statements the theological implications of which, were they but examined, were of the most serious nature. With all of these matters, the Holy Office occupied itself: and, as time went on, its tentacles extended over the whole of Spanish life, secular no less than ecclesiastical.

A problem which was peculiar to Spain, for it was a natural outcome of the Spanish temperament, was that of the Mystics. Not that there was necessarily anything in Mysticism which was repugnant to the Holy Catholic Faith. Many of the greatest figures in the history of Catholicism, indeed, interpreted their religion in terms of mystical experience. But it was a delicate subject, which might easily overstep the borderline between orthodoxy and the opposite: and it is not without its significance that the most eminent Spanish mystics—Raymond Lull, Luis de Granada, Juan de la Cruz, even Santa Teresa herself—at one time or another got into trouble with the authorities. Those who insisted upon the supreme importance of inward light—" *alumbrados*," as they came to be called, the Spanish equivalent of the Italian " *illuminati* "—tended to be contemptuous of ecclesiastical authority and of the function of the priesthood: and their views thus approximated in some respects to the most dangerous of all Protestant doctrines. Another category were the Quietists, who, in complete annihilation of self, abandoned themselves entirely to God, allowing free expression to every idea and impulse which came to them. Akin to them, but even more dangerous, were those who maintained that the body could only receive merit for withstanding temptation if systematically exposed to it, or that the soul could soar above the body only in moments of complete physical abandonment. Mysticism thus descended, by imperceptible gradations, into mere libertinism: sensual priests sometimes exploited their position to manipulate vulgar sexual orgies. Moreover, from time to time religious hysteria or a craving for notoriety (particularly among women) brought about a simulation of sanctity or of supernatural spiritual gifts which sometimes attracted large bodies of credulous followers. After the seventeenth century, all these aspects of mysticism were loosely described as Molinism, after Miguel de Molinos, a Spanish Jesuit, who died in prison in Rome in 1696; for his attempt to reconcile free will with Divine Grace and prescience had led him into the dangerously libertine conclusions of his doctrine of *dejamiénto*—that by annihilating the external world of sense the soul may attain to that perfect detachment in which the word of God may be heard.

It was with the Mystics, then—sometimes for their dangerous approximation to Protestantism, sometimes for extravagant spiritual pretensions, sometimes for unbridled sexual indulgence—that the Inquisition busied itself, more than with any other purely native element in Spain other than the Marranos and Moriscos. As early as 1498, there were complaints against the growth in the country of Illuminism of the Italian type. In 1510, steps were taken against a popular saint known as the

Beata of Piedrahita, who claimed that she was in a very real sense the bride of Christ, in whose arms she was nightly dissolved in love. A little later, a group was discovered in Guadalajara, headed by a certain lay-preacher named Pedro Ruiz de Alcaraz, who taught among other things that sexual union was union with God, that mental prayer was alone necessary, and that confessions, indulgences and good works were superfluous. Though he had deserved burning, according to the Inquisitional code, he was let off with a sentence of scourging and perpetual imprisonment, ultimately reduced to ten years. Some of his followers were punished with him, a few of them being accused in addition of Lutheran heresy.

A more remarkable character was Francisca Hernández, who must have possessed great beauty as well as considerable powers of fascination. She was the leader of a group in Aragon, and her reputation for holiness was such that, when the Inquisitor General, Adrian of Utrecht, was elected Pope in 1522, he instructed his secretary to solicit her prayers on his own behalf as well as on that of the whole Church. She claimed to be the bride of Christ, but nevertheless shewed no taste for monandry. Among her disciples was a youth name Calero, whom she persuaded to sell his patrimony to support her circle, and a student of Salamanca named Medrano, subsequently admitted to Holy Orders. The latter claimed to hold conversations with the Holy Ghost and to be impeccable: but it was rumoured nevertheless that he frequently shared Francisca's couch. Prosecuted in 1530 by the Tribunal of Toledo for the second time, he indignantly repudiated any suggestion of indecency. He was so favoured by God, he claimed, that neither all the evil women in the world nor all the devils in the next could move him to commit carnal sin. He could lie in bed with a woman without feeling desire, and he frequently did so with Francisca, who received both enjoyment and grace from his embraces. Male and female devotees, he asserted, could fondle one another naked without qualms: for it was not clothing but intention that mattered. Medrano escaped burning on the ground that he was more knave than heretic, and suffered only a light sentence. Francisca, it appears, continued in an odour of sanctity to her death.

Some of her contemporaries were not so fortunate. The degree of holiness ascribed to Magdalena de la Cruz was such that her reputation spread far beyond the boundaries of Spain, and both secular princes and ecclesiastical dignitaries solicited her advice and her prayers. But during a severe illness, in 1543, she confessed that all her pretended visions had been due to fraud (or, as she expressed it, demoniacal possession); and, on her recovery, she had to appear at an *auto* as a penitent. A reputation nearly as great was enjoyed by a nun of Lisbon, who claimed to possess the stigmata of Christ. She was unfortunate enough to take the wrong side in international politics, and when proceedings were brought against her it was discovered that the stigmata could be entirely removed with soap and water.

The Jesuits themselves, with their sometimes hysterical piety, were under suspicion of Illuminism at the time of the establishment of the Order; and shortly after 1570, in consequence of the denunciations of a bitter enemy, a group of *alumbrados* inspired by a member of the body was discovered in Estremadura. They all appeared as penitents at an *auto* held at Llerena in 1579. This menacing extension was probably responsible for the fact that in January, 1578, a list of Illuminist errors was added to the Edict of Faith for the information of the faithful, inviting denunciation of those who claimed that inward prayer alone was necessary and public worship superfluous; and that good works, and aids to devotion and the intercession of the saints, were needless, for those who were perfect.

In 1623, stern measures were taken at Seville, in consequence of the discovery of indecent orgies caused by the teaching of a fashionable local priest, named Fernando Mendez, whose congregation would strip naked after he had celebrated Mass and dance together with indecent vigour. Among the penances which he imposed on some of his female votaries was that of lifting their skirts and exposing themselves before him. The discovery from the Edict of Faith that these pleasurable occupations placed those involved within the power of the dreaded Tribunal came as a great shock to many of the stylish ladies of the city, whose coaches sometimes blocked the way to the convent to which he had retired. Hundreds of penitents presented themselves voluntarily to confess their wrongdoing: and for weeks a delegate of the Holy Office was in attendance for eighteen hours a day hearing the applications. The principal person responsible, Padre Fernando, had died just in time to save himself from very serious consequences: but his relics were nevertheless treasured up as holy objects by his disciples. On November 30th, 1624, an *auto* was held at which some of the latter appeared—eight of them confessed impostors. Two years later, two more heresiarchs who had followed Padre Fernando's lead were arraigned. By now, Illuminism had definitely entered the ranks of the more serious crimes: and at an *auto* held in 1630 at the same city eight persons accused of the crime were burned in person, and six in effigy. In 1640-1643, similarly severe measures were taken by the Tribunal of Toledo against the followers of a *beata* named Eugenia de la Torre, accused of similar libidinous orgies with her male adherents, who included more than one priest.

Religious mania could at times express itself even more extravagantly. About the year 1730, a learned Portuguese priest, Father Antonio Guolherme Hebre de Loureyro, was charged by the Inquisition with having proclaimed himself God and the second Redeemer of the human race, as well as with other sins against the principal articles of the Catholic faith. The deluded priest was savagely punished: he was sentenced to wear the *sambenito* and painted mitre in perpetuity, to be prevented from ever exercising the duties of his order, and to be secluded for all time without pardon in the prisons of the Holy Inquisition. It is only when the most secret records of the Holy Office are published—if they are still extant—that we shall know how long his martyrdom endured.

For a century after, similar cases continued to attract the attention of the Holy Office—more particularly the tribunals of the northern provinces, where the tendency in this direction seems to have been greater. As the eighteenth century drew to its close, on the other hand, a more charitable view tended to be taken, such claims to abnormal spiritual powers being ascribed to delusion or insanity rather than to heretical proclivities. A Joanna Southcott, had she appeared in Spain in the sixteenth century, might have been burned; at the end of the eighteenth, she would indubitably have been placed under salutary restraint. It was only in a Protestant country that a woman of this stamp could develop into a major prophet.

One type of Molinist excess was at times not easily distinguishable from the more vulgar crime of solicitation at the Confessional. This was essentially a disciplinary matter. The Inquisition, however, considered it in another light, as a violation or contempt of a sacrament. It therefore took such matters in hand when they came to its notice, removing them out of the jurisdiction of those who might have dealt with them more firmly. For, from the doctrinal point of view, the offence was not a very serious one, and the penalties imposed were generally slight. The records demonstrate nevertheless that the failing was by no means so common, nor was it treated so venially, as Protestant polemists would have one believe. True, it is reported that when in 1563 the population of Seville were requested to denounce confessors who had acted in this manner, there was an astonishing rush of accusers. Twenty secretaries and Inquisitors did not suffice to cope with the situation, and the period for receiving denunciations had to be extended time after time. This account, however, derives from a prejudiced German source, and it is wiser not to accept it unquestioningly. But the priesthood at Seville, above all places, does not appear to have been conspicuously amenable to discipline and decorum; for a brief of Pope Urban VIII. was required in 1642 to forbid them from smoking while celebrating Mass, and from staining the altar-cloths with tobacco.

Occasionally, a more exotic case of heresy would diversify the Inquisitional round. The negro slaves brought home from Africa, and baptised forthwith, could not be expected to forget their former beliefs and practices immediately; and sometimes votaries of hoodoo would be surprised in the very fortresses of Roman Catholicism. In 1731, for example, a group of negro slaves was put on trial at Lisbon for " making a pact with the Demon, whom they recognised and worshipped as God."

A particularly important function was the censorship of literature: for it was notorious that the printing-press had not been without its influence in spreading Luther's damnable heresies, and it was generally believed (not without reason) that Protestants from overseas were attempting to spread their views in the Peninsula by means of smuggled propaganda. When the scare was at its height, Philip II. ordered that no bookseller should sell or keep any work condemned by the Inquisition under penalty of confiscation ánd death. In 1602 the *Suprema* went so far as to instruct their commissioners to seize all new books, or even new editions, and hold them pending a detailed report on their contents.

From books of definitely heretical intentions the purview of the Inquisition extended imperceptibly to those, of blameless origin, which incidentally gave expression to opinions dangerous to the Faith; and hence to obscene works which might have an adverse effect on public morals. Not content with the *Index Librorum Prohibitorum* published under the auspices of the Vatican at Rome, the Spanish Inquisition drew up and periodically reissued its own list of questionable works. Agents were employed to search bookshops and even private libraries, to ensure that no prohibited literature was kept. Finally, notwithstanding the protests of foreign powers, the Holy Office appointed commissioners to search ships which touched at Spanish ports, to discover spiritual contraband: a procedure which, until a few years ago, would have made any modern government the world's laughingstock.

Sometimes, the most blameless and laudable sentiments might be so phrased as to require censure. Thus, certain *Evangelical Discourses* written by Fray Alonso de la Cruz spoke of the love between Saint Andrew and the Cross in such a manner as to convey a distinctly carnal impression. "I desire to court thee, for thou art most fair," the Saint is made to say to the object of his devotion. "How beauteous thou art, killing me with love. . . . If thou dost wish to embrace me, embrace me now, that I may die at once. Thou hast well seen, O Divine Cross, the evil days and worse nights that I have endured to enjoy thee." . . . "What love can compare to that of Saint Andrew and the Cross?" the author went on to observe. "So excessively did they love, that they died locked in one another's arms, as happened to Thisbe and Pyramus, to Hero and Leander." Passages such as this (to which the Inquisition not unnaturally raised objection) help the modern reader to understand how the same Spain could become a byword both for religious zeal and amorous adventure.

With the advance of the eighteenth century, the increased output of books in Northern Europe which were objectionable under both heads (for reasons that is of morality as well as of faith) was so great that this branch of the Inquisitorial activity became heavy. It was simple to decide that the works of M. Voltaire should be excluded, and those of Mr. Locke expurgated. But there were numerous cases in which it was not so easy to come to a decision. A theological expert was frankly in difficulties when he was asked for an opinion about *L'éloge d'ivresse*. "I am horrified to see," he reported, "that this is the third edition of the work; for I never imagined that there could be in the whole world a sufficient number of barbarous idlers to waste their time and their money on anything so ridiculous." One sympathises, too, with the Censor who in 1742 was given a copy of the works of Shakespeare for his opinion. He could find nothing objectionable in them, he reported (it is to be supposed that he could read English), excepting for the presumption that the author was a heretic, having been born in Stratford, one of the '' provinces '' of England infected by heresy.

Even the classics of Spanish literature had to submit to the indignity. Fernando de Rojas' *Celestina y Meliboe* —Spain's greatest contribution to European letters before Cervantes, and one of the sources of inspiration for Shakespeare's Romeo and Juliet; better and more characteristically known as *The Spanish Bawd*—had some of its worst indecencies pruned away, though only in its later editions. (It would have doubtless received earlier and more sedulous attention had the Inquisitors known, as we do now, that the author was a Marrano.) Gil Vicente, the greatest Portuguese satirist, was condemned by the Holy Office after the Spanish occupation of the smaller country.

Even *Don Quixote* was not immune. It will be recalled how at one stage the Knight of the Rueful Countenance tore off the tail of his shirt and tied knots in it to serve as a rosary while he was in the wilderness of the Sierra Morena. Indecent, pronounced the Holy Office: and in the second edition the shirt-tail was transmogrified into a chaplet of cork-tree nuts, to which not even the most pious devotee could take exception. Similarly, in the second part of the work, attention was called to a remark of the Duchess (who should have known better) to Sancho Panza: '' Works of charity done coldly and grudgingly possess no merit and avail nothing.'' This clearly approached the border of Lutheran doctrine, and, after being printed, had to be expurgated by order of the Inquisition. These instances illustrate the statement reported in the name of Cervantes: '' I would have made the book more amusing, had it not been for the Holy Office.'' But he certainly had his revenge: for, fortunately, the Censors do not appear to have recognised themselves in the exquisite vignette of the High and Mighty Inquisition held by the Priest and the Barber on the library of the Visionary gentleman, in order to purge it of its more deleterious works of chivalry. The display of ignorance, credulity and indiscrimination in this is clearly intended to be a satire upon the ecclesiastical censorship, and above all the final conclusion—that, in cases of doubt or when time was pressing, the safest thing (as in our own day) is to commit everything to the flames.

But Art, too, might corrupt Spanish morals; and with this also the Holy Office occupied itself. It was not a question only of suppressing blatant pornography, for which the Holy Office was as well qualified as any other tribunal, but of much more extensive and delicate duties. Books would be deprived of objectionable illustrations: snuff-boxes would be submitted to scrutiny, lest the pictures on their covers should offend good taste: and, in the twilight of its days, the Madrid Tribunal ordered all the hairdressers in the city to remove from their windows, or reduce to decency, the wax busts which they exhibited to advertise their art, on the ground that the over-exuberant display of their charms might prove too tempting to the adolescent mind. In 1796, the Commissioner of the Holy Office at Buenos Aires was much exercised over certain wall-papers received from Barcelona, with mythological figures of questionable nature and in questionable attitudes. At Murcia, in the same year, a perplexing question was presented by reason of a statue of Venus and (presumably) Adonis in one of the public thoroughfares, which clerics affirmed to be libidinously naked, while a Professor of Sculpture certified that, as far as the more important areas were concerned, they were modestly covered. On this occasion, the problem was complicated by the fact that one end of the street was watched over by an effigy of Our Lady of La Fuensanta, and the other by a nunnery! In 1814, Goya himself was called upon to put up a defence of his *Maja Desnuda*, which had been discovered, with other carnal paintings of the same description, among the goods sequestered from (of all places) a convent. It may be recalled that Goya himself (whose master, José Luzan y Martinez, had served as Artistic Censor to the Holy Office) had to leave Saragossa in his youth, when the Inquisition was compelled to take proceedings to stop the unseemly brawlings between the partisans of the two rival Cathedrals. It is believed, too, that in his maturity he suffered from some sort of more direct interference. The above are only a few instances out of a very large number which might be assembled. Here, perhaps, we have the answer to the problem, why it was that Spain never produced a really great artist after Murillo save that astonishing and unrelated prodigy whom we have just mentioned, Francisco Goya.

The first recorded instance of the application of censorship to the motion picture on the score of public morals appears, too, in an Inquisitional report of 1803, when an outraged artist denounced a pleasing novelty recently received from France, and sold widely all over Madrid, called the Magic Lantern of Love, in which were shown figures of a man (in some cases, a Capuchin Friar) performing various indecent acts with a woman.

One of the commonest of all the crimes punished by the Inquisition was that of alleging that fornication among the unmarried was no sin. In almost every *auto de fé*, there figured one or two persons who had uttered this heretical opinion. At Toledo, for example, a larger number of persons were punished for this during the course of the

Tribunal's activity than for all Protestant and similar heresies combined. It would appear an unnecessary subject for theological controversy: but there was obviously something else behind it. We may picture the successive phases: an ardent lover pleading that, as neither party was married, there could be no harm in doing as he suggested: a compliant virgin, yielding to the well-worn argument: a stern or prurient priest, worrying out the truth in the Confessional, and insisting that he who propounded so obviously heretical an opinion must be denounced to the authorities: and finally the arraignment and punishment of the impious Don Juan—not for his immorality, which was a venial offence, but for the arguments with which he had supported it. The penalty in such instances, however, was generally light.

A less logical, and more unusual, object of Inquisitional solicitude was hermaphroditism. This was ascribed, without further ado, to a pact with the demon, and in general the unfortunate individual concerned would be burned out of hand. (The phenomenon involved incidentally contempt for the Holy Sacrament of matrimony, though in view of the heinousness of the other aspect it was hardly necessary for this to be accentuated.) Elvira de Cespedes, whose case was tried by the Inquisition of Toledo in 1588, was comparatively fortunate. At the age of sixteen, while a slave-girl at Jaen, she had been married in right and proper form, and had borne her husband a son. Wearying of the female rôle, she then turned her attention to her mistress, whom she seduced; and, emboldened by this success, she tried her luck, with equal success, on several other women. She then took the business of being a man more seriously, served as a soldier during the Morisco rebellion in Granada, worked in hospital at Madrid and gained a surgeon's certificate. A professional man requires, of course, a regular domestic life. The family of the intended bride was made suspicious by the bridegroom's hairless face and generally effeminate appearance, and had her examined by a doctor. However, the latter granted the necessary certificate, and the marriage was celebrated. Later on, for some reason that is not quite clear, Elvira was again denounced and handed over to the Inquisition, whose physician had no hesitation in declaring her to be a woman. No explanation could be adduced to explain this extraordinary metamorphosis other than that mentioned above—a pact with the devil. Her treatment however was relatively light. She was merely sentenced to abjure *de levi* at an *auto*, to receive two hundred lashes, and to serve in a hospital for ten years without pay. Some amorists might have thought that, considering what she had enjoyed during her metamorphosis, it was worth while.

A conspicuous part of the work of the Inquisition depended to the very end upon the differentiation between "New Christians," whose forebears had been converted from Judaism or Mohammedanism, and "Old Christians," who had no such taint in their ancestry. No matter how long ago the conversion had taken place, the former were suspect, and their orthodoxy considered doubtful. Hence a trifling misdemeanour, condonable in a person of ordinary antecedents, assumed quite a different aspect when a New Christian was in question. This was one reason, and pride of descent was another, which led the Spaniards to differentiate as rigidly as possible between the two categories. In some circles, indeed, it was unwise to pursue such investigations too closely. At intervals, some malicious scribbler would compile a work indicating how the origin of some of the noblest families of the realm was to be traced back to the *judería*: but it was invariably suppressed (a typical example was *El tizon de la nobleza española*, by Cardinal Francisco Mendoza y Bovadilla, which, written in the sixteenth century, only became generally available in the nineteenth).

Meanwhile, Spanish families which prided themselves rightly or wrongly on their purity of blood (*limpieza*, as they termed it) took the greatest pains to preserve it uncontaminated. Various positions and offices (Chairs in the Universities, positions under the Inquisition, and so on) were reserved for them: and the Holy Office derived a considerable revenue from the issue of certificates which enabled the holders to take up such appointments. The Tribunal of Toledo alone conducted 5,000 such investigations, and issued an equal number of certificates during its existence—a figure which exceeded that of all other enquiries which it made added together. Even the lowest classes shared this feeling: it will be recalled, for example, how Sancho Panza prided himself that he was " free from any admixture of Jew or Moor," though whether his master could have made a similar boast is doubtful. It was only after the middle of the nineteenth century that the legal distinction between " Old " and " New " Christians was formally abolished in Spain; yet even after that date, discrimination survived—particularly as regards the Chuetas of Majorca, who (as has been seen elsewhere) were still kept rigidly separated from the other inhabitants of the island. But even now, and even in England, the exploded absurdity is echoed in common linguistic usage. The fact that the veins appear to be of a bluer tinge in a person of fair complexion gave rise to the use of the term *sangre azul* by certain families of Castile who claimed that they were uncontaminated by Moorish, Jewish or other admixture: this in turn being adapted in English in reference to the " blue-blooded " aristocracy.

As has been seen, intermarriage between New Christians and Old was frowned on. Yet interest, romance or reticence were often too much for prejudice. The products of such mixed marriages were termed " Half New Christians "—from Jew or from Moor, as the case might be. If a Half New Christian married a full Old Christian, the offspring would be officially termed " Quarter New Christian." Thus they went on, through minutest modifications, from seven-eighth New Christians down to one-sixteenth New Christians: after which the mathematical computation became too involved, and they were content to register the fact that the person in question " possessed a part of the New Christian." Even this exiguous proportion of infidel blood, however, was sufficient to exclude a man from office, to prevent natural affection from finding its outlet in marriage, or to give a fatal turn to the suspicions of the Holy Office. Until a short while ago, it was possible to speak of this crazy structure with the levity which a dead absurdity deserves. In our own days, however, the entire system has been revived in Central Europe. The main difference is, that instead of the logically defensible term "New Christian," the ethnological absurdity of Aryanism has been called into existence. For the rest, the Half Aryans and Quarter Aryans and so on provide a perfect parallel to the Spanish scene of centuries ago, save that the disabilities from which they suffer are far more extreme. The system lacks even the virtue of originality.

There is one matter, on the other hand, in which the record of the Spanish Inquisition, as compared with the rest of Europe, shews up in a very good light; and this is in the attitude adopted towards witchcraft. To deny its existence outright would have been contrary to the best-informed learned opinion of the day, as well as of Holy

Writ itself, and would have bordered on heresy. But the Inquisition would do nothing on the basis of mere hearsay: it had rules for the evaluation (as well as the extraction) of evidence: and it applied to the conviction of witches and sorcerers the same cold, objective methods as it did to the hunting-down of heretics.

It was only in the sixteenth century that the attack of witch-madness which had affected the rest of Europe a couple of generations before spread to Spain, even so being confined in the main to the extreme north. In striking contrast to its excitable conduct on some other occasions, the Supreme Council of the Inquisition appointed a commission to go into the question. The report recommended that proved instances of witchcraft should certainly be submitted to the jurisdiction of the Holy Office, but that concrete evidence of crime should be obtained before those alleged to be responsible were punished, and that in the meantime the enlightenment of the ignorant rural population in Navarre by properly-qualified preachers would doubtless have salutary results.

The Inquisitor of Navarre, unfortunately, had his own opinions on this matter, and a private witch-hunt in his province resulted in the sentence of a large number of women. It may be pointed out that, in many of these cases, something less than a judicial murder was probably involved. It is likely that in a large number of instances those inculpated actually believed that they could attain supernatural powers and magical qualities which they did not necessarily desire to exercise for their neighbours' good. It would seem that there had survived throughout Europe something of the ancient pre-Christian fertility-cult, of which those accused of witchcraft were the last devotees. Their ceremonies were associated with this: the " witches' Sabbath " was an assemblage to carry out its rites: the Evil One, with whom they were reported to have a pact and to conduct indecent orgies, was the representative of the ancient Pagan deity to whom these rites were originally dedicated, now given by the Church a Christian disguise and identified with Satan.

During the entire course of the sixteenth century, the Spanish Inquisition preserved its balance and its objectivity in this matter. The ignorant peasantry of Navarre, however, retained their own convictions: and evidence accumulated in that province to such an extent that in 1610 the Supreme Council despatched a special commissioner, Fray Alonso de Salazar Frias, to conduct the campaign. Contrary to expectations, his influence was essentially moderating. He decided that at least three-quarters of those hundreds of persons who had come forward to accuse themselves, in obedience to the Edict of Grace which had been published on his arrival, were self-deluded, and that more work required to be done among the population in order to get them out of their credulous state of mind. An *auto* was indeed held at Logroño in the following year, and twenty-nine witches appeared among a total of fifty-three culprits, five being burned. This was a disappointing result, in the eyes of the local zealots, to a campaign which had begun under such auspices: and it marked, not a new beginning, but almost the end.

From that date, comparatively few trials for witchcraft figure in the records of the Inquisition. In the eighteenth century, rationalist England and Scotland (with their estimated total of 300,000 victims in all), and even the American colonies, were cheerfully burning witches, after preliminaries of revolting cruelty, and Sir William Blackstone was laying down the law that "to deny the possibility, nay, actual existence, of witchcraft is at once flatly to contradict the revealed word of God.'' In Spain, on the other hand, the moderating influence of the Holy Tribunal remained preponderant: and, though a few cases were brought before it, conviction ensued in none of them.

For this service to the cause of humanity and truth, the Spanish Inquisition deserves the gratitude of all thinking men. Yet there is an explanation of the prodigy which should not be overlooked. It was unnecessary for the Spaniard to seek an object for his pent-up suspicions, and an excuse for private and public misfortunes, in the absurd activities of a coterie of ignorant beldams: there was an entire category of the population to serve as his bugbear, and through their tribulations the witches were saved.

Male sorcerers also came into the scope of activity of the Holy Office, and were sometimes punished. Generally, this was a mere matter of routine; but there were some significant exceptions. In 1624, for example, a certain Diego de Santa Marta, of Garachico in the Canary Islands, was denounced by the Inquisition as a sorcerer. The proof was plain: for he made a pack of cards obey his will in a most extraordinary fashion, fathoming the thoughts of his audience, anticipating their secret desires, and causing any particular card he desired to emerge at the top of the pack with a truly supernatural docility. Fray Juan de Saavedra was instructed to investigate into the question and to deliver a report. Accordingly, he summoned the accused to give him an exhibition of his skill, in the presence of the Provincial, several Professors of Theology, and the *alguazil* of the Holy Tribunal. Don Diego, unaware that he was practically on trial before this illustrious body, felt highly flattered at the invitation. He excelled himself, performing some surprising card tricks as well as sundry other feats of jugglery. Fortunately for himself, he was somewhat clumsy (due, perhaps, to nervousness), or else the audience was peculiarly sharp-sighted. In any case, Fray Saavedra reported that it was all a matter of sleight of hand, which could be detected by careful observation. Had it not been for this, Don Diego might have been condemned to appear in an *auto de fé* as a penitent, and to end his days in the galleys.

After a prolonged struggle with other authorities, the Inquisition at last established its competence in cases of bigamy, whose votaries made it plain that they despised the Holy Sacrament of matrimony. Few *autos* took place at which there did not figure one or two persons who had " married on two occasions," and were condemned to some supplementary punishment by an unfeeling Tribunal. In 1579, a person accused of this offence at Valladolid shamefacedly confessed that, during the past ten years, he had married no less than fifteen wives. This, in fact, appears to have been the profession on which he relied for his livelihood. He wandered through the country, offering matrimony to any damsel or widow who attracted his fancy, enjoyed her company for a longer or shorter period according to her attraction, and then ran away with any chattels on which he could lay his hands. One of his favourite methods was to impersonate someone who had disappeared, first gathering from the local residents sufficient information to enable him to carry on the deception. This process he repeated no less than eleven times, in some cases establishing by this means a claim to considerable property. The punishment to which he was sentenced fitted the crime. He was condemned to appear at an *auto de fé* wearing a tall cone-shaped mitre decorated with the figures of fifteen women—one for each of those with whom he had lived. In addition, he was sentenced to two hundred lashes and to a life-term in the galleys. This, indeed, was unusually severe for a case of this sort: but it saved the Tribunal from the necessity of deciding the complicated question which would otherwise have confronted it—with which of his fifteen brides he should live on his release.

But there was much else with which the Holy Office occupied itself. In a Latin country, in which normal obscenity assumed a theological form as automatically as it assumes a sexual form in the English-speaking world, the question of Blasphemy was important: and a man who drew doubt upon his faith by shouting *Reniego á Dios!* when he was in a temper often repented it by being lashed through the streets in an *auto de fé*. There was the problem of evil-doers who exported horses to France, possibly for the service of the Huguenot heretics. And, with the advance of the eighteenth century, the problem of the Jansenists, of the Rationalists, and in the end of the Freemasons, became more and more pressing, and ensured that the Holy Office should not run the risk of expiring from sheer inanition.

Not infrequently, the Holy Office intervened in purely political matters. This was the case especially in its last days, when the causes of Revolution and of Irreligion were closely interwoven. Yet the most notorious instance of the sort occurred in the sixteenth century, when Spanish orthodoxy still stood four-square against all the winds of impiety. The most sinister of Philip II.'s Ministers had been Antonio Pérez, the illegitimate son of the Archdeacon of Sepulveda, who was first the protégé, then the successor, of Ruy Gomez, Prince of Eboli. He possessed a considerable amount of ability, of a crude Machiavellian sort, and had a profound respect for espionage and intrigue as instruments of government. Above all, he contributed largely, though in an indirect manner, to the independence of Holland, by fomenting ill-feeling between Philip and his half-brother, Don John of Austria. The latter ultimately sent his personal secretary, Escovedo, to Spain, to urge the necessity of supporting the war more generously if there was to be any prospect of success. Pérez, who had been able to tempt Don John into making certain rash statements, now persuaded the King that the real object of the mission was to stir up a rebellion in favour of Charles V.'s superbly able bastard. Philip was alarmed, and instructed his minister to see that the unfortunate secretary was put out of harm's way.

Pérez obeyed these instructions in the traditional Spanish spirit. From that moment, he knew no peace. His enemies in the Council fostered the report that he was responsible for Escovedo's murder, which Philip blankly disavowed. For some time, he supported his Minister, but in the end suddenly veered round: the reason whispered was that the widowed Princess of Eboli (who was arrested with Pérez), sublimely impartial as between the Arms and the Man, preferred the Minister's embraces to his own. Whether this were so or no (the probabilities seem against it) there can be no doubt that some less personal considerations were also to be taken into account. Pérez was arrested, and, under torture, acknowledged his guilt but at the same time implicated the King. The matter dragged on interminably. In the end, after twelve years, in April, 1590, Pérez managed to escape, dressed in his wife's clothing, and fled into Aragon, where he appealed for justice to the local courts. These, overjoyed at the opportunity of shewing their independence of Madrid, acquitted him.

Philip's slow-moving blood was now stirred, and it became the one object of his life to revenge himself on his former servant. There was only one Court in Aragon which was not completely independent—that of the Inquisition. It was under the control of the *Suprema* at Madrid: and the Inquisitor General issued instructions to the Tribunal of Saragossa to arrest the unfortunate Pérez, on the ground that, on his arrest, he had uttered blasphemous words indicative of heresy. When the news became known in Saragossa, the citizens were wild with anger at this breach of their traditional rights, and rose as one man. The *Justiza* was mobbed, the royal representative killed: and the Inquisitors, in fear for their own lives, restored Pérez to the *Aljafería* or civic prison.

By this action, the people of Saragossa had technically put themselves in the wrong: for their ancient immunities, which they were claiming to defend, did not extend to those charged with so heinous an offence as heresy, and the whole population had subjected themselves to the dire penalties incurred by all who impeded the legitimate functions of the Holy Office. The question of the un-fortunate secretary henceforth was merged in larger political considerations, into which all manner of contending forces entered. The more moderate part of the Saragossan population determined that it was not worth while risking themselves for so unworthy an object, and Pérez was once more handed over to the Holy Office. This however led to a new revolt, which was supported by the new *Justiza*, whose father had just died, and Pérez was once more rescued.

Clearly, there would be no hope for him if Philip regained control. He therefore began to intrigue for the establishment of an independent Aragonese republic, under French protection. Meanwhile, the royal armies were marching from Madrid. The rebels had no troops, and little support excepting from some of the more lawless peasants, who perceived excellent opportunity for reverting to the ancestral profession of brigandage. Accordingly, no organised defence was attempted, and when in November, 1591, Saragossa was reached, the city surrendered without striking a blow. Pérez meanwhile had succeeded in fleeing over the Pyrenees, the Inquisition having the satisfaction of burning only his effigy. For the rest of his life, he remained a stormy petrel of international politics, plotting in every Court of Europe and trying with puny intrigues to avenge himself on his former master. When in 1587 the King of Spain's beard was singed in Cadiz harbour, it was this evil spirit behind the scenes who had prepared the match. Philip, on his side, never gave up his optimistic attempts to secure by treachery what he had been unable to do by any legal process; he pursued his former servant all over Europe, and, when male assassins bungled their jobs, employed a lady of light morals but stern principles for the same purpose.

Aragon meanwhile was under the heel of the conqueror. Together with many others the impetuous young *Justiza* was executed—it was a judicial murder—and the office virtually abolished; the privileges of the Cortes were whittled away almost to nothing; and the country was brought under the direct control of Madrid. Henceforth, though the shadow of constitutional liberty remained, the substance was gone. It was not until three hundred and fifty years had passed that Aragon was able to resume its political identity. In the events which are perplexing Europe at the present day, the curious may still trace the consequences of that ill-starred attempt to champion the cause of a priest's bastard against the Holy Office.

CHAPTER X

NEW WORLDS TO CONQUER

IT is an undoubted fact that the discovery of America in 1492 was, to a large extent, a Marrano enterprise. There is an old legend to the effect that Isabella the Catholic raised the money required by means of her court jewels: but as has been pointed out, it would be more accurate to substitute " Jews " for the last word. Modern Spanish scholars, in a frenzied attempt to vindicate Christopher Columbus as a child of their own country, have evolved the theory that he was in fact a Marrano, and for that reason somewhat secretive as to his origin: and they point to the significant fact that in his will he left money to a Jewish beggar in Lisbon. Be that as it may, there can be no doubt that Marranos had a great deal to do with the genesis of the expedition. It was one of them, Luis de Santángel, who commended the enterprise to the Catholic Sovereigns, actually provided the money for it, and was rewarded by being the recipient of the first report of the discovery of the New World. His colleague and associate, Gabriel Sanchez (whose family, like Santángel's, was also implicated in the plot against Pedro Arbues at Saragossa) similarly played an important part. Indeed, the only high official concerned with the genesis of the expedition who was of " Old Christian " stock had a " New Christian " wife. Of the personnel of the expedition, many belonged to the same category—including Luis de Torres, baptised the day before they set sail, who was both the first European to set foot in the new land and the first to make use of tobacco; and Mestre

Bernal, the ship's physician, who had not long before figured at an *auto* on a charge of Judaising.

In the circumstances, it was not remarkable that crypto-Jews from Spain were eager to seize the opportunity of finding a fresh home and openings in the new continent, where not only was there opportunity for all, but above all the dreaded Inquisition was unknown. The emigration began at an early date, and there were even Marrano *conquistadores* in the little band which followed Cortes to conquer Mexico. But the optimistic hopes which impelled them to cross the Atlantic were ill-grounded: and it was not long before the nightmare of the Inquisition followed them. As early as 1515, a Marrano was brought back from Hispañola with his family to face trial at Seville; and four years later, Apostolic Inquisitors were appointed by the Supreme Tribunal in Spain for the American Colonies. Their powers were deputed in the end to a certain Franciscan Friar named Martin de Valencia. He arrived in Mexico in 1524, amply equipped with authority. He confined his exercise of it, however, to curbing the reprehensible habit of blasphemous swearing in which the gallant *conquistadores* were accustomed to indulge.

It was not until the Dominicans arrived, a few years after, that real heresy-hunting began, though the procedure was apparently somewhat summary. In 1528, the first Act of Faith was held in the New World, and two Spanish Marranos—including one of Cortes' old followers —were burned, in Mexico City, while another was reconciled. Eight years later, proceedings were taken against a Lutheran lapidary named Andres Moral, who was reconciled, as was also a further Jew in 1539. In 1560, an English Protestant, named Robert Tomson, of Wendover, and a Genoese suspect named Boacio, were similarly

penanced, in the presence of a crowd of five or six thou
sand wondering spectators, as heretics and persons
seduced of the Devil. A dozen similar cases followed in
the course of the next decade. The *sambenitos* of all
these victims were duly suspended in the Cathedral
Church for the delectation and warning of the inhabitants.

This sporadic activity, however regrettable to those
who suffered, seemed to indicate that there was no serious
cause for alarm, either for the Faith on the one side, or
for personal safety on the other. In the second half of
the sixteenth century, however, conditions altered. On
the one hand the establishment of the Inquisition in Portugal drove large numbers of suspects to seek their fortune elsewhere—and America combined distance with
opportunity. On the other, Lutheran filibusters—particularly Englishmen—were commencing their ravages on
the Spanish Main, and provided the Holy Office at once
with a pretext and a fresh opening. It thus became
necessary to replace these amateurish endeavours by a
professional organisation—in other words, to extend to
the New World the institution which had been set up, a
century before, in the Old. In 1569-70, accordingly,
Philip II. of Spain secured the establishment in the city
of Mexico of an independent tribunal of the Inquisition,
on the model of those which flourished in his European
dominions, for the purpose of " freeing the land, which
has become contaminated by Jews and heretics, especially of the Portuguese nation.''

It was not however with these that it occupied itself at
the outset, so much as with Protestants—above all the
survivors of Sir John Hawkins' men, who had been
landed to take their chance after the disastrous encounter
at S. Juan de Ullóa in 1568. On February 28th, 1574,

the first *auto* under the new auspices took place, with great pomp; enthusiasts declared that it was the equal in every respect (save for the absence of royalty) to the solemnity which had been staged at Valladolid fifteen years before, when the Spanish Protestants had suffered. A fortnight before, it was announced throughout the city with drums and trumpets, and those living on the Plaza Mayor were deafened by the hammering of the carpenters as they erected staging for the participants and spectators.

On the previous night, a rehearsal (presumably omitting the final stages) was held in the courtyard of the Inquisitional Palace, the participants being munificently regaled at daybreak with wine and a slice of bread fried in honey. There were nearly one hundred sufferers in all—one New Christian, for a minor offence, a couple of persons for blasphemy, three for liberal views on the subject of fornication, and twenty-seven for optimistically considering, before their time, that bigamy was condonable in the New World. But half of the total, including all those who suffered most severely, were Lutherans, mainly English. One of them, a certain Miles Phillips, has left an account of the gruesome affair. Three of his compatriots, he states, were burned, seven sent to enforced service in convents, and some threescore mounted on horseback and scourged through the streets. They were preceded, he tells us, by a crier, calling out " See these Lutheran dogs, enemies of God ": while the familiars of the Inquisition urged the executioners to bear down harder, and harder still, on the English heretics. They were then brought back to the headquarters of the Holy Office, their backs all raw and swollen and clotted with blood, afterwards being despatched back to Spain to serve the rest of their term of martyrdom in the galleys. (The sequel we have already seen.) It was thus that the Spanish government revenged itself for its lost treasure-ships.

Thereafter, the Mexican tribunal shewed an assiduity which might have been envied by Toledo or Seville. For the next decade, *autos* took place almost yearly; then there was a short intermission, until 1590, when they were resumed. English and Irish Protestants, French Calvinists, native suspects, Portuguese Judaisers were arraigned by the score. In 1594, Fray Alonso de Peralta took over Inquisitorial functions, and goaded the Tribunal into even greater activity. In 1596, sixty-six penitents figured at one Act of Faith, no less than twenty-two Judaisers being reconciled, nine burned in person and ten in effigy. Among those relaxed on this occasion was Luis de Carvajal, formerly Governor of the Province of New Leon, who had rendered notable services to the state. With him suffered his mother and three of his sisters, another of whom was reserved for the next great occasion. This was in 1601, when the former figure was exceeded, 120 penitents appearing on one day. No Indians figured as yet. The native population was, in fact, exempt from the jurisdiction of the Holy Office, on the theory (which was used also to justify the atrocities performed against them) that they were too low in the scale of humanity to be capable of properly receiving the Faith.

By 1601, no less than 879 trials had taken place under the auspices of the new Tribunal, in barely a quarter of a century—a remarkable record, rivalling that of the dreaded Inquisition of Toledo, in the heart of the Marrano-infested area at home. No small responsibility for this fact is to be ascribed to the dreaded Fray Alonso de Peralta, who was constantly pressing for fresh violence.

Such was the terror which he inspired in his victims that
Luis de Carvajal, a stout-hearted soldier as well as
administrator, begged that he should not be brought face
to face with the Inquisitor, "because the mere sight of
him made his flesh creep, such was the terror which his
rigour caused." Not long afterwards, proceedings were
brought against Peralta for misconduct in office. By
this time the work of the Holy Office had been performed so thoroughly, that activity diminished henceforth
to a very considerable extent. The heretics had learned
their lesson: and European civilisation had been well and
truly planted in the New World.

Very similar had been the progress of events in the
other parts of the Spanish dominions in America, though
nowhere else did activity reach quite so high a pitch. In
Peru an independent Inquisitional tribunal had been
established in 1570: but, though a French Protestant of
questionable sanity had been burned in the following
year, the number of victims was small until the close of
the century, when Lima began to witness a series of
autos of almost Metropolitan splendour. Thus in 1592,
at least three English Protestants were burned at the
stake, and several more (including three " Pirates " from
Sir Thomas Cavendish's famous expedition for circum-
navigating the globe) were reconciled. Two years later,
as we have seen, Richard Hawkins and his companions
appeared. But the extent of territory which had to be
administered from this centre was so vast that in 1610
another independent tribunal was established for New
Granada, with its seat at Cartagena. Here the populace
seems to have been too uncivilised as yet to appreciate
such an advanced product of European culture. When
the first *auto* was staged four years later, to chastise a
few unimportant offenders, a motley crowd of negroes

and mulattos assembled to pelt the victims with oranges and fruit, and it was necessary to intervene in order to carry out the scourgings with proper dignity.

This period of comparative inactivity was of short duration. One day, in August, 1634, a Lima business-man denounced one of his business-competitors on the ground that he had been unwilling to make a sale on Saturday, besides—horror of horrors!—refusing to eat a rasher of bacon for his breakfast. Under torture, the accused person made admissions which implicated his employer and a couple of other persons. The latter in turn were forced to denounce others whom they suspected of being secret Jews. So the circle widened, and the Holy Office made preparations for its great drive. An inkling was given of what was contemplated by unusual activity in the Inquisitional Headquarters, where fresh cells were prepared to accommodate the expected prisoners. When all was ready the Inquisition pounced. On August 11th, 1634, between 12.30 and 2 o'clock, seven-teen arrests were made, the persons involved including some of the most prominent merchants and business-men in the city. Other arrests followed in the succeeding weeks, until eighty-one persons in all had been lodged in prison, and information collected against at least as many more. Property of immense value was meanwhile seques-tered. The impression created in Lima when the news became known was, according to a contemporary report, like what might be expected at the Day of Judgement; for the best part of the business life of the Colony was in the hands of those implicated. A widespread com-mercial crisis ensued, culminating in the failure of the Bank.

Thus was discovered the *Complicidad Grande*, or Great Complicity—one of the landmarks in the history of Peru in the Colonial period, which was to have its repercussions throughout the New World. It was five years before the trials were completed and the victims delivered from their long agony of uncertainty. The fruits were seen in a great *auto* held at Lima on January 23rd, 1639, at which about sixty Judaisers figured among the seventy victims. Eleven of them were burned—seven alive. These included Manual Bautista Pérez, the wealthiest merchant of the city and a great patron of literature, known among his fellow-Portuguese as the *Capitan Grande*; and Francisco Maldonado de Silva, one of the most notable of all the martyrs of the Inquisition in the New World.

The latter had been a surgeon in practice at Concepcion de Chile, without any interest in or knowledge of any religious system other than Catholicism. At the age of eighteen, the study of a classical work intended to convert the Jews had first awakened in him doubts concerning Christianity. For some years, he kept his secret. At the age of thirty-five however he began to be worried concerning the spiritual welfare of his sister, and tried to bring her round to his way of thinking. A devout Catholic, she was scandalised, and denounced him to the Holy Office. Unlike most others, when he was arrested, he made no secret of his convictions, refusing to be sworn on a crucifix and affirming proudly that he was an adherent to the faith of his fathers. With phenomenal ingenuity, he pieced together out of scraps of paper two books, each of more than one hundred pages, writing in them (with ink made of charcoal, and pens cut out of a chicken-bone) two treatises vindicating his conduct and assailing the Catholic faith. Then, asking for maize-husks instead of his ration of bread, he made a rope from them, by means of which he let himself down from the window of his cell. Instead of making good his escape, however, he visited other prisoners, whom he tried to convert. He had been in prison for nearly thirteen years when he was brought out to be relaxed. As the sentences were being read, a sudden wind tore away the awning from overheard. "This is the Lord's doing," he exclaimed, "that I may look on Him, face to face." His two pathetic paper books were hung round his neck at the last in order to assist the flames.

The next day, the populace were regaled by the spectacle of the public scourging through the street of twenty-nine penitents, men and women, naked from the waist up. General disappointment was however caused by a proclamation of the Inquisition forbidding those who appeared to be pelted by the crowd, as was its usual practice on these occasions. In the following years, the remnants of the *Complicidad Grande* were dealt with, the last survivor suffering as late as 1664. Meanwhile, there had been repercussions at Cartagena, where several persons had been implicated in the confessions which had been extorted from those arrested in Lima. Here, too, there was a sudden raid by the Holy Office, and many persons were apprehended and put on trial. Several figured in public Acts of Faith. There were, indeed, no burnings: but the confiscations which resulted were so considerable as to put the local Tribunal into the possession of vast funds.

The proceedings at Lima had put the Tribunal of Mexico on guard. Here, the first clue was given by the arrest of Gabriel de Granada, a child of thirteen against whom suspicions had been roused for various actions which seemed to savour of Judaism. The poor boy, ruthlessly questioned, was compelled to make admissions which implicated no less than 108 persons in all, includ-

ing his mother and the whole of his family. Wholesale
arrests were immediately carried out, this *complicidad*
constituting for some days the solitary topic of conversation in the city. Meanwhile, an embargo was placed on
the emigration from the province without special licence
of any Portuguese, who were still regarded (not without
cause) as particularly suspect in matters of faith. At the
first sign of danger, a meeting was held by the Marranos
in the house of one of their leaders, a captain in the
Spanish forces, to determine what course of action should
be pursued. It was decided that in case of arrest all
should deny the entire charge categorically, this being the
surest way to avoid implicating others. "My arms are
strong enough to withstand torture," remarked one of
those present, optimistically.

The extent of the danger was not realised. The Inquisition had meanwhile continued its work, with its usual
sinister deliberation. The number of those arrested exceeded all expectation or precedent, and a long series of
autos was necessary to deal with the victims. The climax
was reached in the terrible *Auto General* of April 11th,
1649—the greatest ever known outside the Peninsula.
109 persons appeared—all but one Judaisers—of whom
57 were relaxed in effigy and 13 in person. The spectacle was a magnificent one. A double row of coaches
lined the route along which the procession was to pass,
the occupants remaining in them all night so as to be certain of their positions on the morrow. So many of the
inhabitants of the surrounding villages and municipalities
streamed into the city in order to be present that it seemed
as though all the countryside had been depopulated for
a hundred leagues or more around. The only one of the
victims to hold out to the end was Tomas Treviño, of
Sobremorte whose wealth had made him a particularly

welcome victim. To silence his blasphemies (as they were considered) he was gagged as he was taken to the *auto*, but nevertheless managed to make his views heard. Even the patient beasts of burden, it was afterwards related (though the phenomenon was susceptible of diametrically opposite interpretation) joined the populace in expressing abhorrence of the heretic; for, one after the other, the mules assigned to bear him to the *quemadero* refused to submit to the load, and he was obliged to walk until a broken-down horse could be obtained. An Indian sprang up behind him, and made a final attempt to convert him as they went. Enraged at his failure, he beat the condemned man about the mouth, to stop his replies. On the pyre, Treviño seemed to welcome death, and drew the blazing brands towards him with his feet. "Pile on the wood," he was heard to say. "How much my money costs me!"

This outburst of activity, between 1634 and 1650, seems to have broken the spirit of the Marranos in the New World. Isolated instances of Judaising continued to recur down to the close of the eighteenth century, and to give the Inquisitors some preoccupation: but they were few and, towards the close, confused with political and private considerations. Meanwhile, the English filibusters had become respectable mariners, and another fruitful field of activity was cut off. From the middle of the seventeenth century, therefore, the Inquisition in the New World began to lapse into inactivity, finding its outlet only among humdrum bigamists, sorcerers, *alumbrados* and clerical seductionists, and seldom having the satisfaction of staging a proper Act of Faith, complete with tragic climax.

Judaisers apart, the activity of the South American tribunals was largely concerned with mystical impostors.

Of these, the most remarkable by far was Angela Carranza, whose reputed miracles, ecstasies and revelations deceived the whole of the population of Peru, from Viceroys and Archbishops down to half-starved peasants. Her revelations, to copy which the most learned men of the province considered a privilege, filled fifteen volumes of one thousand pages each. Rosaries and beads which had been in her house, and which she claimed to have taken to heaven to be blessed, were exported in chestloads to Spain, and even to Rome. Garments which she had touched were treasured in the belief that they would become relics of great efficacy. She had a fixed pricelist for intervention with the heavenly authorities to cure sickness, prevent barrenness, or save a wavering marriage. Yet it was alleged that her personal chastity was due only to advancing years, and had by no means been notorious at an earlier stage in her career.

The end of this glamorous activity was heralded in a particularly prosaic fashion. One rainy day, a certain Franciscan friar elbowed her into the mud of the roadway. Such was the indignation that this action aroused that he was sentenced to two months' confinement in the convent prison. He swore to be revenged, and afterwards kept close watch on her. The result was an Inquisitional prosecution, in which all her petty deceits were laid bare, and repudiated in a public *auto*.

The other Spanish dependencies were likewise accorded the inestimable benefits of Inquisitional tribunals. There was one—though it never attained importance or displayed great activity—at Manila, for the Philippine Islands. One had existed in Sicily since the close of the fifteenth century, to deal with the problem of the native New Christians. It relaxed nearly five hundred persons —Judaisers, Protestants, and in the end Molinists—during its three centuries of existence. In Sardinia, where there was in fact very little reason for the existence of the Inquisition in the first instance, the Tribunal lapsed into inanition in the sixteenth century, shewing only by occasional disputes for precedence that it was still alive. There would have been a greater field of activity in the kingdom of Naples, for two centuries under Spanish rule: but the population, while not yielding to any other in Europe in attachment to the Catholic faith, preferred to have heretics burned according to the old-fashioned methods of the Papal Inquisition, and, notwithstanding all the efforts made from Madrid, refused to allow the new Spanish form to obtain a foothold.

Greater activity, coupled with the utmost fidelity to the Spanish example, was observed in the Canary Islands. Here, an Episcopal Inquisition was delegated to deal with fugitive New Christians as early as 1499. As the result of the disclosures which it made, a branch of the Inquisition of Andalusia was set up at Las Palmas in 1504. For the next half century, it was mildly active, a few *autos* being held and several persons relaxed. The results were however considered unsatisfactory at Madrid, and a particularly vigorous Inquisitor was nominated in 1569 to organise a more thorough heresy-hunt. Shortly after his landing, a great *auto* was held, which attracted spectators, not only from the towns and villages of the island, but from the other parts of the group. It was related, indeed, that more than twice as many persons were present as the entire population of Grand Canary.

By now, the direction of activity had changed. To the Judaisers were now added other categories of offenders, above all, Protestants; for Las Palmas was one of the principal ports of call in the Atlantic, and, besides the

traders who put in of their own free will, numerous filibusters were brought in as captives. Hence it was to a
large degree by reports from the Canaries that public
opinion in England was stirred during the reign of Elizabeth and her immediate successors. It may be added
that, here as elsewhere, very few of the sufferers seem to
have shewn much inclination for martyrdom. Most were
willing to make their peace with the Holy Catholic faith,
even though this might entail despatch to Spain to learn
the elements of their new religion: and the name has been
preserved of only one Englishman who submitted himself
to the *quemadero* on behalf of his faith.

The Portuguese Inquisition, too, had an offshoot at
Goa, in India, which attained a great, and deserved,
notoriety. As was the case elsewhere, the original pretext for its establishment was the influx of " New Christians " from Europe, who were dealt with severely,
though summarily, as early as 1543. It was the second
Apostle of India, St. Francis Xavier, the companion of
Ignatius Loyola and the first missionary to the Far East,
who was prime mover in the matter, petitioning as early
as 1546 for the establishment of a tribunal. His wishes
were complied with only fifteen years later, in 1561, the
first *auto* being held in 1563. During the period of office
as Inquisitor of the fanatical Bartholomeu da Fonseca,
the ferocity shewn was outstanding. *Autos* of peculiar
virulence took place in 1575 and 1578: and all told,
down to the year 1623, no less than 3,800 persons were
tried.

An increasingly large proportion of the victims were
from a particularly pathetic class—the native " St.
Thomas " Christians. They had been proselytised,
according to legend, by one of the Apostles, and certainly
well before the tenth century. Generation after genera-

tion, in the midst of a pagan world and completely out of touch with the great centres of the Christian faith, they had managed to preserve their religion, with touching fidelity. But it was not the Roman Catholic religion. Nothing, perhaps, in the history of the Europeans in India, and nothing even in the history of the Inquisition, is quite so discreditable as the attempt made to regiment these Christian loyalists, who had given such outstanding proof of their simple faith, into conformity; for it was among persons of this category that the Goa Tribunal found the majority of its victims.

The most remarkable of all victims of the Inquisition outside Europe was punished neither for Judaising nor for Lutheranism: and he was not Spanish, nor Portuguese, but Irish. Don Guillén de Lampart, they called him—an adroit Hispanisation of the more commonplace William Lamport: but, in moments of greater ebullience, he amplified this into the more impressive Guillén Lombardo de Guzmán. He had been born, according to his story, at Wexford, about the year 1616, his father having been a local Baron and his grandfather Patrick Lamport the Great, who had defended Ireland by land and sea against the English heretics (some little ingenuity, it may be added, is needed to square this account with what is known from the sources ordinarily available of Irish history at this period). His mother, on the other hand, was a Spanish woman, Doña Aldonza de Guzmán, alias Sotem, daughter of Don Eduardo Sotem. This was the account which Don Guillén presented on formal occasions. At other times, however, he gave it to be understood that he was an illegitimate son of Philip III. of Spain by an Irish woman, and half-brother, therefore, to the reigning King.

His career, if his statements are to be believed, had

been a remarkable one. Brought up in England, he had at the tender age of twelve years written a work against the royal authority and the Protestant faith, entitled *Defensio Fidei*. In consequence of this youthful indiscretion he had been forced to flee for his life, and entered the Spanish service. After marvellous adventures in many parts of the world, he was summoned, first to Madrid, where he became a favourite of the great Olivares, and then to the Netherlands, where he assisted the Cardinal Infante in the delicate task of government and won the Battle of Nördlingen, so to speak, single-handed (he would then have been about sixteen). Meanwhile, he had perfected himself (and this was not altogether an exaggeration) in the English, French, Spanish, Italian, Latin and Greek tongues, and had made a profound study of the classical poets, philosophers, theologians and mathematicians, not to mention the Scriptures and the Church Fathers. He claimed, too, that his half-brother, Philip IV., as an expression of gratitude for his remarkable services to the Crown, had raised him to the rank of Marquis and appointed him Viceroy of Mexico—an office to which he certainly held ample patents, presumably forged.

It was this remarkable genius who was arrested by the Mexican Inquisition in the autumn of 1642, on instructions from Bishop Palafox, the acting Viceroy. It was a period of suspicion and perplexity in Mexican politics. Acting under confidential orders from Madrid, Palafox had recently succeeded in ousting from the Viceroyalty the Marquis of Escalona, who was suspected of sympathising with the Portuguese. It is a fatal weakness of Revolutions that they invite imitation: and Don Guillén clearly had hopes of seizing the office, with the assistance of his forged credentials, during the confused period before the next royal nominee took up his duties. But there was even more than that behind his plottings. He was not interested in ruling as an underling. There was as much of the royal blood in his veins, he claimed, as in those of Philip himself, notwithstanding the regrettable absence of marriage-lines: and his real intention, it was alleged, was to sever Mexico from Spain and rule it as an independent sovereign.

There were occasions when the Inquisition had definite uses, and this was one of them. To charge the mad-cap Irishman with treason, at so delicate a moment, was clearly inadvisable. It was not on this charge therefore that the Holy Office had him taken into custody, but because he had consulted an Indian sorcerer and certain astrologers concerning the success of his enterprise. It might be imagined that this would have ushered in the close of the entire affair. But, for some curious reason, the Royal Court of Madrid was interested in him, and it can only be imagined, either that there was some substratum of truth in his preposterous story, or else that he had convinced the King that this was the case. Orders were received from Spain that the case should receive special attention, and that all the relevant papers should be sequestered at the close: and in order to minimise the discomfort of solitary confinement it was suggested that the prisoner should be given a cell-companion if he so desired.

He did so desire: and a certain Diego Pinto was designated for the purpose. Two pairs of hands were better than one, and the immediate consequence was that the two carried out a daring plan of escape. Instead of making his way into safety, Don Guillén spent the night in placarding Mexico City with various manifestos which he had prepared, and sending a communication to the

Viceroy inviting him to arrest the Inquisitors as traitors. He then settled down comfortably to await the result, which he hoped would be a general rising. He was mistaken: and the only outcome of his escapade was that he was taken back to prison and lodged in a specially strong cell, with his feet confined in stocks and his hands in fetters. When the commotion had died down he asked for writing materials, which he employed in composing a slashing attack on the Holy Office. Supplies were now cut off: so, using the sheets of his bed instead of paper, he compiled a similar treatise in Latin verse, which when transcribed covered 270 folios.

This activity hardly endeared him to the Inquisitors, who, seventeen years after his first arrest, determined to make an end of the affair. In the autumn of 1659, sentence was at last pronounced—relaxation, for divination and superstitious cures which indicated a pact with the Demon. The execution was carried out at the *auto* on the following day, after a succession of violent encounters with the priests which had lasted almost all night, and ended only when he covered his head with his bed-clothes and refused to speak. But, at the last moment, he managed to circumvent his tormentors. Sentenced to be burned alive, he threw himself against the iron collar by which he was attached to the stake with such force that it killed him, and only his dead body was a victim of the flames. The most remarkable feature was still to come: for, when the news of his death reached Madrid, the *Suprema* wrote a sharp letter of reproof, asking why this had been done against its express orders. It is obvious that, whatever the reason, Don Guillén was the object of solicitude in the highest possible circles. To us today, he appears one of those exuberant Irishmen who are so typical that they appear caricatures of them-

selves. But, in Mexico, he is regarded to this day as one
of the patriotic forerunners of the independence achieved
two centuries later, and in the present generation the
proposal has been made to commemorate his megalo-
maniac political design by a public monument.

CHAPTER XI

THE AGE OF UNREASON

SPAIN was by now entering upon her decline. Hers was still the greatest empire of the world, whether reckoned in terms of resources or of extent: but for some unfathomable reason, not perhaps unconnected with her mercantile system, it seemed to bring the mother-country little benefit. No *hidalgo* (and a prodigiously large proportion of the inhabitants laid claim to that greatest of distinctions) would soil his fingers with trade. In consequence, it was computed that five-sixths of the home, and nine-tenths of the Indian commerce were in the hands of strangers, while all articles of luxury (which were those most in demand) came from abroad. In the centuries that had elapsed since the days of Ferdinand and Isabella, the population is computed to have declined by 50 per cent., from 12,000,000 to 6,000,000.

No part of Europe was more orthodox: but the orthodoxy, however spontaneous, was minutely regulated. In no country was the nobility more proud, or enjoyed greater privileges: but in none was it so devoid of influence. What was evolved was, in effect, an elaborate vicarious system, involving a rigorous devolution of powers and functions. The common people worked, sweated, and in the last resort paid. Foreigners monopolised business activity. The nobility, exempt from taxation and excluded from authority, enjoyed themselves in their luxurious and absurd local courts. The King and his ministers, when they were sufficiently interested, governed—but not too seriously, unless they were prepared to risk dismissal, and end, like Ripperdá, as Grand

Vizier to the Sultan of Morocco. The Inquisition, in its turn, provided the most popular spectacles (not so frequently, perhaps, as the faithful might have hoped), and told the people what to think.

From time to time indeed there were indications that the Holy Office was not too confident upon this score itself, and that very human jealousies existed even in its own bosom. In fact an internecine quarrel at this period —one of the few of which full details have come to light— did a good deal to undermine its reputation. The last Bourbon King of Spain, Charles II., spent a large proportion of his forty years' almost co-extensive life and reign a fretful and imbecilic invalid. Since it would have been disloyal to attribute this condition to the private lives of his ancestors or to his own not unexceptionable youth, it was convenient to blame it on sorcery. A certain Dominican friar of unenlightened mentality, Froilan Díaz, who had recently been appointed to a place on the *Suprema* in consequence of a Court intrigue, prescribed a characteristic course of action: that certain inmates of a nunnery in Cangas, who were notoriously possessed by demons, should be induced during their moments of aberration to reveal the causes of the royal illness. His advice was followed, and the nuns obediently suggested that, many years before, their sovereign had been bewitched by the Queen Mother by means of a peculiarly revolting potion administered in a cup of chocolate, with a little supplementary assistance some time later from the Queen herself.

This was Maria Anna of Neuberg, a German of phlegmatic tastes, but vindictive temperament, who had succeeded the French princess in whose honour the great *auto* of 1680 had been staged. She promptly entered into the fray. There was much intriguing, and a few providential deaths. But her animosity was directed in particular against Froilan Díaz. The latter had been guilty of some irregularity (though nothing more) by his dabbling in magical enquiry. However, the Grand Inquisitor, Baltasar de Mendoza y Sandoval, Bishop of Segovia, bribed with the promise of a cardinal's hat, proposed to the Suprema that their fellow-member should be proceeded against. The Council was unanimous in deciding that there was no case. Mendoza then hopefully had recourse to the tribunal of Murcia, which he imagined would be amenable to his influence, and then to that of Madrid, but neither would take action. However, he had the satisfaction of seeing Díaz kept for some time in confinement, pending a decision.

Not despairing, the Grand Inquisitor at last appealed to the Holy See, asserting that his colleagues on the Suprema were themselves guilty of grave error—indeed, of heresy—in claiming to have a deciding voice in adjudication on matters of faith. But his influence was on the wane. Charles II.'s life of suffering had by now ended, leaving the throne in dispute. Mendoza had been so unfortunate as to favour the Austrian succession, which would have strengthened Queen Maria Anna's position. Unfortunately for him, the majority of the Spanish people favoured the grandson of Louis XIV. of France; and, though the whole question was for some time in the balance, and fought out (like so many other disputes of a wider importance) on the battlefields of Flanders, there was never any serious opposition in Spain itself. Philip of Bourbon brought to the country new methods and ideas, as well as a new type of physiognomy. Mendoza's Austrian sympathies told against him, and he was dismissed: and Díaz, as well as three other members of the Suprema whom Mendoza had disgraced, were restored to

office. But this unseemly squabble had undermined the
Holy Tribunal. The new king, moreover, while appre-
ciating the uses of the Inquisition as a political instrument, by no means favoured the savage Spanish method
of dealing with heresy. According to precedent, an *auto
de fé* was arranged in his honour a short time after his
accession. To the general amazement, he refused to be
present. Henceforth, the solemnities were shorn of their
greatest éclat.

In Portugal, as in Spain (though to a minor degree),
the exclusive preoccupation of the Holy Office with
Judaisers had somewhat lessened in the course of time.
Ignorance, assimilation, and the continual emigration of
the best brains of the country had sensibly weakened the
force of Marranism. The Restoration of the House of
Braganza in 1648, in which the New Christians had participated to a notable extent, was expected to diminish the
authority of the Inquisition, which had attained particularly great influence under Spanish rule. The new king,
João IV., was reported to be willing to allow freedom of
conscience in the country, and certainly attempted, though
in vain, to modify the severity of the Inquisitional procedure. His liberal tendencies were clearly not very
strong, for in 1642 and 1645 he and his family attended a
series of *autos* held at Lisbon. The Inquisition continued
its activities with undiminished zeal. In 1652 the poet-
statesman, Manuel Fernandez Villareal, was relaxed, notwithstanding the favour which he enjoyed at court. On
June 23rd, 1663, an *auto* with one hundred and forty-two
penitents was held at Evora, and between 1651 and 1673,
no fewer than 184 victims were relaxed in person, and
59 in effigy, by the three tribunals of the kingdom.

Nevertheless, the Court was apparently not unfavour-
ably disposed towards the idea of reform. In 1663,

Duarte da Silva, who had been reconciled eleven years earlier, brought forward from his refuge in London, where his comfits were so appreciated by Samuel Pepys, certain proposals for the amelioration of the position of the New Christians and the limitation of the power of the Inquisition. In return for these concessions he promised the government considerable subsidies in men and ships in the war with Holland for the possession of Brazil. Don Francisco de Mello, the eminent Portuguese statesman and man of letters (himself apparently of Marrano birth), threw the weight of his influence into the scales in favour of these proposals. They were viewed sympathetically by the Court, but before they could be carried into effect the rumour reached the ears of the Pope, who protested vigorously, and with success.

After the death of João IV., in 1656, the Inquisition set about collecting the arrears of confiscation of which it had been deprived for the last half-dozen years. Within the next quarter of a century, the total reached twenty-five millions, of which barely half a million found its way to the royal treasury. In 1671, a great commotion was caused throughout the country by the theft of a pyx containing a consecrated host from the church of Orivellas in Lisbon. The court put on mourning, and it was universally assumed that the New Christians were guilty of the crime. An edict for their expulsion from the country was actually signed, but before it could be put into execution a common thief was arrested near Coimbra, with the stolen article in his possession. Fortunately, no Jewish blood was traceable in his veins, and, though he was burned, the New Christians were saved. An interregnum in the office of Grand Inquisitor from 1653 to 1672, though it did not bring about any decrease in the activity of the Tribunal, did something to lessen its authority.

Meanwhile, the cause of the New Christians had found a champion in no less a person than the celebrated Jesuit Antonio Vieira, known as the Apostle of Brazil. There was a long-standing feud between the Jesuits and the Inquisition, dating from the time of Ignatius Loyola himself; and Vieira was doubtless influenced to some extent by this as well as his own somewhat liberal views. He had already incurred the enmity of the Inquisition by his freedom of opinions, and in the year of the Great Plague had been condemned and formally penanced after a three years' imprisonment. This unpleasant experience increased his sympathy for the oppressed, and he began to urge João IV. to abolish confiscations and to remove the differences which still obtained between the "Old" and the "New" Christians. The Society of Jesus, resenting the treatment to which one of the most distinguished of its members had been subjected, supported him in his efforts. Vieira transferred himself to Rome, where, in the very heart of Christianity, he assailed the Portuguese Inquisition as an unholy tribunal, inimical to the true interests of religion, inspired more by greed than by piety, condemning the innocent as frequently as the guilty, and preying upon persons of New Christian blood. The latter, he maintained, were nearly all fervent Catholics, who were faced with the alternatives of being put to death as *negativos* for denying Judaism, or reconciled as a result of confessing it falsely.

Meanwhile, the New Christians appealed to the Crown, offering an annual payment of 20,000 *cruzados* in return for certain moderate reforms, including the free pardon of those persons then under trial, and the modification of the Inquisitional procedure by the adoption of the more humane forms practised in Rome. They also professed their willingness to maintain a force of 4,000 troops in

India, and to send out each year 1,200 more as reinforcements, with an additional 300 in time of war. The Inquisition protested strenuously against any consideration of this appeal. However, it was supported by many of the greatest magnates of the kingdom, including the faculty of the University of Coimbra and the Archbishop of Lisbon himself. It was accordingly approved, and forwarded to Rome for a final decision. After a prolonged struggle, the New Christians gained the day. On October 3rd, 1674, Pope Clement X. suspended the action of the Portuguese tribunals, evoking all outstanding cases to Rome. The resistance of the Inquisitors, who refused cooperation in the subsequent enquiry on the ground that it would reveal the secrets of procedure, was met by an interdict, and ultimately, on May 27th, 1679, they were suspended from office.

The respite was only momentary. The immediate result of this apparent victory was merely to effect a few unimportant reforms. The suspension of the Inquisitors was removed on August 22nd, 1681, and the resumption of activity of the Portuguese Inquisition was celebrated by a succession of processions and illuminations, followed by a series of brutal *autos de fé*.

Meanwhile, outside the Peninsula, the reaction against the Inquisition had been steadily increasing. The Protestants of northern Europe had long regarded it as the instrument of Anti-Christ. As early as the sixteenth century, works began to appear in England and elsewhere, giving details of the Protestant martyrdoms in Spain, and overlooking of course the fact that the vast majority of those arrested made their peace with the Catholic Church. With the eighteenth century, the tide increased. The anti-Inquisitional writings of a refugee Spaniard of the time of Elizabeth, Reginaldo González de Montés, were

constantly republished.   Michael Geddes, a Scottish
divine, took up the cudgels in London, where he published a couple of striking tracts laying bare the iniquity
of the system.   In one of these, he gives a first-hand
account of a certain "New Christian" acquaintance of
his whose orthodoxy had been unimpeachable until he
was arrested by the Inquisition, but whose sufferings at
its hands turned him into a convinced Judaiser—an
interesting sidelight upon the efficacy of the institution.
Robert Dugdale and John Marchant and a dozen anony-
mous pamphleteers added their voices to the chorus, in
accounts of the "Bloody" Inquisition and of the cruelties
practised by it.   Other contributions came from abroad—
for example, Philip van Limborch's bitterly antagonistic
History, speedily translated from the original Dutch into
English.   Philosophical France thought of the institution
with horror: and Bayle, Voltaire and Montesquieu joined
in the fray with caustic comments, which were received
with almost universal agreement.

Naturally the Jews were not behindhand.   In 1709
David Nieto, Rabbi of the congregation established by the
refugee Marranos in London, and himself of Marrano
descent, published a reply to the sermon preached by
Diogo de Anunciação Justiniano, Archbishop of Cran-
ganor, in India, at an *auto* held at Lisbon on September 6th, 1705.   The sixty-six poor victims had been forced to
listen to a long and brutal invective: "Miserable relics
of Judaism!   Unhappy fragments of the synagogue!
Last remains of Judea!   Scandal of the Catholics and
detestable objects of scorn even to the Jews themselves!
. . .   You are the detestable objects of scorn to the
Jews, for you are so ignorant that you cannot even
observe the very law under which you live."   So sure was
David Nieto of his ground that he had the courage,

unusual in a controversialist, of reissuing with his own work the sermon to which it was intended as a reply. This vigorous but dignified pamphlet, written in Portuguese, was published anonymously, first with the imprint Turin, and then with that of Villa Franca ("The City of Freedom," obviously London), at the Press of Carlos Vero ("Charles Truth"). In 1722, Nieto published also the memoranda prepared by Antonio Vieira for his onslaught on the Inquisition more than half a century before (which even before this time had been in circulation in manuscript) under the title, "Recondite Notices of the Inquisition of Spain and Portugal." In 1750, the work appeared again in Venice, with a slightly different title—this time under Vieira's own name.

This adroit propaganda assisted in undermining the position of the Holy Office, and it was inevitable that ultimately repercussions reached those parts of southern Europe where it still held sway. The beginning was in Portugal. Here Antonio Ribeiro Sanchez, an eminent Marrano physician who had become reconciled to Catholicism, submitted a striking memorandum suggesting the abolition of the distinction between Old and New Christians and the restriction of the power of the Inquisition in the interest of the State. The famous diplomat, Luiz da Cunha, went even further, suggesting that religious freedom should be established in the country. Alexandre de Guzmão, a personage of importance at the court of João V., poured ridicule on the pretensions of certain families to complete purity of blood, pointing out that the total number of progenitors of any person over a period of centuries runs into hundreds. (Indeed, it does into thousands: it has been computed by some mathematical genius that, if we go back to the time of the Norman Conquest, we each had something like one billion ancestors.)

Hence it was impossible to be absolutely certain of all the antecedents of any individual, however much he might boast his unsullied Old Christian (or, as one would say today, "Aryan" or "Nordic") blood. It is a publication which, two centuries old though it is, might be regarded in certain parts of Europe today as a treasonable reflexion upon the fundamental policy of the State.

Exaggerated accounts were still being circulated meanwhile in the outside world of the sufferings endured at the hands of the Holy Office. In 1700 an English balladmonger called upon the public to join with him in celebrating "The Loyal Martyrs, or Bloody Inquisitor. Being a just account of the mercenary and inhuman barbarities transacted in the Inquisition of Spain, shewing how a Gentleman having married a young lady in St. James's Street . . . as they were come into *Spain*, intending to take a view of the place, were both seiz'd by order of the Inquisitor . . . and condemned to be burn't alive." The name of the gentleman concerned (who was the hero of some other similar publications) was Arrowsmith. No record of his process has survived in the Spanish archives, and some doubt may be entertained as to his objective existence. But, by a strange coincidence, there was a martyr to faith of the same name—Edmund Arrowsmith, a Papist burned by pious Englishmen at Lancaster in 1628, whose intercession is subsequently said to have worked miracles. Clearly, though, there was no rational comparison possible between a victim of the bloody Spanish Tribunal and one who suffered at the hands of cool-headed English justice.

Another *cause célèbre* of the period was that of Mr. Isaac Martin, a Protestant merchant living in Malaga, who was haled before the Granada tribunal, and whose trial and subsequent sufferings lasted over a long period.

His tribulations were traceable in the first instance to the fact that his Christian name was Isaac, and his son's Abraham. This circumstance, unusual in Spain, had given rise to the suspicion that he was a Jew: but it was only after he had been imprisoned for six months, and brought up for question on repeated occasions, that the obvious physical examination was made. The result being satisfactory, he was now accused of Lutheranism, and finally condemned to be scourged through the city and then deported. On his return to England, he became a Protestant hero. The story of his experiences, first published in London in 1723, was immediately translated into French and German, and was frequently reprinted. One result of the episode was to revive the anti-Spanish sentiment in England, and to contribute to the atmosphere of suspicion which, in conjunction with the ear of Captain Jenkins, brought about the Anglo-Spanish war of 1739.

Another case which attained international notoriety at the same period was that of a Huguenot named Lewis Ramé, who was tried in Mexico in 1679. Better-known still was that of a certain Dellon, a French Catholic who had fallen foul of the tribunal in Portuguese India, and published at Paris on his release his famous *Relation de l'Inquisition de Goa,* giving a detailed account of his protracted sufferings. This, too, was republished in many languages, time after time. Nor, even at this late stage, were English sailors immune, as was demonstrated by the vicissitudes of William Owen and George Gale, arraigned at Toledo in 1727.

But notwithstanding all the propaganda abroad, and the decline of prestige at home, the Inquisition remained to all appearance as strong and powerful as ever. Nearly three hundred persons in all appeared in the Portuguese *autos* in the period which immediately succeeded the suspension

of 1679-1681. The resumption of activity on the part of
the tribunal at Coimbra reached its climax in the awful
holocaust of November 25th, 1696, when fourteen men
and women were relaxed in person and five in effigy. An
order issued in September, 1683, intensified the sufferings
of those convicted. By this, all persons who had been
reconciled for Judaising had to leave the realm within the
absurdly short period of two months. They were however
to leave behind them all children below the age of seven,
until it was proved that they were living the lives of true
Christians in their new homes. It was not until the outbreak of war with France in 1704 that this measure was
withdrawn.

Throughout this period, the number of victims from
year to year remained appalling. During the two decades
1651-1673, 184 victims were burned in person by the
three Portuguese tribunals, while 59 were relaxed in
effigy and 4,793 were penanced. From 1682 to 1700,
there was a slight remission, only 59 suffering in person
and 61 in effigy, while 1,351 were penanced. However,
after the outbreak of the War of Spanish Succession, the
numbers that appeared were reminiscent of the horrors of
the worst period, the total of the victims and penitents
rising on one occasion, in September, 1706, to as many
as 111, and on another on June 9th, 1714, to 138. In the
first twenty years of the century, 37 heretics were relaxed
in person and 26 in effigy; while in the thirty years or a
little less following this period the total relaxed in person
was 139. The yearly average was thus nearly quadrupled
as compared with the first two decades of the century,
although the total number of penitents was rather less—
a gruesome indication that the temper of the country was
changed, if anything, for the worse.

By this time, the tradition of non-conformity had

apparently been crushed, or else definitely driven below ground, in the more important Portuguese cities, including the capital. The centre of activity was now in the country districts. The vast proportion of the victims were from the northern provinces of Beira and Tras-os-Montes, with a minor centre further south, in Alentejo, where, it was said, whole towns were deserted and prosperous industries ruined as a result of the activities of the Holy Office. It was a systematic war of extermination. In 1718, over fifty natives of Braganza appeared at a single *auto* at Coimbra, and in the few succeeding years that region continued to furnish nine-tenths of the victims of the northern tribunal—805 from the city itself, and nearly 2,000 from the surrounding district. At an *auto* held on May 25th, 1737, at Lisbon (whither it became customary at this period to send persons condemned by the other tribunals, *ad majorem Dei gloriam*), all the twelve persons who were relaxed were from Celorico and Lamego, except one woman. Next it was the turn of the district of Aviz: and in 1744 and the following year, eight out of the ten persons burned were from that region. Again, at the *auto* of October 16th, 1746, all the six persons relaxed, and a majority of those reconciled, came from the same part of the country.

To the middle of the eighteenth century belongs also the martyrdom of one of the most illustrious of all the victims of the Holy Office—Antonio José de Silva, whom one might almost term (making allowances for the difference between the level of imaginative literature in England and her oldest ally) the Portuguese Sheridan. He was one of the most active, and certainly the most popular, playwright of his country at the time, his productions being among those most favoured by the theatre-going public of Lisbon. He belonged to a New Christian family, however, his mother having twice been tried for Judaising. This fact was sufficient to put the familiars of the Holy Office on guard; and already as a student he had been thrown into prison, tortured so mercilessly that afterwards he was unable to sign his name, and reconciled at a public *auto*. In 1757, when he was at the height of his fame, he was again arrested, his mordant pen having gained him many enemies. The principal witness against him was a negro slave-girl, who alleged that he had been accustomed to change his linen, and even to abstain from work, on Saturdays. This, coupled with various details which were discovered by spying on him in gaol, was sufficient to condemn him. Even the intervention of the King himself was now insufficient to save a "relapsed" and "negative" heretic from his fate; and, on October 1st, 1739, he was burned publicly at Lisbon. On the same night, by a coincidence which can hardly have been unintentional, one of his comedies was produced at the principal theatre of the town.

The number of those who suffered the capital penalty in Portugal at this period, it will have been noticed, was appallingly large, marking a retrogression to the worst standards of barbarism. Whereas in the sixteenth century some of the most notable of the *autos* witnessed only one or two relaxations, now the numbers were higher by far. Fourteen persons were burned, as has been indicated, at Coimbra on one day in 1696; twelve at Lisbon (besides two burnt in effigy) at the great *auto* of 1731: the same number in 1737. It is necessary to go back over two hundred years, to the awful days of Torquemada and Lucero el Tenebroso, to find figures rivalling these. Under the circumstances, it is difficult to know whether the greater moderation which began to manifest itself at the middle of the century, when the average number of burn-

ings went down to three or four on each occasion, was due
to greater circumspection on the part of the victims or to
sheer extermination. Of an advance in humanitarian
feeling there is little evidence.

It has been possible to go into some detail regarding the
activities of the Portuguese Inquisition in the eighteenth
century, its records being virtually complete for this period.
Owing to subsequent popular fury, the same is not the
case, unfortunately, with the Spanish tribunals, and it is
less easy to piece together so detailed a picture. The
general tendency, however, was not dissimilar.

The first overt blow at the power of the Spanish inquisition had been dealt, as we have seen, at the beginning of
the eighteenth century, when Philip V., true to his French
upbringing, had refused to grace with his presence the
auto arranged to celebrate his accession to the throne.
Nevertheless, similar ceremonies continued, under less
august auspices, with little intermission.

One of the most notorious took place at Seville on
July 25th, 1720. There were certain cases, indisputably,
where the victims of the Inquisition seem to have been
knaves rather than martyrs. In such instances, they were
generally submitted to lighter penalties: but at least one
who was in this category was condemned to the stake on
this occasion. This was Fray José Dias Pimienta, a
Cuban Friar of "Old Christian" extraction who seems
to have persuaded himself that if he became converted to
Judaism he need have no further worldly worries. At
fifteen, he was a novice in a convent in the island of
Cartagena, but got into such trouble for his precociously
dissolute manner of life that he fled to Curaçoa, where he
became converted to Judaism and married a Jewess.
Finding that his new coreligionists were neither so wealthy
nor so gullible as he had anticipated, he now became a

pirate. Some further trouble, apparently of a highly dis-
reputable nature, caused him to have his nose slit during
a street affray: and, thus adorned, he was handed over
to the Inquisition of Cartagena, which penanced him in
due form and despatched him back to Spain. He nearly
failed to arrive, however, as his imprecations and
grumblings on board were such that the sailors were on
the point of throwing him into the sea.

Arrived at Cadiz, he was handed over to the Com-
missary and put into the ecclesiastical prison, from which
he took the earliest opportunity to escape, making his way
to a convent of his order at Jerez. While living here as a
friar, he entered into relations with the local New Christians, begging money from them and fixing various assig-
nations in which, he explained, he would be easily recognisable by reason of his split nose. Nothing came of this:
and he then wrote to the King offering to conquer Curaçoa
for him from the Dutch, and even to pay for the privilege.
Meanwhile, he spent his leisure in writing an anti-Christian
commentary on the fifty-third chapter of Isaiah, which so
moved him that he ran away from his convent, leaving a
provocative letter behind him stating that he desired to
live and die for Judaism. It was his intention at this stage
to flee to London: but the captain of the English vessel to
which he applied refused to take him, saying that by doing
so he would endanger his ship, his fortune, and his life.

After some further similar adventures, the renegade
gave up hope of escaping from the country, and surrendered himself to the ecclesiastical authorities. Somewhat
to his surprise, they handed him over to the Holy Office.
During his trial, he maintained that he was a Jew, and
was sentenced accordingly to be relaxed to the secular
arm. At the last moment, however, he decided to recog-
nise the truth of Christianity, and thus secured the pre-

liminary grace of garotting instead of being burned alive. His end, at the Seville *auto* of July 25th, 1720, was, we are informed, exemplary, and greatly affected all who beheld it. This was one of the greatest days ever seen in the city, not only because of the great crowd, twelve (*sic*) leagues in circumference, but also because of the merits of the case. The whole city and nobility of Seville assisted, and in their Christian piety ordered an infinite number of masses to be recited for the victim's soul: and all the religious orders, nuns as well as monks, kept great days of penitence, fasting and discipline. If the official account of his physical career and spiritual peregrinations is anything like correct, the victim was certainly not worth such an expenditure of effort. The episode typifies the change in perspective which began in the Spanish Inquisition as the eighteenth century advanced.

In the same year, one of the last *autos* on the grand scale took place at Madrid. At the close of the War of Succession, there had been discovered here a secret synagogue, where for some years past twenty families had been accustomed to assemble for service. Five of those implicated in the affair were relaxed in an *auto* on April 7th, 1720. This discovery roused the other tribunals of the realm to renewed activity, and there was a general recrudescence of persecution throughout the country. In all, during the forty-five years' reign of the first Bourbon ruler of Spain, 1,564 heretics are said to have been relaxed and 11,730 otherwise punished—an appalling total, in the century of enlightenment, when the Encyclopædists were flourishing in France and the breath of religious liberty was sweeping through Europe. The figures have indeed been questioned: yet the indisputable facts shew that they are far from unlikely. In 1722 alone, there were some twenty recorded *autos*, in all the principal cities of the country, and, over the entire period 1701-1746, at least 150 all told. During the six years 1721-7, there were held no less than 64, at which 868 culprits appeared—the vast majority for Judaising: while seventy-five unbelievers were relaxed in person, and an equal number (or rather one fewer) in effigy. Lea, in his classical *History of the Inquisition in Spain*, gives details of a recrudescence in Madrid in 1732, when several New Christians were relaxed on the fantastic charge of having scourged and burned an image of Jesus in a house in the Calle de las Infantas. It is obvious that this is the result of a confusion with the events of precisely one hundred years previous, when a number of persons were punished for having performed a similar outrage in the same city, and at a house situated in a street of the identical name. But there is no need to exaggerate by the addition of fictitious instances. The first half of the eighteenth century saw the Inquisition in Spain and Portugal to all appearance as firmly established and nearly as active as it had ever been. As the contemporary ballad-writer phrased it, expressing the traditional Protestant detestation:

> Of all the nations in the Universe,
>   There's none sure can compare
> With *Spain* for bloody sentences
>   As I'll to you declare.

CHAPTER XII

DECLINE AND FALL

THE Inquisition declined by a process far less spectacular than its rise, and its slow decay was caused by the very success of its labours. As the close of the seventeenth century, it appeared to be at the height of its power. Splendid *autos de fé* were held at frequent intervals in all the principal cities of the Peninsula, vying with bullfights in popularity, and frequently graced by the presence of royalty. Every authority, spiritual and lay, united to approve the scope and methods of the Holy Office, and agreed that it was necessary for the welfare of the country. It was one of the most influential corporations in the land, and its tribunals were housed in magnificent palaces, constructed with the wealth that a long series of confiscations had amassed. Nevertheless, in retrospect, it is obvious that the first traces of decline were already to be discerned. The Moriscos were expelled; the importance of the Judaisers was appreciably diminished, and Spain had never shown any general tendency to turn towards the Protestant heresies. If the *autos* had gained in pomp, they had begun to lose ground as far as numbers were concerned, and this decrease in the total number of victims was bound to continue.

To the new currents of the century of enlightenment Spain remained sublimely impervious. But the Spanish dominions in Europe were not so effectively sealed against outside influence. The War of Spanish Succession initiated a game of General Post among the lesser rulers in the western Mediterranean—or perhaps, since one of the players was occasionally left without a seat, it would be more accurate to term it Musical Chairs. The new brooms began as always by making a clean sweep: and the Holy Office was a natural object of their solicitude. Thus in Sardinia, as soon as the island passed out of the jurisdiction of Spain and into that of the House of Savoy (1708-1718), the Inquisition, which had for some time been quiescent, automatically lapsed. In Sicily, during the brief rule of the House of Austria, a couple of notable *autos* took place, in 1724 and 1732, the expenses being defrayed in the first instance by the King-Emperor himself. But when in 1734 the Infant Carlos of Spain conquered the island, he determined to abolish some of the worst abuses in its administration. The Holy Office was detached from its dependence on the *Suprema* at Madrid, and its authority was curtailed. Though it survived in name for another fifty years, its functions were limited and harmless.

This reforming activity had its repercussions in the Peninsula—not indeed at first in Spain itself, but in her smaller neighbour which, by reason of its maritime connexions, was more susceptible to the influences and opinion of northern Europe. It was in 1751 that Sebastian Joseph de Carvalho e Mello, Marquis of Pombal, and previously Portuguese representative in London and Vienna, was recalled to Lisbon as chief Minister of the Crown. In England, he had been a familiar figure in the most liberal circles, and a refugee Marrano had been his physician. With no army worthy of the name, with her commerce almost entirely in the hands of England, with a corrupt public service and a licentious nobility, with her overseas Empire a profitless millstone, Portugal was a byword for inefficiency throughout Europe. Pombal determined to transform it, single-handed, into a modern state: and the Holy Office was one of the earliest objects of his attention.

Shortly after his accession to power, he decreed that in future no *auto de fé* might be held without the express permission of the civil authorities, by whom all sentences were henceforth to be confirmed. There was of course nothing particularly drastic in this; but it did something to end the secrecy in which the Holy Office had hitherto enveloped its activities, and emphasised its dependence upon the State. For some time to come, nevertheless, its activities continued without any sign of intermission. All told, eighteen persons were burned during the first ten years of the new "liberal" regime—an eloquent testimony to the hold which the institution still had on the country. In Lisbon itself, at an *auto* held on September 24th, 1752, thirty men and twenty-seven women appeared as penitents, besides whom three (all *negativos*, and presumably for that reason burned alive) were committed to the flames. Similar solemnities continued to be held annually in the capital until the great earthquake of 1755, which laid in ruins the whole city, including the Palace of the Inquisition, and according to legend facilitated the escape of many prisoners. The principal seat of activity was now transferred to Evora, where there had been an almost complete cessation since 1686. Now, there was a sudden recrudescence, and eight New Christians were relaxed in four successive *autos* between 1756 and 1760.

Lisbon thus became accustomed to the absence of those public spectacles which had hitherto been the delight of its populace. Nevertheless, even Pombal could appreciate the potential utility of the Holy Office for political objects, and it was upon it that he relied in part in his struggle for the suppression of the Jesuits, whom he hated with a fanatical abomination. A preacher belonging to that order, Gabriel Malagrida, had dared to assert that the recent earthquake was a punishment from heaven for the sins of the country, for which in Jesuit opinion the Minister was so largely responsible. Pombal now forced the Holy Office, a not unwilling accomplice (for, as has been pointed out above, there was a traditional enmity between the two organisations), to show its loyalty. On September 20th, 1761—the exact anniversary of the first Portuguese *auto de fé*—Gabriel Malagrida was burned alive on the Terreiro do Paço at Lisbon.

After this outburst Pombal was content to allow the Portuguese Inquisition to lapse into comparative inactivity. No further capital sentences were henceforth authorised. Malagrida was thus the last of its victims, as well as one of the few of the whole series whose offence was not that of Judaising. The fires of the *quemadero* had been kindled in Portugal for the last time.

The subservience of the Inquisition to the state was now complete, Pombal having secured implicit obedience by appointing his own brother to preside over it as Grand Inquisitor. Only a few further steps were necessary to render it powerless. On April 8th, 1768, the Holy Office was deprived of the powers of censorship, and on November 15th, 1771, orders were given forbidding the celebration of *autos de fé* in public and the printing of lists of those who figured in them. Three years later, there was issued a new code, or *Regimento*, for the Inquisition. This removed its worst abuses, now naïvely attributed to the machinations of the Jesuits, and received the royal approval on September 21st, 1774. In the following years, the various tribunals continued to hold in private occasional *autos*, at which minor punishments were inflicted for technical offences (the latest on record took place at Evora on September 16th, 1781). But it was clear that, in the eyes of the government, this was an entirely ecclesiastical concern which should not be allowed to interfere with the civil life of the country. Henceforth, the dreaded Inquisition of Portugal was almost powerless.

Meanwhile, Pombal had been endeavouring to eradicate the racial prejudice which had been one of the ultimate consequences of three long centuries of religious persecution. The ridiculous differentiation between Old and New Christians, which had been introduced by Manoel I. in direct contravention of his promise at the time of the General Conversion, had caused untold sufferings for those of Jewish blood ever since. Antonio Ribeiro Sanches, who was himself in this category, has left a graphic description of the slights and disabilities which a child of New Christian parentage had to face at every stage of his life, from his school-days upwards. This reads today with a strangely modern accent. In Portugal, it was now recognised to be an antiquated as well as a pernicious system; it has been left to a later period to witness its revival by a great European country, and fortified with all the resources of a muddle-headed science.

Pombal acted with characteristic vigour. First, he ordered the destruction of the registers containing the names of New Christian families. Next, he gave instructions to the heads of all the so-called " puritan " houses (who had hitherto prided themselves on contracting no outside alliances) that within four months they must arrange matches for all their daughters of marriageable age with members of families hitherto excluded from their circle, as being contaminated with Jewish blood. This order, worthy of any Oriental despot, and communicated in private so as to avoid ridicule abroad, was to be enforced by depriving of all their dignities those who refused compliance. A well-known but apocryphal story recounts how the king was by no means satisfied with the policy of his minister, and intimated that if he had his own way he would make all of the descendants of New Christians wear yellow hats, like their unconverted ancestors. On the next day, Pombal turned up at Court with three of the articles in question—one for His Majesty, one for himself, and one for the Inquisitor General!

Finally, on May 23rd, 1773, all legal distinctions between Old and New Christians were removed by law. This measure did not receive anything like unanimous approval in the country. It was actually rumoured that Pombal had received in return for it a bribe of half-a-million *cruzados* from the " Jews," as those who benefited by its provisions were still called. Nevertheless, it was enforced. Thus Marranism was officially abolished in Portugal, and the seal set on the long process of assimilation which the Forced Conversion of nearly three hundred years before had begun.

In Spain too, as the procession of years passed on, the activity of the Inquisition had diminished. This was not at the bottom an outcome of the spread of more enlightened or of more humane views, but of something very different. The inhabitants had been drilled into unimpeachable orthodoxy, and native heretics were become few and far between. On the other hand, the international importance of the country was by no means what it had once been. It had hence become impolitic to interfere with foreign Protestants: it is noteworthy, indeed, that the *causes célèbres* which stirred Europe at the close of the seventeenth and beginning of the eighteenth centuries never ended (with one probably legendary exception) with a capital sentence. The Inquisition was thus left to concentrate its attention upon the same problem as had engaged it at the outset—that of the secret Jews. But, as we have seen, the native Marranos had long since been driven into conformity or across the seas. From the sixteenth century onwards, Portuguese New Christians had taken their place. But in Portugal, too, owing to the combined efforts of persecution, extermination, and emigration, the strength of the New Christians was much diminished: and if those who remained desired to leave, the free and prosperous countries of Northern Europe offered greater attractions by far than their decadent and poverty-stricken neighbour.

The records of the Inquisition of Toledo—the only Spanish tribunal whose archives have remained tolerably complete—give a clear impression of the manner in which the energies of the Holy Office had found their outlet. By far the greatest number of the cases tried—nearly one thousand, that is—were for Judaising. (It may be added that this figure is probably incomplete, in view of the fact that in its earliest days Judaisers formed almost the sole object of Inquisitional solicitude. This offence, moreover, was punished more severely than any other, and the number of relaxations in this section was disproportionately high.) Moriscos numbered 219. Heretics of various sorts—including 39 "illuminists" and 14 Anglicans—totalled only 226 in all. Of the minor categories, there were 188 cases of bigamy, 105 of solicitation in the confessional, 755 of blasphemy, 259 of assertion that simple fornication was no sin, 551 of irreverence and scandalous speeches, and so on. Locally, of course, the relative proportions differed. It was thus natural that in the old kingdom of Andalusia the crime of crypto-Mohammedanism was rather more frequently represented than elsewhere in the kingdom, and that in the far North, where Jews had been few, crypto-Judaism was comparatively weak. But, by now, these categories were both virtually uprooted.

Its former field of activity being exhausted, the Spanish Inquisition became less and less active. It looked about

hungrily for victims, but it became more and more difficult
to find them. Córdova had witnessed *autos* in 1728, 1730
and 1741, twenty-six cases of Judaising being punished
in them: but thereafter there was none for a period of
fourteen years. At Toledo, there was an intermission from
1726 to 1738. At Valladolid, a Judaiser was relaxed in
person in 1745; as were six in effigy, together with the
bones of one dead woman, at Llerena in 1752. These
are almost the last recorded instances of the sort. Crypto-
Judaism in Spain seems in fact to have collapsed. Fourteen cases were taken into consideration at Toledo in 1738:
but there were no fatal conclusions, and thereafter, down
to the close of the series in 1794, there was only one other
accusation of the sort. In the whole country, in the period
after 1780, only sixteen persons were tried for Judaising,
and of these cases two only were of real significance. Some
4,000 in all were examined during this period, indeed:
but few of them (excepting one or two of a political
nature) were serious, and none ended with an *auto de fé*
in the old style.

The Marranos had always provided a majority of the
victims; and, as soon as they disappeared from the scene,
the work of the Inquisition became negligible. From the
middle of the eighteenth century, it constituted in fact little
more than an instrument for the moral policing of the
country, terrible by reason of its reputation and its poten-
tialities (still sporadically exercised) for the suppression
of religious heterodoxy, political insubordination, and
freedom of thought.

A fresh factor had to be considered after 1759, when
Ferdinand VI. (1746-1759) was succeeded by his enlightened half-brother, Carlos III. (1759-1788). The new
ruler, as King of the Two Sicilies, had drawn the teeth of
the local Inquisitional tribunal, as we have seen. Hence

he was not likely to allow the parent-body to attain over-whelming strength in Spain, excepting so far as it suited his purpose. Direct evidence of royal interference is slight; but it is significant that during the thirty years of the reign, there do not seem to have been all told more than twenty *autos*: and they apparently entailed only four relaxations.

Deprived of serious occupation, the Inquisitors began to get careless. Their personal character deteriorated; vacancies were left unfilled; there were widespread com-plaints of negligence. The record of the cases examined eloquently reflects this decline. From the middle of the century, the great Tribunal of Toledo, hitherto one of the most active in the country, despatched on the average only one case a year, trivial solemnities with a single penancing taking the place after 1738 of the great pageants where a half-dozen or more persons were burned alive. In the other tribunals conditions were similar, even though such minor offences as bigamy and blasphemy were certainly no less common than they had formerly been. During the period of office as Inquisitor General of Manuel Abad y la Sierra, from 1792 to 1794, there were only sixteen condemnations to public penance in all Spain. This indeed was largely due to the moderating influence of Abad himself, who planned to take away the sting from the Holy Office by assimilating its procedure to that of the civil courts. However, his design became known, and such still was the power of the Inquisition that he was forced to resign and go into monastic retirement. This was on the specious charge (which, at that time, covered a larger number of alleged sins than Charity itself) of Jansenism.

There seems to have been a growing disinclination at this period to proceed to the last extremity in the case of the "Molinists" and "Jansenists," who with the disappearance of the Judaisers now constituted the majority of the subjects for enquiry. In these instances the Holy Office was predisposed to clemency, and did all in its power to avoid going to extremes. Occasionally it was driven to a relaxation in spite almost of itself. A case in point was that of the *Beata* Dolores, an impostor who had left her father's house at the age of twelve to live with her confessor, and claimed continued and familiar intercourse with the Virgin as well as an early marriage in heaven with the child Jesus, St. Joseph and St. Augustin having acted as witnesses. Every endeavour was made to induce her to profess penitence and thus save her from the agonies of the stake: but she refused to avail herself of the opportunity. On August 22nd, 1781, she was burned, after having secured the preliminary grace of strangulation by a last moment repentance. Not dissimilar from this was the case of the *Beata* of Cuenca, Isabel María Herraiz, who claimed that, in order to be more completely united to her, Jesus had infused his blood and body into hers, so that she was adored as semi-divine by hundreds of followers. She died shortly after her arrest, impenitent: and in accordance with precedent was subsequently burned in effigy, in 1802—almost the last case of the sort on record. Not long before, a Judaiser named Lorenzo Beltran had been reconciled at an *auto* in Seville, on March 31st, 1799. It was fitting that the last effort of the Holy Office against Marranism should take place in the very city where it had begun its operations.

The last *cause célèbre* of the Spanish Inquisition was in itself a demonstration of how far the scope of its activity had altered since the heroic days of its foundation, and illustrated how it had become an instrument for satisfying political and personal animosities. A brilliant and

travelled young Peruvian lawyer named Pablo Olavide
had become interested in the idea of colonising the south
of the country, still suffering from the deportation of the
Moriscos. On the highroad between Madrid and Cadiz,
in a wild and desolate country, arrangements were made
for establishing a settlement of six thousand German and
Swiss Catholics, of which he was to be Superintendent.
He threw himself heart and soul into the project, and success seemed assured. Two vested interests, however,
were concerned—the religious orders, which, for obvious
reasons, were to be prevented from establishing branch
houses in an area which needed repopulation, and the
Mesta, or sheep-owners' association, of immemorial
antiquity, whose grazing-rights would be limited by the
scheme. Olavide was accordingly denounced to the Holy
Office, on a pretext which his foreign travels made both
obvious and specious: that he was an atheist and
materialist, in correspondence with and an admirer of
those arch-unbelievers, Voltaire and Rousseau. In support of these charges, it was pointed out that (in addition
to some more conventional misdemeanours) he had a
rooted objection to the burial of corpses in Church, cham-
pioned the Copernican system, and objected to the ring-
ing of bells as a specific against thunderstorms. His trial
lasted for three years: and at the end in 1778 in a private
auto de fé he was condemned to reconciliation, confiscation of property, and eight years' imprisonment in a
convent.

The offence for which Olavide was condemned was
termed "philosophism" or "naturalism"—a vague
charge, covering any tincture of the new ideas which had
become fashionable on the other side of the Pyrenees. It
was true that they were universally adopted in France,
even in Court circles of immaculate formal orthodoxy.

Yet the Holy Office realised—and, as the event proved, rightly so—that they menaced the very basis of the Spanish scheme of life, and that, once they established themselves in the Peninsula, the system erected by the Catholic sovereigns would be at an end. But the waters rose, more and more menacingly: and in the end not even the pious barrier of an Edict of Faith, signed and countersigned by all the members of the Suprema, could suffice to keep them out.

The outbreak of the French Revolution goaded the Inquisition into a fresh display of nervousness, if not quite of activity. Denunciations became common once more (there were some 5,000 between 1780 and 1820). Three-fifths of them were for " propositions "—that is, liberal ideas which were implicitly or explicitly hostile to the claims of the Church militant or the monarchy absolute. Associated with this was the " crime " of Freemasonry, which was beginning to make slow inroads into Spain notwithstanding the dangers involved. Thus, the Holy Office became more nakedly than at any previous stage in its history little other than a state appanage, with functions pre-eminently political. This very fact rendered possible a complete *volte-face* after the French occupation of Madrid in 1808, when it unblushingly transferred its loyalty to the new regime which it had so persistently vilified. This ingenious procedure did not save it, however: and when Napoleon himself arrived in the capital in the following December a decree was issued abolishing the Holy Office and transferring its property to the Crown.

The accounts of the subsequent proceedings which reached the outside world were as highly coloured as the outside world desired. (It is no new phenomenon, it may be remarked, for news from Spain to be not infrequently of a deplorably tendentious nature.) Some years after the event an English clergyman published what purported to be a Report of the demolition of the Palace of the Inquisition at Madrid, drawn up in 1809 by a certain Colonel Lemanoir of the 9th Regiment of Polish Lancers. The Palace, according to this document, was defended by armed soldiers, who fired treacherously on the three French regiments detailed for duty. This could not of course deter the ardour of the assailants. When the latter had made a breach in the walls, they were greeted in vain with hypocritical blandishments by the Inquisitor General, who sallied forth in his sacerdotal robes. Within, there was unbelievable luxury—marble mosaic floors inlaid with exquisite taste, altars and crucifixes in abundance, and untold treasures. It was impossible however to find the secret dungeons, until one of the French officers ingeniously had water poured on the marble pavements and prised open the flag-stones where it showed a tendency to trickle through.

Below this, the Hall of Judgement and its infamous appurtenances were discovered, including cells still containing human remains, where the victims were immured until death relieved them from their sufferings. They were, it is true, provided with ventilation: but this was not for the benefit of the victims, but so as to ensure that the smell of the decomposing flesh should not offend the Inquisitors' nostrils. In other cells were found about one hundred living victims of all ages and both sexes, all as naked as the day they were born, and in the last stage of weakness. Among the instruments of torture (with which the brave French soldiers made a few interesting experiments on the Familiars and their superiors) was a statue of the Virgin, studded with spikes, which could be made to inflict a fatal embrace on its victims, and so bring about an agonising death. . . .

It is a waste of time to point out the absurdities and incoherences in this egregious account, which was foisted on the horrified public at the height of the period of mid-Victorian respectability. It is, nevertheless, a document of considerable historical value, as an illustration of the Protestant Legend with regard to the Inquisition, which continued to develop throughout the nineteenth century. The same point of view is reflected in Edgar Allan Poe's famous tale, *The Pit and the Pendulum*, which tells how a victim of the Holy Tribunal at Toledo was saved from a remarkably ingenious torture, in the nick of time, by the entry of the French troops into Toledo. As a short story, it is a masterpiece: but it is depressing to consider how many persons must have received their impression of the Inquisition and its practices from this imaginative exercise.

What a foreign autocrat had decided or even carried into effect did not necessarily have much weight with the body of the Spanish people (excepting perhaps persons such as that former parish priest, denounced before the Holy Office about this time, who declared that he would rather be Napoleon than God). In those parts of Spain to which French authority did not reach, the Inquisition continued to function, in name at least, its officials withdrawing from one place to another as the enemy troops occupied their former seat of activity and brought their work to an end. From the autumn of 1810, however, the national resistance was directed by a representative Cortes sitting at Cadiz, filled with liberal-minded men who were honestly anxious that this new Spain of theirs should make a clean break with the abominations of its past.

At the beginning of 1813, after long and at times bitter discussions, the Cortes by a large majority passed a series of resolutions declaring the Inquisition inconsistent with the new constitution of liberal Spain, and recommending that jurisdiction over heresy should be relegated henceforth to the episcopal courts to which it properly belonged. A statement to this effect, and explaining the reasons for the step, was to be read in all parish churches on three consecutive Sundays. There was some criticism of this procedure. The reactionaries continued to maintain that the Holy Office had been necessary, and still was, in order to conserve that which was most essential and characteristic in Spanish life. But the citizens of Madrid congratulated the Cortes on having ended the activities of an institution which for three and a half centuries past had transformed men into tigers and prevented the progress of art and science in the country.

They spoke too soon. The sovereigns of the post-Napoleonic era had a weakness for learning nothing and forgetting nothing. Ferdinand VII. could not bring himself to believe that either the Almighty or the Duke of Wellington had chased the French out of Spain with the intention of leaving anything of their abominable influence behind, and he was determined to restore the old regime down to its last detail. On May 4th, 1814, he declared all the proceedings of the Cortes of Cadiz to be null and void. Since the abolition of the Inquisition had been among the memorable actions of this body, his decision implied that the Holy Office was to be revived. However, he was not content to leave this to logic or imagination, both qualities of which he heartily disapproved. On July 21st of the same year, amid the blank incredulity of Europe, he announced that the tribunals were to resume their functions, on the pretext that the presence of so many heretical foreign soldiers in the country during the War of Independence had seriously affected the religious principles of its simple inhabitants.

In the succeeding period, activity was by no means

great. Possibly, the Holy Office was not desirous of attracting too much attention until its position was more securely established. In any case, it confined its attention to comparatively insignificant doctrinal and disciplinary questions, imposed no particularly severe sentences, and was careful to abstain from staging anything that approximated to a public *auto de fé*. At Seville, for example, a priest was penanced at an *autillo* held on February 27th, 1817, on the charge of having improperly raised the host while celebrating the Mass. This could hardly be regarded as an abuse of functions. Nevertheless, its influence was not minimised abroad: and caricaturists took pleasure in depicting the reactionary Spanish ruler, supported by the devil and an Inquisitor, sitting on a throne precariously balanced on human skulls. "Prisons, Chains, Halters, and the Tortures of the Holy Inquisition for every friend to Constitutional Liberty—Eternal War against Literature and Liberty," the Evil One is represented as saying: while his associate undertakes that the Friars and the Inquisition would support their sovereign as an absolute monarch. The phraseology is certainly lurid: but the sentiments were not far from the truth.

Overseas, a similar change in sentiment had meanwhile taken place. Even more openly than in Spain, the Inquisition had become an instrument of political reaction. This was particularly the case in Mexico, where during the War of Independence of 1805 to 1815, a leading part was played by Miguel Hidalgo, parish priest of Los Dolores. He was a man of advanced views in matters of morality as well as of politics, and in more normal times had more than once been denounced to the Holy Office by reason of his disorderly life. Then, no action was taken: but when he came forward as a revolutionary leader, the matter appeared in a different light, and he was sum-

moned to appear before the Tribunal to justify himself for
the manifold and manifest errors attributed to him in the
past. Not having either the optimism or the opportunity
to present himself, he was tried *in absentia* as a Deist,
Atheist, Judaiser, Protestant, blasphemer and seducer—
a roll of crime which clearly left no loophole for escape.
The quandary of determining on which of these accounts
he should be condemned was however decided by the civil
authorities, who captured the unfortunate insurgent and
had him executed out of hand as an ordinary traitor.

Almost identical was the fate, four years later, of
another insurgent leader, formerly in Holy Orders,
José Maria Morelos, who at one time had been Hidalgo's
lieutenant and ultimately rose to the dignity of Captain
General. In his case, the Holy Office demonstrated that
when circumstances demanded it was capable of expedition. Taken prisoner at the close of 1815, he was brought
to Mexico City on November 21st, brought up for trial
on the 23rd as a Deist, Atheist, Voltairean and Hob-
besean, sentenced on November 26th, condemned and
degraded from Holy Orders at a sumptuous private *auto*
on the 27th, and summarily executed by the civil power
in the following month.

This type of activity did not do anything to endear
the Holy Office further to the more liberal elements
among the population in the New World. Accordingly,
when the news of the Revolution of 1820 and the royal
decree abolishing the Inquisition arrived (a point to which
we shall presently revert) effect was immediately given to
it in Mexico, Peru, and Cartagena. Not long previous,
in 1812, the Inquisition of Goa, which had been suspended in 1774 and reinstated in 1778, was finally
abolished: while the Portuguese Inquisition, which had
survived Pombal's reforms in an emasculated form, and

had unctuously welcomed the French invaders, was finally swept away by a Parliamentary resolution of March 21st, 1821, amid the popular jubilation.

In 1820, Civil War broke out again in Spain: the occasion being the revolt of Ráfael Riego, an Asturian battalion commander of liberal sympathies, who proclaimed the constitution of 1812 and for a time managed to maintain himself in Madrid at the head of a constitutional government. However, a large part of the country refused obedience: and a unified regime was not restored until five years after, when the liberal movement was drowned in blood. Within a decade, civil strife recommenced. The line of demarcation was now nominally dynastic: it was a question of the contending claims of a young Queen who stood in the natural line of succession, against her uncle who claimed that, as the nearest male relative of the deceased sovereign, he was the legal heir to the throne. Behind this, and more important than this, was the constitutional question. Queen Isabella stood, or was made to stand, for a certain degree of Liberalism, the parliamentary constitution first promulgated in 1812, and an enlightened outlook in politics— even in religion. Don Carlos was the representative of the party of reaction, of absolutism, and of reversion to eighteenth-century Bourbonism in Church and State.

The dynastic and constitutional struggle lasted with intervals until 1876. It is possible to say, indeed, that from 1808 to the present day a state of civil war, avowed or suppressed, has existed in Spain for something like half of the total period. The War of Liberation, which from certain points of view was a Civil War, lasted from 1808 to 1814. Riego's revolt and its consequences convulsed the country from 1820 to 1825. The first of the Carlist Wars broke out in 1834, and the last came to an end only in 1876. Thereafter (although a series of military *pro-nunciamentos* punctuated the entire period) there was a qualified tranquillity until the fall of the monarchy in 1931. The sequence of disorder in Spain after that date is not, therefore, such a cataclysm as would have been the case in other European countries. It was in fact a reversion to a state of affairs which, notwithstanding a brief intermission during the previous generation, had been endemic in the country almost since the year of Trafalgar.

The Spanish Civil Wars, moreover, have constantly repeated the same features. What have elsewhere been considered atrocities have there been commonplace amenities of political intercourse. It has always been a regrettable weakness of Spanish political enthusiasts that, instead of putting their opponents into gaol, they have often preferred to stand them up against a wall, and put an end to their rhetoric and their idealism for good. The reactionaries have always had delight in burning municipal offices, and the liberals have shewn their eman-cipation from religion by conscientious attempts (not without a haunting expectation of Divine vengeance) to burn churches. At intervals, the mob have broken into the gaols and massacred those political prisoners of whose views they disapproved—a procedure which caused as much horror abroad in 1835 as it did in 1936. The change between now and one hundred years ago is not one of temperament. The only outstanding difference is that, with the advance in civilisation, instruments of destruction have attained so devastating a degree of per-fection.

Even in the details of military operations, Spanish history shews a remarkable tendency to repeat itself. The Carlists more than once reached the gates of Madrid, but in spite of what was generally anticipated never mastered the city. Nor is it generally realised that the Republic of 1931 was the second to exist in Spain, an earlier experiment having begun under the most promising auspices in 1873 and continued for nearly two years.

The international repercussions have been similar. Foreign contingents have fought in the Spanish civil wars, and on more than one occasion have turned the tide of battle; foreign powers have intervened to secure the establishment of their own particular ideology; and in the nineteenth century, too, there was danger more than once of the Spanish dispute developing into a European war, and suggestions were made for the establishment of a *cordon sanitaire* by the Concert of Europe to localise the bloodshed. The main difference between the two periods has been that a conservative government in France shewed more eagerness to fish in the troubled waters than a Socialist one in our own day, and that a century ago liberal opinion in England considered that foreign support, when it was a question of reinforcing the popular cause against reaction, was less preposterous than a hundred years later, when circumstances were reversed.

It was during this period of qualified anarchy that the Spanish Inquisition finally came to an end. At the beginning of Riego's liberal administration, sullenly yielding to force of circumstances, the King renewed his oath to the Constitution of 1812, and simultaneously, on March 9th, 1820, issued a decree abolishing the Inquisition. But the new government, as is so often the case in Spain, found difficulty in maintaining order: and three years later, a French army under the Duc d'Angoulême crossed the Pyrenees, with the approval of the more noisy instruments in the Concert of Europe, to restore what they called "order," but liberals dubbed "reaction." The King immediately issued decrees invalidating everything that had been done since March, 1820, and, by implication, restoring the Inquisition once again. His French allies were strongly opposed to anything of the sort. Chateaubriand, for example, who had been principally responsible for the expedition, protested vehemently at the prospect of tarnishing the wilted Restoration laurels by any such procedure. It was therefore considered tactful to say nothing at all about the Holy Office. But events shewed that the Royalist party considered it to be fully reinstated. This was proved by an event which took place on July 26th, 1826, at Valencia, where a human life was sacrificed in order to demonstrate to the world that heresy was still a capital offence in Spain. A poor schoolmaster of blameless character, named Cayetano Ripoll, was arraigned before an Episcopal *junta de fé*, or Council of Faith (not quite, therefore, an Inquisitional tribunal in the old sense), on a charge of professing and teaching Deist principles. He was condemned to death, and garotted forthwith. Public opinion was no longer capable of supporting the idea of a public burning. Instead, the body was encased in a barrel on which scarlet flames were painted, so that the traditional penalty might be carried out symbolically at least: it was then buried in unconsecrated ground.

The news was received abroad with a shudder of horror. But it was impossible at any time to speak or think moderately of anything in which the Inquisition was concerned. In contemporary reports, accordingly, the unhappy victim was made a Jew (for it was notorious that the Inquisition existed in order to burn Jews): and journalists embellished the story, giving a lurid account of the proceedings at the *auto*, of the agonies of the victim as he was being burned alive, and of how the monks led the assembled multitude in singing hymns in order to drown the despairing shrieks from the middle of the flames. But even this was not enough, for later on historians collated the two accounts and determined that two victims figured on that occasion—a Deist schoolmaster and an unfortunate Jew!

It seems that this sudden display of ferocity was staged for no other purpose than to vindicate the rights of the ecclesiastical authorities and the attitude of the country towards religious non-conformity. For it was isolated. Ripoll thus had the distinction of being the last victim of the Inquisitional system in Spain. Thereafter, the activity displayed was insignificant, as it had been during the previous period of reaction between 1814 and 1820. But let there be no mistake. We know today that the last victim of the Holy Office perished in 1826. No one did then: and it seemed that the dreaded organisation was still couchant, biding its time for another terrible onslaught. No man of tolerant views or open mind could feel entirely secure until it was rendered harmless.

Hence the abolition of the Holy Office became part of the liberal creed in Spain, and the progressive leaders never wearied of pressing for it to be carried into effect. They had to wait until Ferdinand had passed away, on September 29th, 1833, and (in his own words) the cork was removed from the fermenting and surcharged bottle of Spain. There was another way of expressing the same truth, as a contemporary did with biting sarcasm: " That king, who deceived his parents, his masters, his friends, his ministers, his partisans, his enemies, his four wives, his people, his allies—all the world, in fact—deceived also death, who thought to make us happy in delivering us from such a devil: for he left us his brother and his daughter, who kindled a dreadful war, and the legacy of misery and scandal is yet unexhausted.''

Yet for the moment it was believed that with Ferdinand VII. had passed also the last relic of eighteenth-century obscurantism. There was now an interlude of reform under the child-queen Isabella II. and her mother, Cristina, who for some years acted as Regent. The Inquisition was among the very first objects which the new government took into consideration. On July 15th, 1834, notwithstanding the protests of a superannuated minority, the Queen Mother issued an edict finally and definitely abolishing the Holy Office and all its powers, direct and indirect, without reservation or qualification. Its property was appropriated to the extinction of the public debt; its former employees were given compensation for their lost emoluments: the right of the bishops was recognised as to censorship over writings on religion, morals and discipline. But the essential part of the decree was contained in the first clause, which summed up in nine words, with commendable brevity, the end to which Spanish liberals had for so long been striving: *'' It is declared that the Tribunal of the Inquisition is definitely suppressed.''*

AFTERMATH

A CAREER of blood which had persisted for three and a half centuries was ended at last. Yet, though the Inquisition was abolished, its shadow still remained heavy over the land. Until the century was well advanced, the *Sambenitos* of those condemned and the accompanying portraits still remained hanging in many parish churches. In some cases they were renewed from time to time and painted over in oils, to bring everlasting shame on the descendants of the heresy-hunts of miserable victims of many generations before. Nor was there any question as to their object: down to a period almost within living memory, lists of families of tainted descent were posted up on the church doors, so that the faithful should be warned against intermarrying with them. As regards the *Chuetas* of Majorca, discrimination survived to our own day, and they are still treated (or were until very recently) as a race apart. All this was spasmodically condemned by the central authorities. Nevertheless, even on the mainland the prejudice lingered on, proof of unsullied lineage being required of aspirants to many offices, and certain professions. It was only as late as 1860 that the official distinction between Old Christians and New was finally abolished, by a resolution of the Cortes which made it unnecessary henceforth for candidates for admission to the Corps of Cadets to produce certificate of *limpieza*, or purity of blood " from any admixture of Jew and Moor," or from such as had been condemned by the Holy Office.

Nine years after this, on June 6th, 1869, the principle

of religious toleration was incorporated in the Spanish constitution. Lord Malmesbury, a former British Foreign Minister, was in Madrid at the time, and gave in his *Memoirs* an account of the attendant circumstances. " A most curious discovery," he writes, " has been made at Madrid. Just at the time when the question of religious liberty was being discussed in the Cortes, Serrano had ordered a piece of ground to be levelled, in order to build on it, and the workmen came upon large quantities of human bones, skulls, lumps of blackening flesh, pieces of chain and braids of hair. It was then recollected that the *autos de fé* used to take place at that spot in former days. Crowds of people rushed to the spot, and the investigation was continued. They found layer upon layer of human remains, showing that hundreds had been inhumanly sacrificed. The excitement and indignation this produced among the people was tremendous, and the party for religious freedom taking advantage of it, a Bill on the subject was passed by an enormous majority."

Religious liberty in Spain was not however equivalent to religious toleration. Though dissenting forms of public worship were no longer prohibited, they were performed on sufferance only, with less approach to broad-mindedness on the part of the majority than had been the case in the Middle Ages. It was not until the Revolution of 1931 that religious equality became part of the Spanish constitution, and Torquemada's work was at last undone —finally, as one may hope, though one does not dare to prophesy.

*   *   *   *   *

One Friday in August, 1763, a representative assortment of humanity set out from London in the Harwich stage-coach. There was the inevitable elderly gentlewoman; a Dutch youth of undecided character: a short-sighted, middle-aged individual with many unpleasing mannerisms and no manners: and a Scotsman in the early twenties, who treated the former (who was seeing him off to Holland) with pathetic reverence, and called him " Doctor Johnson " with a deferential persistence which permitted no one to overlook the fact.   In the afternoon, the conversation turned on Spain, and the lady spoke vio-lently against the Roman Catholics and the horrors of the Inquisition.   To the amazement of all present except his faithful acolyte, Dr. Johnson argued the point.   "False doctrine," he thundered, "should be checked on its first appearance. The civil power should unite with the Church in punishing those who dare to attack the established religion.   And such only are punished by the Inquisition."

This has been from the beginning a main line of argu-ment of those who champion the Holy Office.   It is of course weakened (as Dr. Johnson of all men should have realised) by the fact that it implies unquestioned recogni-tion that what is not at the moment the doctrine of the Church and State is, necessarily, false doctrine.   All the great religions of today, after all, began as dissenting movements, and none would now be in existence had a ruthless and effective Inquisition flourished at the time of their birth.   The theory of the Inquisition postulates, in fact, exclusive possession of the knowledge which leads to eternal felicity.   Question this, and its *raison d'être* dis-appears.   And even if it be admitted, this does not neces-sarily imply a recognition of the efficiency of the prac-tice; for proveably the Inquisition sometimes defeated its own ends.

The Blood of Martyrs is the Seed of the Church in a sense rather different from that in which the phrase is generally intended.   It is natural for the human mind to brood over that which it is constantly told to avoid, and sometimes to be attracted by it. A study of the original processes of the Inquisition shews that this was frequently the case in Spain. Many an accused person, in the course of his examination, admitted frankly that he had known nothing of the heresy or misdemeanour with which he was charged, until his attention was drawn to it by the insistence with which it was denounced by the Holy Office. New adherents were attracted sometimes because of the heroism which the martyrs shewed at the last; and Marranos, brought up in complete ignorance of the religion of their fathers, sedulously studied the Edicts of Faith and the sentences of the condemned in order to learn something of Jewish practice. It is on record too that perfectly innocent persons, quite sincere in their orthodoxy, were sometimes so scandalised at the inhumanity with which the Holy Office treated them once its suspicions were aroused, that they would subsequently go over whole-heartedly to the heresy of which they had been falsely accused.

In recent years, with the nominal acceptance of the doctrine of religious tolerance, the traditional defence of the Inquisition has been clothed in slightly different terms. In a state in which religion and society were co-extensive, heresy was anti-social, and had to be repressed and punished in the same way as any other crime against the majority. It is a somewhat dangerous contention: for the definition of an anti-social crime is somewhat vague, and in our own days has received an alarming extension. Moreover, granted the premise, the savageness of the procedure even so remains unjustified and unexplained.

It must be borne in mind, too, that the activities of the Inquisition were not confined in fact (as distinct from theory) to those who were endeavouring to undermine the fabric of Roman Catholicism. It was founded to deal with, and the greatest part of its energies were directed against, a different category—forcible converts from Judaism and Islam, who had not desired to enter the Catholic Church, who had little knowledge of Catholic ceremonial and doctrine, but whom the Inquisition tried to force into conformity with blood and fire. That other categories of offender were subsequently dealt with does not in the least affect the fact that in the Inquisition's heyday and in the period of its greatest ferocity, the victims were in the main claimed among persons who, from the social point of view, owed no allegiance to the established Church.

Another defence sometimes put forward of late is empiric, but slightly revolting. It suggests, in effect, that the victims of the Holy Office were of slender importance — crypto-Jewish pedlars and crypto-Moslem peasants, whose loss was anyhow of minor consequence. This method of argument has in its favour the universal historical phenomenon, that a thing cannot both be and not be at the same time: and that, when a student or cleric was burned in his middle twenties, it is impossible to affirm with certainty that he would have been a great luminary in letters or in philosophy had he been allowed to live another thirty years. Nevertheless, it is possible to draw up an impressive list of persons of real eminence whose activities were cut short in the fires of the *quemadero*: of others, who were proceeded against, submitted to indescribable suffering, and narrowly escaped with their lives after years of imprisonment: of others, again, who were arraigned after death, and whose bodies were dug up and burned, as they themselves would have been had they lived a little longer: and finally others who avoided arrest and condemnation only by a timely flight, and were "relaxed" *in absentia*. One name only, in each category, need be mentioned here. Antonio José da Silva, burned at Lisbon in 1739, was the most popular Portuguese playwright of the time. Garcia d'Orta, whose bones were exhumed and burned after his death in India, in 1580, was the greatest Portuguese scientist of the Renaissance, and founder of the study of tropical medicine. The jurist Francisco Velasco de Gouvêa, subsequently to use his pen to vindicate the right of the House of Braganza to the Portuguese throne, was under trial by the Holy Office for five years, from 1626 to 1631. And, at the great *auto* held at Seville in 1660, among the thirty persons burned in effigy were two at least of the highest reputation in intellectual circles—Doctor Melchor de Orobio, Professor of Medicine in the University of Seville and subsequently physician to the King of France, and Antonio Enriquez Gomez, a prolific writer and rival of Calderon for the favours of the theatre-going public of Madrid. The extirpation, expatriation, or stultification of intellects such as these, spread over a long period of years, cannot but have had a deleterious effect on Spanish and Portuguese cultural life. One may go even further: it was a crime against the human race as a whole.

But there is yet a further consideration, more important still, and fraught with a special significance at the present time. Those who suffered from the effects of the Inquisition were not only those whose conduct gave grounds for suspicion, or whose ancestors belonged to a particular ethnic or religious minority. They comprised every inhabitant of the country—all those who had to be circumspect in speech, lest an Inquisitional spy were within hearing; all teachers who were compelled to weigh every word carefully, lest they gave expression to some idea which could not bear close examination from the point of view of the accepted conventions; every writer, who had to scrutinise and rescrutinise each line before it was sent to the printer, for fear that some unguarded phrase or ill-considered witticism might cost him his liberty for months or years, or even bring upon him a worse fate.

The effect of all this was not to be discerned in a few months, or years, or even generations. It is with justice that historians point to the fact that Spain's great age came after the establishment of the Inquisition, when the *auto de fé* was an established institution and Palaces of the Holy Office adorned most of the principal towns. It was then that Cervantes wrote, that Velasquez painted, that Santa Teresa dreamed, that Spanish galleons sailed in every sea and the Spanish flag was triumphant in every continent. All this is true. But the Dead Hand of the Holy Office was pressing slowly on the vital arteries of Spanish intellectual life, and the cumulative effect was felt at last. The fall of Spain was even more catastrophic than its rise was sudden. After the middle of the seventeenth century, the desiccation began, and it proceeded relentlessly. Before long, the country's downfall was complete: and any contributions it was henceforth to make to the common heritage of Europe, were insignificant or incoherent. It took the Holy Office two hundred years perhaps to complete its work. But, by the middle of the eighteenth century, it was possible to see the result: a country drained of its inspiration, of its genius, of its wealth—of everything in fact but its orthodoxy and its pride.

The Spanish Inquisition has been extinct, now, for a little more than one hundred years. Its spirit has recently been revived outside Spain, and in certain parts of the world has achieved in the course of the present generation a triumph ostensibly more instantaneous and more remarkable than Torquemada could ever have hoped. But, if history has ever a lesson to teach us, it is to warn us against being overawed by the clattering of a bully's sabre, even if the scabbard is still bedecked with stolen finery. The essential greatness of a country does not depend on the extent of its empire nor on the number of its armed forces nor on the efficiency of its military machine, but on the free spirit of enquiry which enables the patrimony of the past to be retained, consolidated and extended. The example of Spain is enough to warn us that it matters not that a nation gain the whole world if it lose its soul.

APPENDIX I

THE TRIAL OF DIOGO HENRIQUES

THE best manner of obtaining an idea of the Inquisitional Process is to read the full record of some specific trial. Of these, a few of special interest have been printed, and one or two even translated into English. They are not available however to the ordinary reader. For that reason, the following excerpts of a case of 1646-8 before the Lisbon Tribunal are published here. They are by no means exhaustive, the original being of considerable bulk. Nevertheless, the passages quoted sum up in a so-called " voluntary " confession the information elicited by various means during the long examination which had preceded, and illustrate in a remarkable fashion the Inquisition's deadly but petty curiosity. They are of special interest as illustrating the curiously wide-spread ramifications of a family broken up by the Holy Office, from America to Italy. The original is to be found in the State Archives of the Torre do Tombo at Lisbon, Inquisição de Lisbõa, processo 1170. It will be noticed that for illustrative purposes the Portuguese Inquisition, with its virtually complete records, is in many respects more convenient than that of Spain in its stricter sense. The supplementary documents are in this case particularly interesting, giving as they do a picture, not only of the mechanism and procedure of the Holy Office, but also of its less grim aspect.

GENEALOGY AND SENTENCE

Names other persons and declares his genealogy

On the 19th day of December, 1646, in Lisbon, in the first Audience Hall of the Offices of the Holy Inquisition, his Worship Inquisitor Melchior Dias Pretto, holding the morning Audience, summoned to appear before him Diogo Henriques, with whom this Process deals, he having asked for an audience, who, being present, said that he had asked for an audience, in order to name other persons with whom he remembers he had communication, when in error. And that he might in all things speak the truth, and preserve secrecy, he was told to take oath on the Holy Gospels on which he placed his hand, and having taken oath accordingly under seal thereof: He said that having reached the country of Brazil, five years ago or thereabouts, he became acquainted in Pernambuco with Manoel Nunes, does not know his native city, but who lived for some time in Madrid, and deponent has heard that he fled from thence to France fearing the justice of the Holy Office, and then proceeded to Pernambuco, where he followed the profession of surgeon; he was married to Catherina da Costa, who, deponent has heard, was burnt in effigy, in Madrid. And the said Manoel Nunes appeared to be about forty-five years of age and spoke Portuguese, and confessant saw him attending the Sinagogues and publicly professing belief in the Law of Moses, as he did also when his profession brought him to confessant's house, and he was accustomed to seeing him in the sinagogue where they assembled, and on various occasions they declared to one another their belief in the aforesaid Law, in which Law Catherina da Costa, wife of the aforesaid, also lived publicly.

Further declares that at the same time he was acquainted with Abraham Israel, whose name as a Catholic he does not know, native of Portalegre, cousin of Luis Mendes, of whom confessant has spoken, and confessant has heard the said Abraham Israel say that he left this kingdom and went to Holland, for fear of the justice of the Holy Office; and in Pernambuco, where confessant knew him, the said Abraham Israel publicly professed his belief in the Law of Moses, and attended the sinagogue in confessant's company in the manner customary to Jews; and the said Abraham Israel would be about forty at the time, tall, and stout, and followed the calling of barber, besides having certain commercial dealings; and he said that he was married to a niece of his, who was also a Jewess by belief, and lived in Amsterdam.

Further says that at the same time he was acquainted in Pernambuco with David Zuzarte, whose name as a Catholic he does not know, native of Thomar, married in Amsterdam, but does not know to whom; and at that time he appeared to be about forty years of age, short and black bearded; and he also publicly professed the Law of Moses, continuing in the belief and observances thereof, attending the sinagogues in company with confessant. And all the said persons were in Arrecife at the time confessant was brought to the Fortress of the River of San Francisco, and further saith not, and has nothing to declare as to good or ill will. And since he had nothing further to say the usual questions as to his genealogy were put to him.

Asked his name, age, race, native town and place of residence: Says, he is named Diogo Henriques, is of the race of New Christians, native of Medina de Rio Secco in Castile; is twenty-six years of age or thereabouts; that his father was named Pedro Henriques, and his mother Anna Vas; he does not know, and does not remember having been told, the names of his paternal or maternal grand-parents, nor where they were born; and that on his father's side he had four uncles, though he has never heard any but Antonio Henriques spoken of, who, as deponent has already said, left this kingdom for Italy.

And that the said Antonio Henriques was married to Fillipa de Mesquita, sister to confessant's mother, who had one daughter only, also named Fillipa de Mesquita, married to Francisco Alvares, of whom he has spoken, and he does not know whether they have any children. And he does not know the names of his other uncles, nor whether they were married, since he has never known children of theirs, nor has he any information concerning them, but has heard his father say that he had four brothers; and he now remembers that his said father had a sister named Isabel Henriques, who lives in the town of Padua, widow, and deponent does not know when she married; and she has two sons, one a Doctor of Medicine, and the other also follows a learned profession, but does not know which; both sons unmarried; he does not know their names.

And that on his Mother's side he has one uncle only, Francisco Vas by name, of whom deponent has spoken, and who was married to Beatriz Rodrigues, deceased, by whom he had two daughters, who have remained un-married, the oldest is named Fillipa de Mesquita, he cannot remember the name of the other.

And this deponent has three brothers, namely, Antonio, João and Fernando, all unmarried and younger than deponent; and two sisters, namely, Violante Henriques, married to Isaac Baru, of whom deponent has spoken, and they have no children, and Catherina Henriques married to Jacob Vas, whom deponent spoke in his confession, and they, also, have no children.

And that this deponent is unmarried, and, as he has said, he was baptized in the Church of Santa Maria Maior of Medina de Rio Secco, but he does not know by whom, nor who were his godparents, and that he is not confirmed. And that notwithstanding his being baptized, he did not at any time go to Church, as Catholic Christians do, nor perform any action or work as such, because from his earliest years he was instructed in the ceremonies and beliefs of the Law of Moses, having no knowledge whatever of the mysteries of our holy faith: and in this blindness he ever persisted, for the reason that he did not know the prayers of the church, nor was he at any time instructed therein, but on the contrary his said parents warned him that the Law of Moses forbade any knowledge of the Law of the Gospel. And he only knows how to read, write and count as much as is needed for his business and commerce. And that he has nothing further to say concerning the faith other than what he has already declared before this Tribunal, and does not know of any relation of his being brought before the Inquisition, or who was arrested or penanced by the Holy Inquisition.

Asked whether he, the prisoner, has understood the reason why he was summoned before the Inquisition and detained, says, that he was brought here as a Jew, and that he was detained because the fact of his having been baptized was known. He was informed that the Holy Office has sufficient reason to detain him, without which it is not customary to take proceedings against any person whatever; and that since God, Our Lord, through this detention has granted him the special privilege of realising his errors, and has given him understanding to bring him to repentance of them, which is necessary for the salvation of his soul, since the Law of Moses was ended by the promulgation of the Law of Grace, he is exhorted, therefore, after rendering thanks to that same Lord for so great a privilege, to persist most firmly in his resolution, being certain that only in the belief of our holy faith lies salvation, and that for his benefit it is necessary he should declare before this tribunal all that he further remembers concerning his faults or the questions which have been put to him; and in particular whether before or after following the Law of Moses, he had received instruction or had knowledge of the matters and mysteries of our holy Faith, as all the aforesaid is necessary for the better discharge of his conscience, and the despatch of his cause: And as he said that he would render thanks to God our Lord for the favour granted him, and that he had never at any time received instruction in the mysteries of our holy Faith, in which he earnestly begged to be instructed, and that should he remember anything further touching his errors he would come to declare it before this tribunal, the session was read to him, the which having heard he declared it to be well and truthfully written, and signed with his Worship, whereupon he was formally admonished and sent to his cell.

Belchior Dias Pretto.
Diogo Henriques.

Written by Gaspar Clemente.

DIOGO HENRIQUES

The Inquisitors in ordinary and Deputies of the Holy Inquisition are agreed:

That taking into consideration these autos, errors and confessions of Diogo Henriques, new Christian, unmarried, son of Pedro Henriques, native of Medina de Rio Secco, Kingdom of Castile, resident in Pernambuco, State of Brazil, the prisoner here present:

By which is shown that being a baptized Christian, and as such obliged to hold and believe all that the Holy Mother Church of Rome holds, believes and teaches, he acted to the contrary and since the last General Pardon, finding himself outside of this said kingdom and circumcised, he took the name of Abraham Bueno, and being persuaded and instructed in the false doctrine by certain persons of his race, he adopted the Law of Moses, and publicly professed it, even holding it to be good and true, hoping to be saved therein, and not in the Faith of Christ, Our Lord, in whom he did not believe, nor hold Him to be true God, the Messiah promised in the Law, but still waited for Him, as do the Jews: and believed only in the God of Abraham, Isaac and Jacob, Creator of heaven and earth, who gave the Law to the people of Israel, and to Him he commended himself by Jewish prayers; and in observance of the said Law he kept the Sabbath beginning on Friday afternoon, doing no work on that day, wearing his best clothes and clean linen; celebrating the Jewish holy days, and in particular the feast of Peça in memory of the exodus of the people of Israel from Egypt, eating unleavened bread at that time, doing no work for eight days, keeping them as days of festival; observing also the festival they call Jacoth in commemoration of God's mercy to the said people in bringing them to the Promised Land: And another festival known as Salvuoth (*sic*) in commemoration of the aforesaid Law, which lasts for two days; and keeping also, in observance of the said Law, the feast of Kippur, vulgarly known as the Pardons, which falls in September, remaining on that day without food or drink until the rising of the star; also that of Thebeth observed in the same way; and that of Purim in memory of Queen Esther, remaining without food or drink for twenty-four hours; Observing also another fast, which they name the three weeks in memory of the people of Israel, and another in memory of the destruction of the Temple (*casa Santa*).

Publicly attending the Synagogues, observing therein all further rites of the aforesaid Law: speaking of these things publicly more especially with other observers of the Law, to whom he declared himself to be a Jew. Behaving in Catholic countries only exteriorly as a Catholic, in dissimulation and conformity whilst among them, attending the churches, and performing acts and outward observances of a Catholic Christian; knowing and understanding that the aforesaid Law of Moses was contrary to that which the Holy Mother Church of Rome holds, believes and teaches; persevering in his belief of the aforesaid errors, until he made his confession before the tribunal of the Holy Office.

All of which being considered, as well as what further appears from the autos, they declare:

That the offender Diogo Henriques was a heretic and apostate from our holy Catholic faith, and that he has incurred the sentence of major excommunication and confiscation of all his goods to the Royal Fisc and Treasury, and all other penalties as by law established in similar cases: But seeing that following better counsel he confessed his faults to the tribunal of the Holy Office with signs of repentance, asking pardon and mercy; and taking into account what further appears in the Acts, they receive the offender Diogo Henriques into the fold, and into union with holy Mother Church, as he asks: And in penalty, and in penance for his faults they command that he shall appear in the Auto da Fe in customary manner; and hear his sentence, and shall formally abjure his heretical errors; and they assign to him a prison, and he shall wear a penitential habit perpetually; and in prison he shall receive instruction in matters of our holy Faith necessary to the salvation of his soul. And he shall perform all other spiritual pains and penalties that may be imposed on him. And they command that he be absolved from the major excommunication, which he has incurred, according to ecclesiastical custom.

(*Signed*)   LUIS MARTINS DA ROCHA.

The above sentence was read to the offender Diogo Henriques in the public Auto da Fe celebrated on the Terreiro do Paço of this city of Lisbon, on Sunday, 15th day of December, of 1647.

Written by Gaspar Clemente.

Formal Abjuration

I, Diogo Henriques, in presence of your Worships, take oath upon the Holy Gospels, on which I place my hand, that of my own free will, I do anathematize, and reject every kind of heresy that has been or may be put forward against our holy Catholic Faith and the Apostolic See, especially those into which I fell, and which have been here read to me in my sentence, which I hold to be here repeated and set forth, and I swear ever to hold and to keep the holy Catholic Faith, as it is held and taught by the holy Mother Church of Rome, and that I will ever be most obedient to our most holy Father, Pope Innocent X., at present presiding over the Church of God, and to his Successors, and I confess that all who rebel against that holy Catholic Faith are worthy of condemnation; and I do swear never to join with them, but to pursue them and to make known any heresies I know anyone to hold, to the Inquisitors, or the Prelates of holy Mother Church; and I do swear and make promise to fulfil as far as in me lies the penance which is, or may be, imposed on me; and should I fall again into these errors, or into any other heresy whatsoever, I desire, and it is my pleasure that I shall be held to be relapsed, and punished in conformity with the law, and if at any time anything should be proved against me in contrary to my confession sworn before your Worships, I desire that this absolution be of no avail, but I submit myself to the severity and correction of the Sacred Canons, and I request the Notaries of the Holy Office to issue an Instrument accordingly, and those here present to be witnesses thereof, and to sign with me:

Joao Mendes de Vasconcellos, and Francisco Dias Castro signed as witnesses.

Written by Gaspar Clemente.
Diogo Henriques.

Deed of Secrecy

On the 10th day of the month of December, of 1647, in Lisbon, in the Casa do Despacho of the Offices of the Holy Inquisition, their Worships the Inquisitors holding their morning audience, summoned to appear before them, from the Penitential Cell, Diogo Henriques, with whom these Acts deal, to whom being present oath was administered on the Holy Gospels on which he placed his hand, under seal of which he was charged to keep secrecy as to all that he might see or hear in these prisons, and might occur with reference to his process, and neither by word or writing or any other method whatsoever to disclose the same, under pain of severe punishment, all of which he promised under seal of the aforesaid oath, whereupon this document was issued by order of their Worships aforesaid, the which he signed.

Written by Gaspar Clemente.
Diogo Henriques.

Deed of Penance

On the 11th day of the month of January, 1648, in Lisbon, in the Casa do Despacho of the Offices of the Inquisition, their Worships the Inquisitors holding their afternoon audience, summoned to appear before them Diogo Henriques, prisoner with whom these Acts are concerned, who being present, was informed that in penalty and for penance for his offences he must perform the following spiritual acts: Namely, he shall go to confession on the four principal festivals of the year, Christmas, Easter, Pentecost and the Assumption of our Lady, but shall not receive Communion without licence from this Tribunal; he shall recite every Saturday the Rosary of Our Lady the Virgin Mary, and on one Friday in the month he shall fast in honour of the Passion of Christ, all this during the coming year, at the end of which he shall send a certificate to this Tribunal in witness of having done so, to be annexed to his Process: and this city is assigned to him as prison, from which he may not absent himself without licence from this Holy Office; and on Sundays and Holy Days he shall attend the principal Mass in the Church of São Lourenço, wearing his penitential habit, until it is removed by order of the most Illustrious Lord Bishop, Inquisitor General; all of which he promised to perform, whereupon this Deed was drawn up by order of the Worshipful Inquisitors, and signed by Domingos Esteves, notary of the Holy Office, who wrote it, and by the prisoner Diogo Henriques.

Most Illustrious Lord,

Diogo Henriques, a poor youth, a wanderer in this Kingdom, who appeared in the last Auto, as a Judaizer, and who was ordered to attend the principal Mass in the

Church of São Lourenço, wearing a penitential habit, the which he has done up to the present, suffering much distress both from sickness and want of necessities, which distress he cannot remedy during the period in which he must wear the said penitential habit. For which reason he addressed two petitions to your Lordship's tribunal, neither of which was granted, and since he is still suffering from the aforesaid distress, with none to succour him, he begs your Lordship and the most Reverend Senate, by the death and passion of our Lord Jesus Christ, to take compassion on his distress and poverty, and to give order that his penitential be removed, which will be a great charity. R. M.

Let the Inquisitions be informed of the decision:
Lisbon, 28th February, 1648 (a rubric).

The Bishop, Dom Francisco de Castro, Inquisitor General of the Kingdom and Dominions of Portugal, and member of his Majesty's Council of State, etc. We make known that the above petition of Diogo Henriques reconciled in the last Auto-da-Fe, and the information given by the Inquisitors being taken into consideration:

We think fit to dispense the aforesaid for the period remaining for the performance of his penance. And we command that the penitential habit be removed, and we commute the said penance to any spiritual penances which their Worships the Inquisitors think necessary for the salvation of his soul, which he shall perform, as well as all else contained in his abjuration: this shall be annexed to his process, with the deed of Admonition made to him, and the declaration of the penances imposed on him. Given in Lisbon over our Seal only this 4th day of March, 1648.

Written by Diogo Velho.
Dom Francisco de Castro, Bishop.

Your Lordship thinks fit to dispense Diogo Henriques, reconciled, for the period remaining for the performance of his penance.

*   *   *   *   *

On the 4th day of March, 1648, in Lisbon in the Casa do Despacho of the offices of the Holy Inquisition, their Worships the Inquisitors, holding their morning audience, summoned to appear before them Diogo Henriques, who was reconciled in the last Auto, who, being present was informed that his illustrious Lordship has shown him mercy, and taking into consideration the time during which he has performed his penance, and the information given by this Tribunal, has thought fit to dispense him for the period remaining for the fulfilment of his penance, and has given order for his penitential habit to be removed, which was done, and his sentence commuted to such spiritual penances as were imposed on him in the first instance, which he must perform for another year, and must further comply with all else contained in his abjuration, the which he promised to do; whereupon their Worships the Inquisitors gave order for this deed to be issued, the which he signed.   Diogo Henriques.

Domingo Esteves, who wrote this deed.

APPENDIX II

A "LISTA" OF 1731

THE scope, methods, pettiness and vindictiveness of the Holy Office cannot be better illustrated than by the perusal of an original Inquisitional Programme, or Lista. One only has been available hitherto in English—that of the Lisbon *auto* of May 10th, 1682, published by Michael Geddes in a very rare contemporary tract. The text appended is half a century later, referring to an *auto* in the same city on Sunday, June 17th, 1731. It will be seen that no less than twelve persons—four men and eight women—were "relaxed" to the secular arm to be burned; and, according to the indications given, it would appear that the majority of them were burned alive. In addition, seventy-one other persons appeared as penitents. The first few cases illustrate the range of the Holy Office at this period and the comparative weight which it attached to various species of misdemeanour. The original is a printed broadsheet of four folios, published to be distributed and studied during the course of the proceedings like a modern race-card.

LIST OF PERSONS

who were summoned, penalties which they received and sentences that were read in the public *auto-da-fè* which took place in the Church of the Convent of Santo Domingo located in the western quarter of this city of Lisbon, on Sunday, June 17, 1731.

Inquisitor General

The most eminent and most reverend Senhor

NUNO DA CUNHA

Cardinal of the Holy Church of Rome known as Santa Anastasia and member of the Council of State of His Majesty.

———————

MEN

A Person Who Neither Abjures Nor Wears The "Sambenito"

Case 1. Duarte Navarro, age 83, one quarter New Christian, rentier, native of the town of Guimaraens in the Archbishopric of Braga and resident of Trancozo in the Bishopric of Vizeu, who was reconciled for the sins of Judaising by the Council of the Holy Tribunal of the Inquisition in Coimbra on September 25, 1683. Held again for relapsing into the same sins.

Sentenced to life imprisonment and five years in the Castro-Marim.

Those Who Made Light Abjuration

Case 2. Antonio Guedes, age 21, servant, single, son of Manoel Simoens, shoemaker, native of Granja which is the new name of the town of Ucanha, expelled from the monastery of Salzedas and residing in the western quarter of this city of Lisbon, for participating in the occult practices.

Sentenced to two years' banishment from the eastern and western quarters of Lisbon.

Case 3. Father Antonio Morinho, age 47, a priest of the order of San Pedro, native of the town of Freyxo de

Nemão in the Bishopric of Lamego, and resident of the
eastern quarter of the city of Lisbon, for sins of Molinism
and soliciting.

*Sentenced to permanent suspension of the right to con-
fess and eight years' deprivation of the practices of his
order in the Kingdom of Algarve; prohibition from entering in future either this patriarchate or the Archbishopric
of the eastern quarter of the city of Lisbon.*

Case 4. Father João Alvares of Nazareth, age 40, sub-
deacon of the order of San Pedro, native of the city of
Funchal and resident of this western quarter of the city of
Lisbon, for confessing without being a priest.

*Suspended forever from the practices of his order and
disqualified for promotion in said order; also sentenced
to five years in the galleys.*

Case 5. Domingos Luis Leme, age 43, without a trade,
native of the city of São Paulo and resident of the town of
Nossa Senhora do Bom Successo in the Bishopric of Rio
de Janeyro, for marrying a second time when his first and
legal wife was still alive.

Case 6. Francisco Soares, age 38, seaman, native of
the city of Funchal and resident of the town of Fayal in
the Bishopric of Angra, for the same sin.

Case 7. Domingos Peres de Gusmão, age 31, servant,
native of the town of Santa Ursula, Canary Islands, and
resident of the eastern quarter of the city of Lisbon, for
the same sin.

Cases 5, 6 *and* 7 *sentenced to whipping and five years
in the galleys.*

Case 8. Jozeph Mendes Gago, age 31, without a trade,
single, son of Manoel Gago, chief receiver, native of the
city of Beja in the Archbishopric of Evora and inhabitant
of the eastern quarter of Lisbon, for saying mass without
being a priest.

Disqualified for promotion in his order; also sentenced to whipping and six years in the galleys.

Persons Who Have Not Abjured And Who Wear The "Sambenito"

Case 9. Rafael Mendes do Valle, age 58, New Christian, rentier, native and resident of the western quarter of this city of Lisbon, who was pardoned for the sins of Judaising in the public *auto-da-fè* held in the market-place of San Miguel in the city of Coimbra on May 9, 1728; held again for disturbing and interfering with the righteous and free exercise of the Holy Tribunal.

Case 10. Luis Cordeyro do Valle, age 32, New Christian, lawyer, native of Villa-Real in the Archbishopric of Braga and resident of the western quarter of the city of Lisbon, pardoned for the sins of Judaising in the public *auto-da-fè* held in the market-place of San Miguel in the city of Coimbra on May 29, 1729; held for the second time for disturbing and interfering with the righteous and free exercise of the Holy Tribunal.

Cases 9 and 10 sentenced to two years' banishment from the cities where the Tribunal of the Inquisition resides.

First Official Abjuration for Judaising and Other Sins

Case 11. Diogo Dias Correa, age 21, New Christian, without a trade, single, son of Antonio Dias Fernandes, business man, native of the town of Freyxo de Nemão and resident of the eastern quarter of the city of Lisbon.

Case 12. Pedro Fernandes, age 30, New Christian, barber, native and resident of the town of Monsanto in the Bishopric of Guarda.

Case 13. Francisco Lopes Cazado, age 26, New Christian, single, son of Jozeph Rodrigues, locksmith, native and resident of the town of New Idanha in the Bishopric of Guarda.

Case 14. Luis Vaz de Oliveyra, age 24, half New Christian, dealer, single, son of João Sanches Maioral, apothecary, native of Saoselle in the Kingdom of Castile and resident of the Mines of Ribeyrão do Carmo in the Bishopric of Rio de Janeyro.

Case 15. Manoel Henriques, age 35, New Christian, blacksmith, native of New Idanha and resident of Monsanto.

Case 16. Francisco Nunes de Payva, age 22, New Christian, without a trade, single, son of Francisco Nunes de Payva, surgeon, native and resident of the town of Covilhã.

Cases 11, 12, 13, 14, 15 *and* 16 *sentenced to imprisonment at the option of the Holy Office and wearing of the " sambenito " at the auto-da-fè.*

Case 17. Miguel Fernandes Vicente, age 28, philosophy student, single, son of Francisco Fernandes Vicente, writer, native of the village of Serezeda, suburb of the town of Miranda del Castañal in the Bishopric of Salamanca, Kingdom of Castile, with no definite residence, for falling into the errors of the Lutheran sect.

Sentenced to imprisonment at the option of the Holy Office and wearing of the " sambenito."

Case 18. Manoel da Costa Espadilha, age 42, New Christian, storekeeper, native of the town of Penamacor in the Bishopric of Guarda and resident in the Minas do Ouro (gold mines) in the Bishopric of Rio de Janeyro.

Second Abjuration for Judaising

Case 19. Manoel Rodrigues Franco, age 67, New Christian, shoemaker, native of the town of Penamacor and resident of Covilhã in the Bishopric of Guarda.

Case 20. Gaspar Mendes Morão, age 28, New Christian, single, gunsmith, son of Gaspar Mendes, blacksmith, native of the town of New Idanha and resident of the village of Fundão, suburb of the town of Covilhã.

Case 21. Manoel Henriques da Fonceca, age ..., New Christian, cane sugar worker, born on the sugar plantation of Inhobim and resident of Rio do Meyo, district of the city of Paraiba in the Bishopric of Pernambuco.

Case 22. Belchior Mendes Correa, alias Antonio Cardozo Porto, age 61, New Christian, merchant, native of the town of Celorico in the Bishopric of Guarda and resident of the city of Bahia.

Case 23. Francisco Nunes, age 42, New Christian, shoemaker, native and resident of the town of New Idanha.

Case 24. David Mendes da Sylva, age ..., New Christian, business man, single, son of Gregorio da Sylva, dealer, native of Villa-nova de Fascoa in the Bishopric of Lamego and resident of the Mines of Serro-frio in the Bishopric of Rio de Janeyro.

Case 25. Estevão de Valença Caminha, age 28, New Christian, business man, single, son of Luis de Valença Caminha, cane sugar labourer, native of the New Sugar Plantation and resident of the Old Sugar Plantation in the district of the city of Paraiba.

Third Abjuration for Judaising and Other Sins

Case 26. Antonio Rodrigues de Campos, age 49, New Christian, labourer . . . , native of the town of Almeyda in the Bishopric of Lamego and resident of the village of Irara, suburb of the town of Santo Amaro in the Archbishopric of Bahia.

Case 27. Luis Nunes da Fonceca, age 66, part New Christian, tobacco labourer, native of the village of Poxim and resident of the New Sugar Plantation in the district of the city of Paraiba.

Case 28. Diogo Mendes, age 28, New Christian, shoemaker, native and resident of Fundão.

Case 29. Diogo Rodrigues, age 57, New Christian, shoe-maker native and resident of the town of Monsanto.

Cases 18, 19, 20, 21, 22, 23, 24, 25, 26, 27, 28 *and* 29 *sentenced to imprisonment and perpetual wearing of the " sambenito."*

Case 30. João Pereyra, age 32, half New Christian, mule driver, single, son of Francisco Pereyra Dias, tenant, native of Molelos and resident of the town of Tondella in the Bishopric of Vizeu.

Sentenced to perpetual wearing of the " sambenito" and imprisonment without remission; also five years in the Kingdom of Angola.

Case 31. Diogo de Lima Cordeyro, age 35, quarter New Christian, rentier, single, son of Antonio Cordeyro de Lima, also a rentier, native and resident of the village of Raiz do Monte, suburb of Villa-Real in the Archbishopric of Braga.

Sentenced to the same punishment as Case 30, *plus five years in Cabo-verde.*

Case 32. Father Antonio Guilherme Hebre de Loureyro, age 37, priest of the order of San Pedro, and Bachelor of Arts in Canon Law, native of the eastern quarter of the city of Lisbon and resident of the town of Tondella in the Bishopric of Vizeu, for proclaiming himself a God, second Redeemer of the human race, and for affirming and introducing other sins against the principal articles of our Holy Catholic Faith.

Sentenced to perpetual wearing of the "sambenito" and imprisonment without remission; also to wear a painted pasteboard mitre with the mark of a heretic and a dogmatist, to be prevented from ever exercising the duties of his order and to be secluded without pardon in the prisons of the Holy Inquisition.

Fourth Abjuration for Witchcraft and Judaising

Case 33. Jozeph Francisco Pereyra, age 26, Negro, single, slave of João Francisco Pedrozo, native of Inda Costa da Mina and resident of the western quarter of Lisbon, for the sin of witchcraft and for making a pact with the devil whom he recognised and worshipped as God.

Case 34. Jozeph Francisco, age 19, Negro, single, slave of Domingos Francisco Pedrozo, business man, native of Inda Costa da Mina and resident of the western quarter of the city of Lisbon, for the same sin.

Case 35. Manoel Delgado, age 42, Negro, slave of Captain Jozeph Rodrigues de Oliveyra, native of the Island of S. Thomè and resident of the western quarter of this city of Lisbon, for the same sin.

Cases 33, 34 *and* 35 *sentenced to perpetual wearing of the "sambenito," also a painted pasteboard mitre with the mark of witchcraft; to be whipped, to spend five years in the galleys and never again to enter the eastern and western quarters of the city of Lisbon.*

Case 36. Manoel da Piedade, age 27, Negro, single, slave of Captain Gaspar de Valladares, native of the city of Bahia and resident of the eastern quarter of the city of Lisbon, for the same sin.

Sentenced to the same punishment as the above and also prohibited from ever again entering the city of Porto and its environs.

Case 37. Sebastian Ferreyra, age 47, half New Christian, merchant, native and resident of Villa-Real in the Archbishopric of Braga.

Case 38. Diogo d'Avila Henriques, age 31, New Christian, merchant, single, son of Jorge Henriques Moreno, tenant, native of the village of Azevo in the Bishopric of Lamego and a resident of the city of Bahia.

Cases 37 and 38 sentenced to perpetual wearing of the " sambenito " with marks of fire and imprisonment without remission and five years in the galleys.

WOMEN

Persons Who Have Not Abjured and Wear the " Sambenito "

Case 1. Maria Henriques, age 22, New Christian, single, daughter of Simão Rodrigues, shoemaker, native of the town of Penamacor and resident of Covilhã, who was pardoned for the sins of Judaising in the public *auto-da-fè* which was held in the Church of the Convent of Santo Domingo of this city on October 13, 1726; held again for committing the same sins.

Sentenced to perpetual wearing of the " sambenito " and imprisonment.

Case 2. Isabel Nunes, age 27, New Christian, single, daughter of Simão Rodrigues, shoemaker, native of the town of Penamacor and resident of Covilhã, pardoned for the sins of Judaising in the public *auto-da-fè* which was held in the Church of the Convent of Santo Domingo of this city on October 13, 1726; held again for committing the same sins.

Sentenced to perpetual wearing of the "sambenito" and imprisonment without remission with seven years in the Kingdom of Angola.

First Abjuration for Judaising

Case 3. Jozepha Maria, age 26, half New Christian, married to Jorge Nunes, shopkeeper, native and resident of the town of Alpedrinha in the Bishopric of Guarda.

Case 4. Violante Rodrigues, age 44, three-quarters New Christian, married to Henrique Froes, apothecary, native of the town of Monsanto and resident of the village of Teyxozo, suburb of the town of Covilhã.

Case 5. Maria Rodrigues, age 47, New Christian, married to Matheos Rodrigues, shoemaker, native and resident of the town of Monsanto.

Case 6. Brites Nunes, age 73, New Christian, widow of Antonio Fernandes, shoemaker, native and resident of the village of Fundão.

Case 7. Isabel Henriques, age 44, New Christian, married to Braz Nunes, merchant, native and resident of the city of Guarda.

Case 8. Leonor Maria, age 27, New Christian, single, daughter of Antonio Henriques, a trader, native of the city of Guarda and resident of the village of Teyxozo.

Case 9. Leonor Henriques, age 51, New Christian, married to Francisco Nunes de Payva, surgeon, native of the town of New Idanha and resident of Covilhã.

Cases 3, 4, 5, 6, 7, 8 *and* 9 *sentenced to imprisonment at the option of the Holy Office and wearing of the " sambenito " which will be removed at the auto-da-fè.*

Second Abjuration for Judaising

Case 10. Micaela Joanna, age 32, New Christian, single, daughter of Francisco Lopes Preo, physician, native and resident of the village of Fundão.

Case 11. Roza Maria, age 29, New Christian, married to Jozeph Mendes, merchant, native and resident of the city of Guarda.

Case 12. Mecia Lopes, age 52, New Christian, widow of Francisco Rodrigues, blacksmith, native and resident of the town of Alpedrinha.

Cases 10, 11 and 12 sentenced to imprisonment and wearing of the " sambenito " at the option of the Holy Office.

Case 13. Maria de Valença, age 32, New Christian, married to Antonio de Fonceca Rego, cane sugar labourer, native of the Central Sugar Plantation and resident of the Old Sugar Plantation in the district of the city of Paraiba.

Case 14. Anna Henriques, age 20, New Christian, single, daughter of Simão Gomes, merchant, native and resident of the town of Covilhã.

Case 15. Clara Henriques, age 71, New Christian, widow of Antonio Dias Pinheyro, sugar plantation master, native of the village of Cucau and resident of the Sugar Plantation of Santo Andrè in the district of the city of Paraiba.

Case 16. Guiomar Henriques, age 27, New Christian, single, daughter of Jorge Rodrigues, blacksmith, native of the village of Fundão and resident of the town of New Idanha.

Third Abjuration for Judaising

Case 17. Anna da Fonceca, age 52, New Christian, single, daughter of Luis Nunes da Fonceca, sugar cane worker, native of Paraiba and resident of the New Sugar Plantation in the district of said city.

Case 18. Branca Rodrigues, age 48, New Christian, married to João Rodrigues Morão, blacksmith, native of the town of Monsanto and resident of Covilhã.

Case 19. Guiomar Nunes Bezerra, age 49, partly New Christian, married to Luis Nunes da Fonceca who is mentioned on this list, native of the Sugar Plantation of Inhobim and resident of the New Sugar Plantation in the district of the city of Paraiba.

Case 20. Ignes Nunes, age 62, New Christian, married to Diogo Rodrigues who is mentioned on this list, native of the town of New Idanha and resident of Monsanto.

Case 21. Joanna do Rego, age 42, New Christian, married to Manoel Henriques da Fonceca who is mentioned on this list, native of the village of Poxim and resident of the Middle Rio district of the city of Paraiba.

Case 22. Anna da Sylva, age 42, New Christian, widow of Diogo Alonso, barber, native and resident of the town of Covilhã.

Case 23. Guiomar de Valença, age 24, New Christian, married to Henrique da Sylva, sugar cane worker, native and resident of the Old Sugar Plantation in the district of the city of Paraiba.

Fourth Abjuration for Judaising

Case 24. Antonia Maria de Carvalho, age 15, New Christian, single, daughter of Simão Gomes, merchant, native and resident of the town of Covilhã.

Case 25. Felippa da Fonceca, age 60, New Christian, married to Luis de Valença Caminha, sugar cane worker, native of the Sugar Plantation of Poxim and resident of the Old Sugar Plantation in the district of the city of Paraiba.

Case 26. Anna Maria, age 43, New Christian, married to Jozeph Rios, shopkeeper, native and resident of the town of Covilhã.

Case 27. Leonor Henriques, age 72, New Christian, married to Antonio Rodrigues de Campos who is mentioned on this list, native of Villa-nova de Fascoa in the Bishopric of Lamego and resident of the village of Irara, suburb of the town of Santo Amaro in the Archbishopric of Bahia.

Case 28. Mecia de Chaves, age 34, New Christian, single, daughter of Francisco Lopes Preto, physician, native and resident of the village of Fundão.

Case 29. Leonor Henriques, age 38, a quarter New Christian, married to Francisco Vaz da Fonceca, nick-named Tomba, quartermaster in the Cavalry, native and resident of the town of Pinhel in the Bishopric of Vizeu.

The above seventeen cases sentenced to perpetual wearing of the " sambenito " and imprisonment.

Fifth Abjuration for Judaising and Witchcraft

Case 30. Violant Maria, age 31, a quarter New Christian, single, daughter of Antonio Cordeyro de Lima, a rentier, native and resident of the village of Raiz do Monte, suburb of Villa-Real in the Archbishopric of Braga.

Sentenced to perpetual wearing of the " sambenito " and imprisonment without remission; also five years in the Kingdom of Angola.

Case 31. Maria de Sousa, age 39, partly New Christian, married to Caetano Tavares, a rentier, native and resident of the town of Trancozo in the Bishopric of Vizeu.

Sentenced to the same punishment as Case 30 with five years in S. Thomè.

Case 32. Jozepha Maria, age 31, single, daughter of

Jozeph Ribeyro, farmer, native of the village of Alqueydão, suburb of the town of Ourem in the Bishopric of Leyria and resident of the eastern quarter of the city of Lisbon, for the sins of witchcraft and for having made a pact with the devil whom she recognised and adored as a God.

Sentenced to imprisonment and wearing of the " sambenito" at the option of the Holy Office; also the painted pasteboard mitre with the mark of witchcraft, whippings and five years in the Kingdom of Angola with one of seclusion in the prisons of the Holy Tribunal.

Case 33. Maria da Incarnação, age 34, widow of Manoel . . . , a leather-dresser, native and resident of the eastern quarter of the city of Lisbon, for feigning to have received divine revelation so that she might be held and esteemed as a saint, and for the sins of witchcraft and for having made a pact with Satan whom she recognised and worshipped as God.

Sentenced to perpetual imprisonment and wearing of the " sambenito" and the painted pasteboard mitre, and holding a candle; also imprisonment at the option of the Holy Office in the prison of the Holy Inquisition; five years in the Kingdom of Angola and never again to enter the eastern and western quarters of the city of Lisbon.

Case 34. Isabel Luis Simoa, age 34, part New Christian, single, daughter of Simão Luis Ramalho, adjutant, native and resident of Villa-nova de Fascoa in the Bishopric of Lamego.

Sentenced to imprisonment and perpetual wearing of the " sambenito" without remission with the insignia of fire; also seven years in Benguela.

Persons Handed Over in the Flesh

Case 1. Miguel de Mendonça Valhadolid, age 37, New Christian, dealer, native of the city of Valhadolid, Kingdom of Castile, and resident of the territory of Nossa Senhora de Penha de França, district of the city of São Paulo in the Bishopric of Rio de Janeyro, convicted, lying, dissembling, inadequate confession and impenitent.

Case 2. Alvaro Rodrigues, age 57, New Christian, shoemaker, native of the town of New Idanha and resident of Covilhã, convicted, lying, dissembling, inadequate confession, inconstant, recanter and impenitent.

Case 3. Felix Nunes de Miranda, age 62, New Christian, business man, native of the town of Almeyda in the Bishopric of Lamego and resident of the city of Bahia, convicted, lying, dissembling, inadequate confession, impenitent and relapsed.

Case 4. Francisco da Sylva, age 28, part New Christian, tobacconist, single, son of Francisco Soares, merchant, native of the town of Guimaraens in the Archbishopric of Braga and resident of Muimenta da Beyra in the Bishopric of Lamego, convicted, refused to confess, obstinate and relapsed.

Case 5. Anna Rodrigues, surnamed Cossaria, age 78, part New Christian, widow of João da Costa, shoemaker, native and resident of the city of Lamego, convicted, lying, dissembling, inadequate confession and impenitent.

Case 6. Maria Ribeyra, age 55, part New Christian, married to João de Abrunhoza, barber, native of the town of Trancozo in the Bishopric of Vizeu and resident of Castello-melhor in the Bishopric of Lamego, convicted, lying, dissembling, inadequate confession and impenitent.

Case 7. Agostinha Baptista, age 63, part New Christian, married to Manoel da Costa, surnamed Cossario, adjutant, native and resident of the city of Lamego, convicted, lying, dissembling, inadequate confession and impenitent.

Case 8. Ignes de Mesquita, age 56, part New Christian, widow of Manoel de Almeyda, dealer, native of Villapouca de Aguiar in the Archbishopric of Braga and resident of Freyxo de Nemão in the Bishopric of Lamego, convicted, lying, dissembling, inadequate confession, inconstant, recanter and impenitent.

Case 9. Maria Henriques, age 41, one-quarter New Christian, married to Luis Pereyra, shoemaker, native of the town of Pinhel in the Bishopric of Vizeu and resident of Freyxo de Nemão in the Bishopric of Lamego, convicted, lying, dissembling, inadequate confession, inconstant, recanter and impenitent.

Case 10. Guiomar Nunes, age 37, New Christian, married to Francisco Pereyra, tinsmith, native of Pernambuco and resident of the Sugar Plantation of Santo Andrè in the district of the city of Paraiba, convicted, refused to confess and obstinate.

Case 11. Maria Mendes, age 29, New Christian, married to João Terrones, without a trade, native of the city of Beja in the Archbishopric of Evora and resident of the village of Moncarapacho, suburb of the city of Tavira in the Bishopric of Faro, Kingdom of Algarve, convicted, refused to confess and obstinate.

Case 12. Felippa do Valle, age 65, New Christian, single, daughter of Diogo Lopes, tenant, native and resident of Villa-Real in the Archbishopric of Braga, convicted, refused to confess and obstinate.

Persons Dead in Jail, Handed Over in Effigy

Case 13. Diogo de Avila Sexas, New Christian, merchant, native of the town of Celorico in the Bishopric of

Guarda and resident of Vouzella in the Bishopric of Vizeu, convicted, refused to confess, obstinate and relapsed.

Case 14. D. Anna Maria Nogueyra, part New Christian, single, daughter of Manoel Rodrigues Nogueyra, business man, native and resident of the western quarter of this city of Lisbon, convicted, refused to confess and obstinate.

SELECT BIBLIOGRAPHY

I.—Manuscript Authorities, etc.

Besides the printed works listed below, manuscript authorities from the following collections have been utilised in the preparation of this volume :

The British Museum.
Bodleian Library, Oxford.
State Archives of the Torre do Tombo, Lisbon.
National Archives, Madrid.
State Archives of the Frari, Venice.
Library of Jewish Theological Seminary of America, New York.
Library of University of Pennsylvania, Philadelphia.
Library of the Author, London.

Contemporary printed *Listas* and similar records in the above collections (all of the utmost rarity, and some possibly unique) have also been largely utilised.

II.—Printed Works.

H. C. Lea, *A History of the Inquisition in Spain.* 4 vols. 1906-7. (Fundamental.)
> *The Inquisition in the Spanish Dependencies.* 1908.

E. N. Adler, *Auto de Fé and Jew.* 1908.

J. A. Llorente, *Historia Crítica de la Inquisición de España.* (Frequently translated and reprinted.)

W. T. Walsh, *Isabella of Spain.* 1931.

A. Herculano, *Historia da origem e estabelecimento da Inquisição em Portugal.* (English translation, 1926.)

A. Baião, *A Inquisição em Portugal e no Brasil.* 1921.
> *Episodios dramáticos da Inquisição Portuguesa.* 3 vols., 1919-1937.
> *A Inquisição de Goa.* 2 vols., 1930.

A. J. Moreira, *Historia dos principaes actos e procedimentos dā Inquisição em Portugal.*

R. Sabbatini, *Torquemada and the Spanish Inquisition.* 1913.

A. S. Turberville, *The Spanish Inquisition.* 1932.

A. B. Wallis Chapman, *English Merchants and the Inquisition in the Canaries.* 1912.

Genaro Garcia &c., *La Inquisición de Mexico.* 1906
    Autos de fé de la Inquisición de Mexico. 1910.

C. Roth, *History of the Marranos.* 1932.
    Large numbers of independent articles in *Revue des Etudes Juives, Transactions of Royal Historical Society,* &c.

B. Braunstein, *The Chuetas of Majorca.* 1936.

V. La Mantia, *L'Inquisizione in Sicilia.* 1904.

F. Garau, *La Fee Triunfante.* 1691. (Reprinted 1931.)

J. T. Medina, *Historia de la Inquisición de Lima; de Chile; de la Plata; de Cartagena de las Indias; en las islas Filipinas.* 6 vols., 1887-1899.

A. J. Texeira, *Antonio Homem e a Inquisição.* 1895-1902.

V. Vignau, *Catalogo . . . de la Inquisición de Toledo.* 1903.

J. del Olmo, *Relacion Historica de Auto General de Fee que se celebró en Madrid este Año de 1680 con Assistencia del Rey.* 1680.

J. Baker, *History of the Inquisition.* 1736.

History of the Inquisition from its origin under Pope Innocent III till the present time. Also the private practices of the Inquisitors, the form of trial and modes of torture. 1814.

J. Marchant, *A Review of the Bloody Tribunal . . . of the Inquisition.* 1770.

A. Puigblanch, *La Inquisición sin Máscara.* 1811.

Gonzaléz de Montés, *Discovery and Playne Declaration of Sundry Subtile Practices of the Holy Inquisition of Spayne.*

Ludovico à Paramo, *De origine et progressu Sanctae Inquisitionis.* 1598.

J. M. Marin, *Procedimientos de la Inquisición.* 2 vols., Madrid, 1886.

I. de las Cagigas, *Libro Verde de Aragón.* 1929.

R. Cappa, *La Inquisición Española.* 1888.

L. González Obregón, *D. Guillén de Lampart: La Inquisición y la Independencia.* 1908.

A. Paz y Mellia, *Catalogo abreviado de Papeles de Inquisición.* 1914.

308   THE SPANISH INQUISITION

G. R. G. Conway, *An Englishman and the Mexican Inquisition*. 1927.

D. Fergusson and C. Adler, *The Trial of Gabriel de Granadā by the Inquisition in Mexico*. 1899.

A. F. G. Bell, *Luis de Leon*. 1925.

Getino, *Vida i Procesos del Maestro Fray Luis de Leon*. 1907.

Madeleine Jouve, *Torquemada*. 1935.

Sir Alexander G. Cardew, *A Short History of the Inquisition*. 1933.

G. G. Coulton, *The Inquisition*. 1929.

M. Kayserling, *Ein Feiertag in Madrid*. 1859. (And other works by same author.)

Mémoires instructifs pour un voyageur dans les divers états de l'Europe. 1738.

Ramon de Vilana Perlas, *La Verdadera practica apostolica de el S. tribunal de la Inquisición*. (Spanish and Italian.) 1735.

F. Freire de Mello, *Representação ás Cortes e invectiva contra a Inquisição*. 1821.

H. B. Piazza, *A Short and true account of the Inquisition and its Proceeding*. (English and French.) 1722.

J. Lucio d'Azevedo, *Historia dos Christãos Novos Portugueses*. 1921.

A. L. Maycock, *The Inquisition*. 1926.

Jean Marx, *L'Inquisition en Dauphiné*. 1914.

Hoffmann Nickerson, *The Inquisition*. 1932.

Conde de Castellano, *Un complot terrorista en el siglo XV: los comienzos de la Inquisición aragonesa*. 1927.

De Gray Birch, *Catalogue of a collection of original MSS., formerly belonging to the Holy Office of the Inquisition in the Canary Islands*. 2 vols., 1903.

A. S. Turberville, *Mediæval Heresy and the Inquisition*. 1920.

Bernard Gui, *Manuel de l'inquisiteur*. 2 vols., 1926-7.

L. Tanon, *Histoire des Tribunaux de l'Inquisition*. 1893.

INDEX

A

B